The Jewish Family
in a Changing World

# The Jewish Family in a Changing World

*Edited by*
Gilbert S. Rosenthal

Thomas Yoseloff
*New York* • *South Brunswick* • *London*

ISBN: 0-498-07679-2
Printed in the United States of America

*For the Six Million,
who exemplified the
finest values in the
Jewish family.*

# CONTENTS

# FOREWORD

Since 1955 a truly unusual organization has been in existence in American Jewish communal service. I refer to the Commission on Synagogue Relations of the Federation of Jewish Philanthropies of New York. The Commission brings together the ablest leadership of our congregational life and the most gifted architects of Jewish social service in our city. The aim of the Commission is the building of a bridge between Federation, the house of *Tzedakah*, and the synagogue, the house of prayer.

The need for the Commission derived from the erosion of the traditional role of the synagogue in philanthropy and the building of a wall of separation in American Jewish life between the synagogue and the Jewish communal institutions. Thus, the two most creative forces in our community, the synagogue and the social service agency, have gone their separate ways, with relatively little rapport between them.

The Commission sought to put an end to this dichotomy and to bring together the synagogue and our social work institutions in an effort to create cooperation instead of continuing the chaos that has existed.

The Commission is engaged in projects and programs whose aims are to interpret the needs of the synagogue and the religious Jew to the Federation and its affiliated institutions. On the other hand, through the work of the Commission, we are able to interpret the needs of our communal institutions to the synagogue world in order to gain support for Jewish communal service from the synagogue.

During these past years of fruitful cooperation, we

have addressed ourselves to the many problems which the synagogue and the Jewish communal institutions share in common. We have been fortunate enough to produce a significant body of literature in a pioneer field that has grown out of discussions between rabbis, synagogue lay leadership, and experts in social work.

Through our Committees, the Commission has sponsored conferences, workshops, and dialogues dealing with every aspect of Jewish communal life. As a result, significant and original papers have been written for the Commission in the areas of intermarriage, divorce, drug addiction among Jewish youth, the unwed Jewish mother, the problems of the black Jew, the role of the synagogue in communal affairs, arts and literature in Jewish life, the relationship of the rabbi to the Jewish social worker, and many others.

We have been fortunate to have some of our material printed in permanent form. A volume on *Jews and Divorce, The Rabbi and the Jewish Social Worker, A Hospital Compendium—A Guide to Jewish Moral and Religious Principles in Hospital Practice,* and several others have been published and widely circulated in the United States as well as abroad. Graduate students from all over the world have utilized our publications and papers as research sources. Several years ago we were pleased when Thomas Yoseloff published our volume *Judaism and the Community* (New Directions in Jewish Social Work) edited by Dr. Jacob Freid. The essays which appeared in the volume provided authoritative insight into the problems which beset Jews in their individual, family, and community life. In his introduction to the volume, Dr. Freid stated: "During the present transitional stage of urban and suburban Jewish life, the Federation of Jewish Philanthropies contains the foremost peripatetic university of social welfare, health, and communal expertise in the United States of America, and, indeed, the world. This is a contemporary storehouse of knowledge, information, insight, and guidance into the crucial problems and anxieties and pressures of contemporary urban life waiting to be tapped by the Jewish community for its guidance and benefit. Their professional knowledge and experience gives guidance to our Greater New York Jewish community and to all Jewish metropolitan communities upon those matters which so profoundly concern us in our world today."

The present volume, edited by the young, energetic, and able Rabbi Gilbert S. Rosenthal, contains the search and striving for the meaning of Jewish life today, with particular stress on the Jewish family. In this volume the reader will find original papers which have appeared nowhere else, dealing with every facet of the Jewish family today.

The Commission on Synagogue Relations will continue in all of its work to underscore the Jewish component in social service and to accentuate the need to stress Jewish values in all organized Jewish activities.

In the opinion of Commission leadership, the sole rationale for Jewish communal service is the enrichment of Jewish life. This, then, is the purpose of this volume and to this end the Commission dedicates itself in the future.

RABBI ISAAC N. TRAININ

# ABOUT THE CONTRIBUTORS

*Isaac N. Trainin,* rabbi and social worker, is Director of the Commission on Synagogue Relations of the Federation of Jewish Philanthropies of New York. He is the author of numerous papers and articles on Jewish communal life and Jewish family institutions, and he has lectured on these subjects throughout the United States. Rabbi Trainin has pioneered in the programs of Federation to join the disciplines of the rabbinate and social work and he has been responsible for numerous conferences, symposia, and volumes that have dealt with the American Jewish community and its problems.

*Gilbert S. Rosenthal* is rabbi of the Oceanside Jewish Center, Oceanside, New York. He taught Bible at the Women's Institute of the Jewish Theological Seminary of America and lectured at the Theodor Herzl Institute. He is the author of *Banking and Finance Among Jews in Renaissance Italy; Generations in Crisis; Maimonides: His Wisdom for Our Time,* and many articles and reviews published here and in Israel. Dr. Rosenthal is Chairman of the Publications Committee of the Commission on Synagogue Relations of the Federation of Jewish Philanthropies of New York and he edits the Commission's magazine, *News and Views.* He received the Commission's Israel Cummings Award in 1969. He is also editor of the *Bulletin* of the New York Board of Rabbis.

*Louis Birner* is a practicing psychologist in New York City and is a member of the American Psychological Association and the National Association for Psychoanalysis. He is a consultant to the Commission on Synagogue Relations of the Federation of Jewish Philanthropies of

New York on the problem of intermarriage. Dr. Birner is on the faculty of the Metropolitan Institute for Psycho-analytic Studies and he was a clinical supervisor for the Metropolitan Center for Mental Health.

*Meyer H. Diskind* is Assistant Commissioner of the Narcotic Addiction Control Commission of New York State and former Director of the New York State Parole Narcotic Treatment Bureau. He is the author of two books and numerous articles in professional journals on addiction and its treatment. He is a member of the Academy of Certified Social Workers, member of the Board of Directors of the New York City Chapter of the National Association of Social Workers, and he was a panelist at the White House Conference on Drug Abuse in 1962.

*Stanley Einstein* is a clinical and social psychologist and is Executive Director of the New York Council on Alcoholism. He is the founder and Executive Director of the Institute for the Study of Drug Addiction and is the founder and editor of the *International Journal of the Addictions*. Dr. Einstein has taught about the problems of addiction at New York Medical College, New York University, and Fordham University. He has lectured nationally and internationally on the addiction problems and he is a member of the International Council on Alcoholism and Addiction, a non-governmental agency of the United Nations.

*S. P. Goldberg* has been associated with the Council of Jewish Federations and Welfare Funds since 1945. He is the author of "Jewish Communal Services," a review of the year's highlights, which appears annually in the *American Jewish Yearbook,* and of "The American Jewish Community," published by Women's ORT. He is a contributor to the *Encyclopedia of Social Work* and to *Encyclopedia Judaica* and was formerly a member of the Columbia University School of Social Work.

*Irving Greenberg* is rabbi of the Riverdale Jewish Center in New York and is Associate Professor of History at Yeshiva University. He has taught at Tel Aviv and Brandeis universities and has authored many papers and studies that have appeared in scholarly journals. Dr. Greenberg is a member of the Advisory Board of the National Religious Jewish Students Association and is a member of the Board of Directors of the Religious Education Association.

The late *Henry Enoch Kagan* was rabbi of Sinai Temple, Mount Vernon, New York, and was professor of Pastoral Psychology of the Graduate School of Pastoral College at Iona College. He was a practicing psychologist and directed the Counseling Center of the New York Federation of Reform Synagogues. Dr. Kagan was the author of *Six Who Changed the World; Changing the Attitude of Christian Toward Jew: A Psychological Approach Through Religion,* and *Judaism and Psychiatry,* as well as many papers on psychology and religion. He received the Israel Cummings Award.

*Bernard Kligfeld* is rabbi of Temple Emanuel in Long Beach, New York, and is Chairman of the Committee on Child Guidance and Welfare of the Commission on Synagogue Relations of the Federation of Jewish Philanthropies of New York. He received the Israel Cummings Award of the Commission. Rabbi Kligfeld has written several papers on intermarriage, bereavement, and Jewish sexual norms.

*Florence Kreech* has been Executive Director of the Louise Wise Services for over twenty years and is a recognized expert in the field of adoption and child welfare. She is a board member and consultant for Standard Development for Adoption Service, Child Welfare League of America, and is a board member of the Community Council of Greater New York. In 1966 she received the Naomi Lehman Award of the Federation of Jewish

Philanthropies and the Certificate of Honor from her Alma Mater, Western Reserve University School of Applied Social Sciences, "in recognition of outstanding achievement and service in the field of social welfare." She received the Israel Cummings Award of the Commission.

*George Krupp* is a psychiatrist in Rockville Center, New York, and is the author of numerous articles that have appeared in popular and scholarly journals. For nine years he was Assistant Professor of Psychiatry at Adelphi College School of Social Work and he has been a consulting psychiatrist for Hillside Hospital, Montefiore Hospital, and the Rockville Center School System.

*Norman Lamm* is rabbi of the Jewish Center in New York City and Erna Michael Professor of Jewish Philosophy at Yeshiva University. He was founder and first editor of the magazine *Tradition* and he is the author of *A Hedge of Roses* and numerous essays.

*Sarah Lederman* is District Director of the Jewish Association for Services for the Aged and has been a social worker for over thirty-five years. Miss Lederman is a board member of the Central Bureau for the Jewish Aged and was a recipient of the Israel Cummings Award.

*Arnold Mendelson* is assistant Borough Supervisor of the Bronx Jewish Family Service. Prior to that he was a caseworker in the Bronx Veterans Administration Hospital and at the Jewish Family Service.

*Mark Jay Mirsky* teaches English at the City College of New York. His first novel, *Thou Worm Jacob,* was published in 1967, and a second novel, *Simcha,* will shortly appear.

*Victor D. Sanua* is Associate Professor in the Department of Social and Psychological Foundation of the School of Education at New York's City College. Prior to that he taught at Yeshiva University and the University of Paris. He has written many scholarly papers.

*Richard Schachet* is a rabbi and a social worker. He is Director of a project run by the Federation of the Handicapped at the narcotics unit at Manhattan State Hospital and was Associate Director of the Good Samaritan Halfway House for Addicts.

*Alvin I. Schiff* is Professor of Education and Chairman of the Department of Jewish Education at the Ferkauf Graduate School of Yeshiva University. He is also a visiting professor of Social Science Research at Queens College. Dr. Schiff is the author of *The Jewish Day School in America* and numerous studies in the field of Jewish education, and he is associate editor of the *Jewish Education* Quarterly.

*Manheim S. Shapiro* is Executive Director of the Bureau for Careers in Jewish Service and is a well-known sociologist. He has authored numerous papers on Jewish sociology in various professional and lay journals.

*Rav A. Soloff* is rabbi of East End Temple in New York City and teaches at the School of Education of the Hebrew Union College in New York. He is Vice President of the Commission on Synagogue Relations of the Federation of Jewish Philanthropies and received its Israel Cummings Award.

*Bernard Warach* is Executive Director of the Jewish Association for Services for the Aged and was formerly General Director of Associated YM-YWHA's of Greater New York. He was a welfare official with the displaced persons program of UNRRA in Europe and he lectured at the Schools for Social Work of Adelphi and Hunter Colleges and New York University.

*Adolph E. Wasser* is Director of the East New York YM-YWHA and is a professional social worker. He has authored many articles on Jewish social services that have appeared in professional journals. He was a recipient of the Israel Cummings Award and is a member of the Commission on Synagogue Relations.

# INTRODUCTION

## Gilbert S. Rosenthal

### The Uniqueness of the Jewish Family

"The society of scholars and the family are like a stone roof," observed the sages of Israel. "Remove a stone and it collapses; add burdens and weights and it endures solidly and firmly." This perceptive passage from the Midrash sums up the unique character and quality of the Jewish family. For if there has been *one* salient feature about the Jewish civilization it is this: the Jewish family has been exemplary—the pride of the Jewish People and a model to the gentile world. The Jewish home has become synonymous with loyalty and love, decency and devotion, kindness and consideration.

Why? What has been so unique about the Jewish family? What characteristics have been typical of the Jewish home?

Perhaps the most striking attribute of the Jewish family has been its cohesiveness. The Jewish family has always been a close-knit unit. Each member was bound to the other with bonds of love; each person was filled with a sense of duty and responsibility toward the other. This sense of responsibility extended beyond the nuclear family. It encompassed sisters and brothers, cousins and *landsleit,* distant kinsmen and Jews who happened to come from the same *shtetl* in the old country.

This tightly woven family unit was held together by common bonds: bonds of blood, bonds of heritage, bonds of history, bonds of suffering. And it was pulled together, too, by family rituals—usually of a religious nature—that brought the family members together in communion. At the Friday-night table, at the Passover Seder, during the High Holiday season—the family in its broadest extension came together to join in precious family rituals that cemented indissoluble bonds.

The second feature peculiar to the Jewish family was that traditionally each member had a clearly defined role. Father was the dominant factor and discipline figure; mother dished out milk and honey. Children knew their place in the scheme of things; grandparents played their roles, too. There were even the marginal members of the *mishpahah* (family) who had their niche: the widowed aunts, the bachelor uncle, the greenhorn cousin from the Old Country who boarded at the homestead. Each knew his place, his duties, his job. Some were disciplinarians; some dispensed love; all were expected to display *derekh eretz* (respect) to parents and elders. Each component part fit perfectly to shape the whole. In the apt words of the tuneful song, "Tradition," from the Broadway hit *Fiddler on the Roof,* "Because of our tradition, everyone here knows who he is and what God expects him to do."

Another striking feature of the Jewish family was its rich religious tradition. Jewish rituals and norms were—until relatively recently—integral parts of the Jewish home. *Mitzvot,* laws, folkways, customs, and Jewish values served as the centripetal force to counteract the centrifugal force of assimilation and apostasy. As long as the home was a kosher one, Sabbaths and festivals were observed punctiliously, laws of family purity were cherished, prayer and Torah study revered, and intermarriage disdained, few Jewish children could or would stray from the fold. The Jewish home was a "miniature sanctuary" in which the finest ideals and noblest expressions of the civilization of the Jew were concretized and sanctified in day-to-day living. And consciously and unconsciously, the

Jewish child was conditioned to be a loyal Jew and a decent human being.

A corollary to the role played by Jewish traditional values was the philosophy of marriage in the typical Jewish household. Marriage was sacred, holy, *kiddushin*—a heaven-made, divinely blessed institution sanctified not by man nor by rabbi but by God himself. Consequently, such an institution had to be revered and cherished, handled with dignity and respect, reverence and awe. It was not a casual thing to be undertaken or dissolved cavalierly or casually.

Another corollary of the religious value system of the Jewish family was the philosophy of sexuality. To the traditionally oriented Jew, sex was never viewed as dirty or profane, taboo or sinful. Rather, the sexual impulse was seen as a divine force—"the flame of God," in the words of Song of Songs. Like a flame, it could warm and illumine; like a flame, it could sear and destroy. Sexual matters were handled chastely and delicately—if at all. Lewdness and obscenity were strictly taboo; pornography was unheard of. Only in the yeshiva were sexual matters dealt with in the frank, but delicately contrived, academic discussions. Adultery and immorality were rare; perversions almost unknown. True, there were cuckolds and libertines in medieval Jewish communities. But they were the exception of the general rule that religious standards and conditioning engendered chaste and pure men and women in the Jewish community.

One facet of the Jewish home that stood out was the enormous altruism, self-sacrifice, and intensiveness with which the Jewish parent raised his offspring. One of the common Yiddish expressions was: "Everything for the children." And it was not a mere expression: It was a philosophy of life, a mode of living, a pattern. Parents would sacrifice everything and anything to make their sons rabbis, doctors, lawyers, accountants. They would go to any length to assure a good *shidukh* (match) for their daughters. Such intensiveness and smothering devotion may have created some neurotics and misfits; but it also produced Nobel Laureates and leaders in arts, letters, and industry.

Parental control was never lacking in the Jewish family. Parents showed an inordinate amount of care, concern, and control. Parents invariably chose the mates for their children; they usually directed the sons into a field of endeavor or profession. In the classic Jewish family, there was little *laissez faire* and much benevolent tyranny.

Finally, the Jewish family was profoundly shaped by its reaction to the hostility of an alien world and an enemy environment. In the face of a Christian or Moslem society that prayed for and worked for its demise via conversion or physical annihilation, Jews withdrew from society. Buffeted about on an alien, hostile sea of enmity and hatred, mistrust and contempt, the Jewish family became inner-directed. Rejected by its neighbors, the Jewish community turned in unto itself; it scorned the environment; it withdrew into its cocoon-like ghetto and isolated and insulated itself. Intercourse with the outside world was limited to casual or peripheral contacts; limited interchange of ideas or ideals took place. Why should it have? What could the Jew learn from the drunken, illiterate peasant or the brutal, venal nobleman? How could the Jew ever coexist with a world intent on annihilating every vestige of Judaism? Predictably, the Jewish family became an isolated organism—an undiluted entity in a sea of hostility. And this, too, helped it preserve its unique character and its singularly Jewish values.

All of these factors made for a uniqueness that was so extraordinary in the Jewish family.

The Jewish family had a low divorce rate and a negligible infidelity rate.

It had little incidence of alcoholism or drug addiction.

It knew of almost no wife-beating or child-molestation.

It boasted of an inordinately low rate of crime and juvenile delinquency.

In a word, the Jewish family has been as stable and enduring and secure as the Rock of Gibraltar. And this is the reason for the legendary character of the Jewish family.

## The Changing World and the New American Family

That we live in a rapidly changing world cannot be gainsaid. The pace of scientific and technological advances is breathtakingly rapid. In this process of revolution, old values and norms have been discarded and new notions and ideals are replacing them. The new world in which we live is witness to phenomenal developments in science and medicine, communications and transportation, technology and industry. But this revolution is not an unmixed blessing; new problems and tragically unforeseen consequences have developed. The American family is changing—and the changes are, regrettably, not for the better.

There is a lack of cohesiveness and adhesiveness in the American family. The components no longer interlock as in the past; people go their separate ways.

The family has achieved an unprecedented mobility. Formerly, families were born, lived, and died in the same neighborhood—frequently in the same house. Today families scatter to the four winds and once powerful fraternal bonds are frayed and broken.

In addition, the normal family roles are confused, ill-defined, obscured. The father is emasculated, often absent, frequently in default. "Momism" has afflicted too many homes; in the absence of strong male figures, mother has taken over new and unfamiliar functions in decision-making. Children are enjoying the fruits of parental default and a "teenage tyranny" is running too many American homes. Grandparents and old folks—once permanent and honored denizens of the home—are shunted aside, ignored, degraded, put away in institutions.

Obviously, religious norms have declined in significance. True, over 90 percent of Americans declare a belief in God. But less than half of Americans attend church with any regularity and fewer and fewer take their religious traditions seriously. Protestants have little regard for the commandments of their religion; Catholics (formerly so zealous in their faith) are defecting in increasingly large numbers. The college campuses where about six million of our boys and girls spend four of the most critical years of their lives have become a spiritual wilderness and a cemetery for religious values.

The mood and temper of Americans seem to be different from the past. Hedonism, egoism, selfishness, and the pursuit of pleasure are rife. The "Playboy" philosophy is widespread; the commercial use of sex is common. Sacrifice and altruism are obsolete and idealism (except in some circles on the campus and in hippieland) is passé. Far too many Americans are guided by a self-seeking, pragmatic, pleasure-gratifying philosophy that demands: "What's in it for *me*?"

Finally, a new spirit of liberalism has gripped the land. Liberalism in politics, liberalism in sex, liberalism in the media, liberalism in economics, liberalism in the matter of censorship of prurient matters. Today, scenes are acted out on stage or in movies that would have been considered obscene and liable to criminal prosecution a mere ten years ago. Today, families break up over minor infractions, whereas a generation back couples would grit their teeth and endure the worst indignities. Today, interreligious and interracial marriages are no longer viewed with horror in most circles while a generation ago such actions were adjudged sinful and revolting—or worse.

The results of these new changes in the values of the

American family are startling—and not a little alarming.

Americans divorce at a rate of over 400,000 annually—half the world's total! Between one-third and one-fourth of American marriages eventually break up.

Infidelity is no longer seen as sinful. Nor are premarital sexual acts or sexual perversions condemned with the old vigor. The Kinsey Reports have documented the changing sexual mores. A recent Gallup Poll showed that 55 percent of female collegians see nothing wrong with premarital coitus; 72 percent of the males took the same view. We have tripled the number of illegitimate births since 1940 and venereal diseases rose 230 percent from 1956 to 1965.

Juvenile delinquency has risen to shocking proportions. Over half the federal prisoners in America are under 21 and there are about 700,000 court referrals of minors each year. In 1964, 37 percent of all perpetrators of crimes were under 18 years of age and over 2.5 million children (ages 10 to 17) have police records.

The use of habit-forming drugs is soaring. Alcohol is still the chief poison of over five million addicts in this country. But now we are witnessing a new phenomenon as drugs are beginning to crowd out liquor from the campuses. A study of several Long Island colleges indicated that drugs are readily obtainable and openly sold. Many high schools report the same situation. Figures on drug usage and addiction are contradictory, but the most recent Gallup Poll indicated that at least one million collegians have tried drugs at least once. In Westport, Connecticut, 18 percent of the 1,396 students acknowledged at least one experiment with marijuana, and 69 percent of the students at Columbia University's Law School made a similar confession. Whereas drug usage was once basically limited to criminal classes and deprived ethnic groups, it is widely found today among so-called respectable middle- and upper-class whites and collegians. The soaring crime rate is doubtessly due, in part, to the proliferation of drug use and addiction.

America is also witnessing a new role for its ever-increasing aged population. In 1967, there were more than eighteen million Americans over 65 and, by 1980, 9 percent of our population—24.5 million—will achieve the magic number. But longevity has not proved to be a clear-cut blessing. Greater leisure time has engendered its problems: boredom, *ennui,* and a sense of uselessness afflict many retired citizens. And then there is the question of health: The older the person is, the more frequent the bodily breakdowns and the mental and physical illnesses. And what of the residences for our older citizens? Formerly, the old folks lived with children and formed an integral part of the family unit. Today it is not so simple: There is inadequate room in the cubicle-like apartments, and it is not easy to run a home dispensary for sick old folks. It is certainly more expedient to shelve an old, senile, feeble parent in a custodial institution, senior citizens' hotel, or home for the aged.

In sum, the changing world has changed the American family—changed it radically. The family unit is coming apart at the seams; it is shaky, tottering, unstable, insecure. And once the nuclear element of society crumbles, society itself is in peril. Clearly, the new world for which we hoped is not quite the Utopia for which we prayed.

## The Impact of the Changing World on the Jewish Family

There is an old saying, *"Vie es Christelt sich, so Judelt es sich"*—"As the Christians go, so go the Jews." There is much to commend itself in this aphorism. True, Jews before the French Revolution and ensuing Emancipation were relatively isolated from the gentile world and insulated against its blandishments. But it is a mistake to conclude that *no* interaction ever took place between the two worlds. Historically, Jews did learn from and interact with their Christian and Moslem neighbors. After the emancipation of European Jewry, that process was speeded up considerably. Since the nineteenth century, Jews have become assimilated at a faster rate than ever before in their long history. This process has been alarmingly rapid in America where Jews enjoy a unique and unparalleled degree of economic, political, social, religious, and cultural freedom.

Predictably, therefore, the Jewish family has absorbed much of the new behavior patterns of the American Christian family. The cohesive Jewish family is unraveling. Jewish families are mobile and are dispersing rapidly. The old Jewish domestic roles are blurred. Religious observances are at an unprecedentedly low level; family rituals and home observances are adhered to by a minority of America's 5.7 million Jews. Hedonism and pleasure-seeking are the favorite pastimes of America's Jews, too. *Avant-garde* liberalism has gripped our collegians. (And why not? After all, weren't we Jews traditionally the liberals of the world? Why should we, who gave mankind Moses and Jesus, Hillel and Maimonides, Marx and Freud and Einstein, take a back seat at this juncture in human history?)

And the results? To a lesser degree, the results are precisely the same as in the Christian community. The impact of the times is felt in the Jewish family as well.

Although our divorce rate is lower than that of our Christian neighbors it is climbing perceptibly.

The virus of infidelity is beginning to attack the Jewish home. Sexual aberrations are proliferating. The sexual revolution also has its Jewish accent.

Juvenile delinquency is making its mark, too. Jewish chaplains are seeing an alarming increase of young Jews in their prisons.

Drug usage and addiction were almost nonexistent ten

years ago. Today, every rabbi whose head is out of the sand will attest to this new phenomenon in Jewish life. Who would have thought that a volume on the Jewish family would include five papers on drug usage among Jews? But here is such a symposium in this volume!

Who would have dreamed two decades ago that intermarriage would pose a threat to the very survival of American Jewry? Yet the formerly low national figure of 7 percent of intermarriage has soared to probably 17 percent. In Washington, D.C., the rate of native-born Jews who intermarry is 17.9 percent; in Iowa it is a stupendous 40 percent. At Columbia University in the center of the largest Jewish concentration in the world, 33 percent of Jewish collegians interdate and over 15 percent consider it likely they will intermarry. And worse: 70 percent of the children of intermarriages are lost to Judaism!

What expert would have foreseen thirty years ago that the position of the aged would change so radically in such a short time?

And how many observers of the American-Jewish scene in the 1930's would have prophesied that 80 percent of Jewish youths of college age would be on campus in the 1960's and that 300,000 Jewish collegians would be ensconced in America's colleges and graduate schools? Moreover, who could have predicted that the colleges would become the graveyards of Jewish traditions and values and that the disaffection rate would erode the ranks of the promising Jewish youth of tomorrow?

Clearly, the new society in which Jews live is making its impact felt on the Jewish family. The Jewish family is in a changing world and not all of those changes are beneficial. In fact, if present trends continue, the Jewish family of tomorrow is likely to bear little resemblance to the family of yesteryear and many of the cherished values and ideals of the Jewish home are likely to be discarded. If this is to be the shape of things for the future, the Jewish

People is going to be confronted by a tragedy of major magnitude. For once the Jewish home becomes "an empty purse," to borrow Franz Rosenzweig's formulation, we cannot be sanguine about preserving the classical Jewish beliefs, practices, and norms that have shaped this unique phenomenon called the Jewish People.

What is to be done about reversing the trend? How can we salvage the integrity of the Jewish family from the wreckage of the American home?

We must, first of all, have the facts. For we cannot act rationally on the basis of hearsay or folk legend.

Second, Jews must gather together and talk; we must plan and program rationally for the future.

Finally, we must act—without panic, without partisanship, without overheated emotion—but coolly, rationally, soberly and intelligently.

This volume is an attempt to present the facts in a scientific and dispassionate way. It does not seek to preach or frighten; it does seek to sound the alarm and alert the Jewish community to some real and immediate perils. For if the Jewish family goes bankrupt, what hope can we hold for the future?

It is because we believe in the absolute necessity of building tomorrow on the foundation of a healthy Jewish family that this volume has been undertaken and produced.

The Jewish Family
in a Changing World

*Part I*
# The Child

# 1

# THE DEMOGRAPHY OF AMERICAN
# JEWRY

## Manheim S. Shapiro

Our subject, in plain language, is the number and kinds of
Jews there are in America. We will also consider their
marital status, the number of children they bear, how
much and what kind of education they acquire, where they
live, how they earn their livings and what their incomes
are likely to be.

Data on these subjects, for all American Jews, are
limited. There is no single, complete process equivalent to,
let us say, the decennial U.S. Census, which would give us
certain, authoritative and exhaustive information about
every Jew in the United States. Indeed, the opposition of
Jewish organizations, along with that of others who fear
breaches in the wall of separation between church and
state, has inhibited the Census Bureau from taking a
count of the religious affiliation or identification of those
it tallies. The Council of Jewish Federations and Welfare
Funds is engaged in developing a nationwide survey of the
Jewish population. Even when that is completed, however,
it will have had to rely on sampling techniques rather than
on a total census and it will be subject to the margins of
error such a process implies.

Nevertheless, in spite of these limitations, there is a
surprising amount of information we do have. It comes to
us from a variety of sources. There are the estimates
(combined with research data where they exist) which

form the bases for the analyses of Jewish population published annually in the *American Jewish Year Book*. In almost every instance when these estimates have been tested by actual research, they have turned out to be remarkably accurate.

In 1957, the Census Bureau surveyed a sampling of some 60,000 heads of household and included religious identification of those in the sample. That survey provides us with indices to some of the tendencies among Jews.

There are available reports of a number of studies of the Jewish populations of particular communities in the United States. These vary in date, type of information sought, methods used, and extensiveness. But in spite of the variations among them, these studies do provide, cumulatively, indications of what is probably true for American Jews at large. They are sufficiently scattered and diverse in size, region and community character to overcome the hazard that they cover only Jews of cities of a particular size, region or type.

Lastly, there is information acquired in the course of studies or surveys intended to obtain primarily other kinds of information. Such studies were sponsored both by Jewish bodies and by others. Whatever their purpose, however, they have often incidentally picked up information relevant to this discussion.

According to the best available estimates, as this is written, there are in the United States over 5,720,000 Jews. They are dispersed throughout the country. They tend to be concentrated, however, in particular cities, types of cities, and regions.

Approximately one-half of all American Jews live in the Greater New York Metropolitan Area (New York City proper, Westchester, Rockland, Nassau and Suffolk counties in New York State and the northeastern counties of New Jersey). About two-thirds of all American Jews live in the northeastern states: New England and the

Middle Atlantic region. Looking at the map of the United States, the Jewish population tends to be concentrated in three major areas: the states along the Eastern Seaboard from Maine to Florida; the states bordering on the Great Lakes (New York, Pennsylvania, Ohio, Indiana, Illinois, Michigan, Wisconsin, and Minnesota); and the states along the Pacific shore from southern California to Puget Sound.

American Jews tend to be not only urban but super-urban; that is, they are likely to be living in major metro-politan centers. Over 90 percent of all American Jews live in metropolitan areas with total populations of a quarter million or more. Three quarters of all American Jews can be found in the metropolitan complexes of ten major cities; New York, Los Angeles, Philadelphia, Chicago, Boston, Washington, D.C., Cleveland, Detroit, Baltimore, and San Francisco. Yet, the remaining quarter are scattered widely over the rest of the United States, in cities both large and small. There are communities of a hundred or more Jews in cities like, for example, Kokomo, Ind., Anchorage, Alaska, Muscatine, Ia., Billings, Mont., Keene, N.H., or Las Cruces, N.M. There is also a small, almost statistically negligible, proportion of Jews living on small farms but these, too, tend to be concentrated in particular areas and are diminishing.

It would be misleading to report this tendency toward urban dwelling among Jews without at least mentioning in passing that the tendency is for all Americans to become increasingly urban. At one time, in various contexts, it was fashionable for social analysts to describe the typically urban character of Jews as an "abnormal" trait. Increasingly, however, probably in most developed countries but certainly in America, to be urban tends to being the archetype of the general population. In this, as in various other social characteristics, Jews seem to have done sooner what the entire population is tending to do.

As one analyst put it, Americans generally are becoming more like Jews.

Concerning such coinciding tendencies, it should be pointed out, too, that Jews like other middle-class Americans have tended to become suburban; that is, they have migrated, especially since the end of World War II, to the satellite communities of the urban centers. There are indications that some families, particularly middle-aged or older couples whose children have grown up and left home, return to the center cities. There is no sign, however, that this is in any sense a massive movement and its future course is obviously tied to the critical questions of the rehabilitation of the major urban centers and the facilities they provide. Whether young Jewish families, for example, will choose to reside in center cities will depend to a large extent upon what happens to the schools in those centers.

Jews are more likely to marry than Americans generally are. In a number of cities where surveys were made of the Jewish population, as much as 98 percent of the adult Jewish population had been married at least once. This is a far higher rate than is true for the general population. Like the general population, however, wives tend to outlive husbands. In some of the surveyed cities, for example, in the higher age brackets, there are twice as many widows as widowers. Above the age of 70, the number of surviving males is almost negligible as compared to the surviving females. Thus, in a Detroit survey in 1963, for example, 13 percent of the Jewish women were widows as compared with 2 percent of the men who were widowers. That survey describes the prospect of "a decade of widowhood for the average Detroit Jewish woman." In Milwaukee (1964), 30 percent of the women over the age of 65, were widowed as compared to 15 percent of the men.

This phenomenon must, though, be coupled with another: that in almost every age bracket, there is a substantial number of formerly married women but only a small or nonexistent number of formerly married men. This suggests that formerly married men are more likely to remarry than their female counterparts, that they marry younger women, or, possibly, that they leave town once they have been divorced or widowed. Those who have surveyed individual communities tend to offer this last explanation as one of the reasons for the disparity between the number of formerly married women and that of formerly married men. If this is so, however, they must go to large urban centers, where their presence would be statistically insignificant, because they do not turn up in the surveys of other small or medium-sized communities.

Closely related to this is another relatively frequent phenomenon: that in most cities surveyed, in the 20-30 age group, there is a significant excess of married women over married men. In the same Detroit survey mentioned earlier, for example, 60 percent of the women between the ages of 20-29 were married, as compared to 34 percent of the men in this age category. A number of inferences may be drawn: that women marry earlier, that they marry older men, and that men are more likely to defer marriage, probably while acquiring education, training, or occupational stability.

We have referred to the "formerly married" without specific reference to separation and divorce. Hard facts about the incidence of divorce, especially within ethnic or religious groupings, are hard to come by. (There are problems of definition and relationships to time which make this an extremely elusive statistical problem.) Nevertheless, there seems little doubt that the rate of divorce among American Jews has been rising although it has probably not yet reached the level of divorce in the general population. A Greater Boston Jewish population survey (1967), for example, reports 1 percent of the Jewish adults as divorced, as compared with 6 percent of all adults in the area. However, the Boston figure refers only to marital status *at the time* of the survey and does not account for those who may have been divorced and then remarried. (An interesting project for the future might be an effort to discover whether, as compared to the greater tendency of Jews to marry generally, divorced Jews are more or less likely than other divorced persons to remarry.) An interesting clue is found in the Milwaukee survey (1964), which shows that 8 percent of the Jewish women between the ages of 35 and 44 are divorced, but only 1 percent of the Jewish women between the ages of 45 and 64 are divorced. That sharp drop may reflect the possibility that a larger proportion of the 45-64 group were foreign-born, who were less likely to be divorced; or, it may mean that the 35-44 age group were old enough to have been divorced, but not yet old enough (and possibly with young children, who are a deterrent) to have been remarried.

Certainly it is true that the Jewish immigrants were less likely, for a variety of reasons, to be divorced than their American-born children and grandchildren. As these foreign-born Jews tend to become a smaller part of the total Jewish population—or to disappear entirely—we may anticipate, if present trends continue, an upward trend in the number and percentage of Jewish marriages which end in divorce. The significance of this possibility for family stability—and for traditional Jewish attitudes —is one which merits fuller exploration in a more speculative rather than descriptive examination.

The decreasing proportion of immigrant Jews among the total Jewish population is a phenomenon of major import for a great variety of manifestations among Jews. (In our own surveys of the attitudes of Jews in four different American cities, for example, we found that the sharpest divisions in attitude toward many aspects of being Jewish, including those toward intermarriage, came between the foreign-born or those with foreign-born parents as compared with the native-born of native-born parents.) In any case, the proportion of American-born Jews has been increasing rapidly and is continuing to increase.

All the studies of Jewish communities, especially when related to the time of the surveys, reveal this upward tendency of the American-born as compared with the foreign-born; for example, the proportions of American-born for some selected cities are as follows: San Francisco (1958) 77.2 percent; Los Angeles (1959) 75.2 percent; South Bend (1961) 79.7 percent; Trenton (1961) 85 percent; Pittsburgh (1963) 88 percent; Greater Boston (1967) 85 percent. There are some statistical phenomena that are worth noting. Some cities, for example, tend to have had a much larger proportion of foreign-born than others. Thus, Rochester, N.Y., and Providence, R.I., tend to have still a relatively larger proportion of foreign-born than, let us say, Camden, N.J., or Pittsburgh. Even more interesting is the fact that there are notable differences in these proportions among the various communities in a given metropolitan area. Thus, the Boston survey of 1967 divides its total Jewish population into nine community divisions in which the proportion of immigrant population varies from 4 percent (Framingham-Natick) to 37 percent (Dorchester-Mattapan and Chelsea-Malden).

In any case, the tendency is clear. It is perhaps best summed up in this comment from the Milwaukee survey (1964) : ". . . the foreign born are almost entirely over 45 years of age, and . . . over half are already over 65 years of age. This means the next twenty-five years will witness the almost complete demise of the foreign-born group and that by 1990 the community will be composed almost entirely of persons native to the United States."

This means the gradual emergence and ultimate predominance of a new kind of Jewish aged in the United

States: American-born, American-educated and with their outlook and interests shaped by the American experience. Nor will this group be inconsequential in the determination of American Jewish group characteristics and outlook; for the Jewish group in America tends to be, as a group, older than the general population.

American Jews have, for some years, been more amenable to family planning—and to the use of the most effective methods of birth control—than has been true for the American people as a whole. Although Jews did, like other Americans, experience a "baby boom" at the end of World War II, this tapered off rapidly. Jews have neither had, nor do they seem likely to have, a "population explosion." With the extension of life expectancy at the further end of the scale, the group has tended to be more heavily weighted with the elderly. This has pushed the median age for the group toward the early forties, considerably higher than for the general American population.

As indicated, both the birth rate and fertility rate for American Jews have been lower than that for the general population. While most Jewish couples do have children, the tendency is to limit the family to two children, on the average. The major deviations from this general principle come at the lower and upper ends of the socio-economic scale; that is, for the current composition of the group, those with low incomes and those with high incomes are more likely to have more children. This is not sufficient, however, to overcome the rather static tendency of the great majority of Jews.

This means that at the present rate the Jewish group is just barely producing sufficient children to reproduce itself. If one adds to the scales the potential losses to the group which come about through intermarriage and other processes of attrition, there is a possibility that over the long run the Jewish group may dwindle, at least numerically. If this is coupled with the tendency in recent years for a rapid expansion in the general population, there is the inference to be drawn that Jews will become a smaller proportion of the whole population and one of the clear statistical facts about Jewry in Western society is that the rate of intermarrying is in inverse proportion to the relative proportion of Jews in the total society; the greater the percentage Jews form in the whole community, the less the tendency toward intermarriage.

All the above is, of course, based on the premise, "if present trends continue." Present trends may not continue. It is possible that with greater affluence, and with suburban living, the family size of Jews may increase. Even more likely is the possibility that current tendencies in the general population will be reversed. Here again it is possible that Jews have only arrived earlier at tendencies which others will manifest soon. Certainly with the dissemination of family planning information—indeed, propaganda—to groups which formerly did not receive it, with the continuous improvement of birth-control methods and devices, and with the loosening of the restraints upon birth control imposed by some church authorities, we may well see in the relatively near future a reduction at least in the rate of acceleration in the growth of the American population. If so, the sharp disparity between the rate of numerical growth of Jews and that of Americans as a whole will be dulled. Nevertheless, the numerical factor is a serious one especially when coupled with a seeming tendency for an unmeasured (though possibly substantial) falling away of Jews from identification as Jews. There is a possibility that the cries of those who advocate replenishment of the group through active programs of proselytizing may achieve greater cogency as time elapses.

As concerns general education, Jews tend to be among the most highly educated—if not the highest—of all ethnic or religious groups in the country. Perhaps their only rivals in this regard are the Episcopalians, who tend to be among the highest of all religious denominations with respect to socio-economic status and education. Virtually all Jewish children attend high school and almost all complete it. The most recent studies and estimates have shown that close to 85 to 90 percent of Jewish young people of college age are, in fact, in college. This compares to the 30 to 40 percent of this age group in the general population who attend college. The often-repeated joke is that a Jewish dropout is one who doesn't go all the way to his Ph.D.

This is, of course, the current pattern and refers to the age group currently of high school and college age. When we take the Jewish population as a whole, of course, and include the elderly, the foreign-born (whose education often cannot be evaluated by the standards of American education) and women, the averages drop, although they still represent a high proportion of educational achievement as compared with the general population or with ethnic or religious segments of that population.

Let us take a few examples: In the Detroit survey of 1963, it was found that 75 percent of the Jewish males under 45 had attended college as compared with 24 percent of that age category in the general population. For the total Jewish male adult population 54 percent had attended college as compared with 20 percent of the total male adult population of Detroit. In Greater Boston, 44 percent of all Jewish adults had attended college, as compared with 27 percent of the adults in the general population. Of the 21 to 29 age group (including women) among the Jews of Boston, 78 percent have attended college; of the total Jewish group in this age category, 16 percent have received a graduate or professional degree of some kind. In the Milwaukee study (1964), among Jewish males in the 20 to 34 age group, there are none who have not attended high school; 43 percent have been to college and another 43 percent have also been to graduate school. In short, the tendency is clear. American Jews are at the stage where the percentage of young people who attend college is rapidly approaching the 100 percent mark; it is likely, if present trends continue, that in the relatively near future virtually all Jewish young people will attend college and a majority of them will also obtain postgraduate training of one sort or another.

(We leave to speculation or further research the question of whether this is "good for the Jews," at least with respect to the amount of commitment to Jewishness. There have been assertions, and even some research evidence, though not definitive, that the college period is the one in the lives of young Jews when they detach themselves from Jewish associations and often articulate disaffection from Judaism and from the Jewish community. There is, however, another question buried within this, for which only time or ingenious research may provide the answer; viz., whether it is the college as such which produces this effect or whether it is merely the fact that this period coincides with the departure from home and the freedom from parental and communal controls which permit already existent attitudes to be expressed and acted out. Research designed to test these factors will have to test also the question of the extent to which the return to the community overcomes this attitude or, perhaps, reimposes communal expectations which have the effect of restoring Jewish involvement.)

This education pattern among Jews is an index to their occupational choices and achievements, for the employment distributions of American Jews are closely associated with high educational attainment. In general, American Jews tend to be employed predominantly as proprietors and managers, sales personnel, professionals and white-collar workers. The factory worker, the unskilled laborer and domestic employee are tending to disappear from among American Jews. Here and there (generally in those communities where there is still a relatively larger proportion of foreign-born Jews) one finds a small percentage of such workers but this is a vestige of an earlier period with the tendency clearly for no new or young worker to become occupied in such areas of employment.

The above is a relatively gross description of the occupational patterns of Jews. More specific analysis reveals some interesting changes. The large proportion of "professionals," for example, in some communities as high as 40 percent of the employed adult males, does not represent an increase in the number of Jews in the "traditional" categories of law, medicine and dentistry; rather, the increases seem to have come in such so-called "secondary" professions as optometry, pharmacy, or chiropody. Even more noteworthy is a relatively large increase in such professional occupations as engineering, scientific research of various types, and college teaching; mostly these are occupations which have comparatively recently been opened to Jews.

Again, there is a relatively high proportion of Jewish managerial and self-employed persons. In Pittsburgh (1963), for example, 30 percent of the Jewish population fell into this category as compared with 12 percent of the general population residing in the same census tracts. Again, however, there are facets which must be noted for the pattern to become clear. The large incidence of Jewish "proprietors" in studies of, say, a generation ago generally reflected a large number of personally owned businesses: "mom and pop" stores, small personal service establishments like cleaning or tailoring establishments, and small contracting businesses such as painting and paperhanging, glazing and plumbing. This occupational distribution, however, is tending to be on the way out. Such small businesses, in conformity with the general American economic patterns, are tending to become obsolete. It is unlikely that when the present older owners of such businesses die their children will maintain the businesses.

On the other hand, where small businesses became large businesses and developed into corporate entities, often with public ownership of stock, the original owners and their children have often ceased to regard or describe themselves as "owners" and tend to think of themselves as "executives" or "managers." The children, indeed, are often trained in managerial skills (such as business administration, or special fields of knowledge like merchandising or particular categories of science) so that they may take their places in what was originally a family-owned business as "executives." Still another "hidden" category is that of what might best be called "financiers"; those who have, through financial skill, amassed substantial interests in or control of corporations; such persons might classify themselves as "businessmen," as "managers," or as "executives," without describing themselves as "proprietors," which, in a technical sense, they are not.

Still another category which is showing marked changes is that of white-collar worker. This category, today, for Jews, is much more likely to refer to sales personnel than to clerks. For Jewish men, to the extent that they are engaged in "clerical" categories, they are more likely to be accountants and controllers than they are to be bookkeepers. The white-collar Jewish male is more likely to be an insurance agent than a mail clerk; an advertising salesman than a proofreader.

"Skilled workers," too, are diminishing as a proportion of the Jewish population. The children of linotypers or cigarmakers have not, by and large, entered these fields; indeed, the fields themselves are being replaced by machine processes. Even in labor unions, Jews are now more likely to be in the union management, or research or education or welfare directors, rather than organizers or shop stewards.

Finally, there is an emerging category whose impact has not yet been felt in most surveys: the educated woman who has borne and reared her children, who returns to school to refurbish or expand her education, and then seeks employment in a professional or semiprofessional category. This is a phenomenon increasingly characteristic of middle-class women for all America, but to the extent that Jews are more consistently middle class than the American populace as a whole, this pattern tends to be more frequent for Jewish women as a group.

The incomes of American Jews, as might be expected from their levels of education, their occupations, and their "achievement-orientation," are comparatively high. In the middle fifties, the U.S. Census Bureau sampling of heads of households revealed that the median income of Jewish heads of households was considerably higher than that of either Protestant or Catholic heads of households. Those were, of course, gross figures. The margin of difference would have been reduced had the comparison been made with "white Protestants," or, better still, with "urban white Christians." Nevertheless, almost all surveys do show a tendency for Jews to earn more than their equivalent Christian peers.

Even apart from the comparative level of income, however, is the absolutely high income figures of American Jewish households. Thus, the Milwaukee study (1964) revealed that the median income for all Jewish families was $9,485, as compared with one of $7,900 for the Milwaukee population at large. Strikingly, fully 27 percent of the Jewish families had an annual income of $15,000 or more. (It is to be assumed both that families tended to under-report income and that incomes have increased substantially since 1964.)

Bearing in mind the tendency for Jews to achieve higher education, that survey made an interesting correlation between college training and earnings. Thus, 85 percent of those earning $15,000 to $19,999 had been to college. The tendency, therefore, for almost all Jews to attend college makes it more than likely that as time goes on, the income level of Jews as a group will continue to rise. This conclusion is strengthened by the awareness that the older segment of the population is also likely to include that segment of the Jewish population which was restricted in economic opportunity by being foreign-born and less well educated and by discriminatory patterns which are less oppressive today.

The Milwaukee figures of relatively high income levels for American Jews are consistently repeated, without the necessity to repeat them here, by all surveys in other cities where income was included in the study. However, an important qualification must be noted here. While it is true that the income picture for Jews *as a group* conveys an image of general affluence, this should not be misconstrued to imply that *all Jews* are affluent or even well-to-do. Thus, for example, the 1967 survey of Greater Boston reveals that 8 percent of the Jewish families had incomes under $3,000 and another 21 percent had incomes under $6,000; in other words, almost a third of all the Jewish families in the Greater Boston area had incomes under $6,000. This compares relatively favorably with the fact that 41 percent of all Boston families fall in this level. But that 29 percent of the Boston Jewish population with relatively low incomes, some below the government definition of poverty, is a significant corrective to the tendency to think of all Jews as economically successful and free of care.

True enough, a large proportion of that low-income group consists of the elderly and the infirm. They are likely, with time, to disappear. Yet, they are with us. Their ultimate disappearance, while it will raise the statistical picture of American Jewish income level even higher, is of small relevance to an accurate picture of what prevails today.

## SUMMARY

There are in America today some five and three-quarter million American Jews. They tend to cluster in the East, the upper Middle West, and along the West Coast. Nevertheless, there are Jews in virtually every part of the United States. They are super-urban and suburban rather than rural.

They are more likely to be married than are Americans generally, but seem to be approaching the level of the whole population in the incidence of divorce among them. They bear relatively fewer children than the American population as a whole although there are some indications that this difference may be reduced, more likely by a reduction in the rate of general American population expansion than by a sharp increase in Jewish reproduction. Because of the low birthrate, American Jews tend to be a relatively older segment of the whole population.

Jews have a high level of educational attainment and are tending toward virtually total college education for Jewish young people. This tendency is associated with a parallel tendency to increasing proportions who obtain postgraduate and professional training.

Occupationally, Jews tend to concentrate in the ownership, management, professional, and white-collar categories although the concentrations within these categories are shifting from generation to generation and as new categories open in the economy. (We may expect in the near future a relatively large concentration of Jews in computer-related occupations.)

Incomes of Jews are relatively high, as might be expected from the occupations in which they are found. However, there remains a substantial proportion of poor Jews.

In describing human phenomena, it is hazardous to make predictions. Nevertheless, unless there should be some sudden, cataclysmic events in the society as a whole, or for Jews in particular, it is likely that the tendencies described above will continue for the foreseeable future: a static, or only slowly increasing, Jewish total population; high levels of education, high income and concentration in major urban population centers, though not in city centers.

# 2

# ADOPTION AND THE JEWISH COMMUNITY

## Florence Kreech

Adoption has become increasingly popular in the United States. In 1967, 158,000 children were placed for adoption. Thirty-five years ago the number placed was 16,000. In earlier years adoption agencies had to seek families who might be interested in adoption. There were many who looked rather skeptically at the idea. Later the picture changed and agencies became concerned about having to turn away many couples who wished to adopt. Most nonsectarian agencies throughout the country reported a ratio of at least ten applicants for each white child on referral for adoption.

The situation was especially difficult for Jewish families. The ten to one ratio was applicable only to the Jewish agency in New York City. In other cities the ratio was much larger and in many it was just not possible to adopt a Jewish child at all.

About five years ago the situation changed. The ten to one ratio disappeared. Some nonsectarian agencies reported a ratio of two to three families for each child; others reported more children than families. This situation has always existed for black children; for white children it was a new phenomenon. More children could be placed for adoption because of the increase in the number of children born out of wedlock. Also, the more flexible attitude on the part of agencies made it possible to place many children for adoption who were formerly considered unadoptable. Another factor in the change of ratio between families and children was the increase in withdrawals by couples because of pregnancy. The medical field has become increasingly successful in helping couples faced with the problem of infertility.

Jewish agencies were not faced with the problem of having more children than families. The number of Jewish families applying to adopt still outnumbered the Jewish children who could be placed. However, there was a decided increase in the number of Jewish children for adoption. For the first time Jewish couples had a better opportunity to adopt. The New York agency's ratio was no longer ten to one; it became three to one. Jewish agencies that formerly had no children for adoption were able to place several each year. In some cities the number of Jewish children increased from five a year to 25 or 30. There were even some Jewish agencies that began to wonder whether they, too, might eventually be confronted with an insufficient number of families.

In those states where the law permits placement across religious lines, more Jewish families were adopting non-Jewish children. Faced with an insufficient number of adoptive homes, nonsectarian agencies in such states welcomed the opportunity of placing with Jewish families. Also, where not prohibited by law, non-Jewish unmarried mothers surrendered their children to Jewish agencies for adoptive placement.

## The Current Picture

The current situation shows another drastic change. All over the country agencies report a decrease in the number of white children surrendered for adoption. Once again Jewish couples are finding it increasingly difficult to adopt. There has been a nation-wide decrease in adoptive placements of Jewish children since 1965. In a recent survey by the Council of Jewish Federations and Welfare Funds most Jewish agencies reporting an increase stated that this was due to the fact that a number of non-Jewish children were placed with Jewish families.[1]

## Adoption and Religion

The decrease in the number of Jewish children limits the opportunity for Jewish families who wish to adopt. If the current pattern continues, in the future even fewer Jewish families will be able to become parents by adoption. The number could increase some if adoption laws relating to religion were changed in those states that still restrict placements to families of the child's religious faith. In addition to laws that prohibit placements across religious lines, there are also agencies with rigid policies in relation to religion. As a result, there are large numbers of children denied adoption because of religion.

The Standards on Adoption of the Child Welfare League of America state:

> It is not in the best interests of the child if requirements for religious matching, as determined by state laws, agency policies, or the obligation to respect wishes of parents, work to deprive any child of the opportunity for adoption. In those instances where religious matching is required by law, it may be possible to make legal provision, through use of waivers, for parents who wish to do so, to give the agency permission to place the child in a family of another religion or in the best available home.

The Standards further state:

> The family selected for a child should be one in which the child will have an opportunity for religious or spiritual and ethical

---

[1] *Survey by the Council of Jewish Federations and Welfare Funds*, 1968 (unpublished).

development; but religious background alone should not be the basis for the selection of a family for a child.[2]

## Adoption of Interracial Children

Adoption of more interracial Jewish children and non-white children of other religions would also increase adoption opportunities for Jewish families. Experience has shown that there are many families who can successfully adopt a child of a race different than their own. The Louise Wise Services in New York City has had the most experience of any Jewish agency in the placement of non-white children. It placed almost 500 nonwhite children for adoption in the past sixteen years. The majority of these children were interracial, born to white Jewish mothers and black fathers. Most were placed with black families, but there has been an increase in the number of white families, Jewish and non-Jewish, applying for these children. In addition, Louise Wise Services has placed 53 American Indian children with white families, Jewish and non-Jewish.

Both black and white people have raised questions with regard to transracial placements. Some have asked if it is fair to the child to place him with a white family. To answer this question we need to look at the alternatives. There is a dearth of adoptive families for black and interracial children. Is it, therefore, "fair" for a child to remain in a foster home or institution rather than be placed with a family of another race? Also, in the case of children of two races, should we always decide to consider only one race in selecting a home for him?

Louise Wise Services does not seek white families instead of black. For interracial children of the black and white races, black families are the most suitable for the

---

[2] *Child Welfare League of America Standards for Adoption Service*, pp. 18 and 35 (Revised printing, 1968).

majority of the children. White families simply increase the adoption possibilities. The need is so great that families of all races and religions should be considered.

Louise Wise Services recognizes the many questions that must be faced in transracial placements, especially with regard to the future of these children and parents. Nobody has the answers. More experience is needed. Most of the families who adopt children of races other than their own attend discussion groups at the agency where they have the opportunity of discussing with other families their experience with adoption and questions that have arisen with regard to their child's race. Approximately twenty white families who adopted interracial children during the past four years are participating in the agency's follow-up study of transracial placements. This will continue for several years.

*Agency Services For Adoptive Parents*

As was stated before, it is more difficult for a Jewish than a non-Jewish family to adopt because there are relatively fewer Jewish children available. Beyond that there are no essential differences between Jewish and non-Jewish adoptions. There are differences between biological parents and adoptive parents which are shared by Jew and non-Jew alike. It is here that social agencies can be most helpful.

Selection of the family is only the first step in adoption. Living together and becoming integrated as a family is adoption in a broader sense. Adoptive parents are like all parents in most ways. There are some things that they share in common only with other adoptive parents. Being adoptive parents adds something extra to the difficult job of parenthood.

Many who adopt because of their inability to have a child by birth struggle with their feeling about this. For some there is conflict about the natural parents of their adopted child and the fact that he was born out of wedlock. Most adoptive parents have questions and need help with regard to explaining adoption to family and friends, and to their adopted child.

The adopted child also has special needs because of the social and emotional implications of being an adopted child and the deprivation he may have suffered in the earlier loss of the biological parents. He needs help in understanding the reasons why he was given up for adoption; that it was because of concern about his well-being and not because he was not wanted.

Adoption agencies cannot give formulas to adoptive parents for handling questions such as how best to help their child understand adoption. Agencies can only give general guides and can try to help adoptive parents develop an awareness of their own feelings. Most people who adopt wish that their child had been born to them and that they would not have to tell him about adoption. It is helpful to them to learn that such feelings are shared by most other adoptive parents; that this does not indicate failure and that they do not need to feel guilty about it.

It is important for adoptive parents to know of the agency's readiness to be of help prior to legal adoption and also afterward. For many parents group discussions can be meaningful in giving them the opportunity for sharing with and learning from each other. Therefore, individual counseling and group meetings, before and after legal adoption, should be offered as part of an adoption service.

## The Unmarried Parents

Adoption deals with three groups of individuals: children, adoptive parents, and the unmarried parents. Frequently, when Jewish people speak of adoption, they tend to relate only to the families wishing to adopt and do not think about the natural parents of the child placed for adoption or the families of these unwed parents. Surprise is sometimes expressed that Jewish young women also become pregnant out of wedlock and that they represent a cross section of the entire Jewish community. Hundreds of Jewish families each year are faced with the problem of their daughter becoming pregnant out of wedlock or of their unmarried son impregnating a young woman. Sexual mores are changing, but it is doubtful that out-of-wedlock births are acceptable to most families. The increasing number of interracial children born to Jewish unwed mothers has added a further problem for the family. Likewise, the fact that an increasing number of white unmarried mothers, Jewish and non-Jewish, keep their children affects Jewish family life. (It is also a factor in the decrease in the number of Jewish children available for adoptive placement.)

The figures on out-of-wedlock births have shown a steady increase. In 1966, there were 302,400 out-of-wedlock births in the United States. It is estimated that by 1970 this figure will rise to 350,000. It is interesting to note that although there has been a decrease in total births, statistics show a continuous increase in out-of-wedlock births. The figures for New York City on total births and out-of-wedlock births in a three-year period were as follows:

| Total Live Births In N.Y.C. | Out-of-Wedlock Births In N.Y.C. |
|---|---|
| 1965—158,815 | 1965—20,980 |
| 1966—153,334 | 1966—22,714 |
| 1967—145,802 | 1967—24,336[3] |

In spite of the increase in out-of-wedlock births, in the

---

[3] Report from the City of New York Department of Health, Bureau of Records and Statistics, September 19, 1968.

white as well as in the black group, agencies report a decrease in the number of white unmarried mothers applying for agency help. Many people assume that the "pill" is responsible for this decrease in the number of white mothers applying to agencies. The "pill" is undoubtedly a factor in the decrease of total births, and may also account for the decrease in the number of college girls applying for help. However, since out-of-wedlock births continue to increase, in all races and religions, the "pill" is not the answer.

Significant changes are noted by agencies serving unmarried mothers. Residence facilities are used for shorter periods of time than in the past and a larger number of young women remain in the community throughout their pregnancy. Agencies also report an increase in the number of white mothers keeping their babies.

In order to meet the present needs of unmarried parents, agencies need to evaluate their programs to determine whether they have adapted their service to the changing mores and changing needs. Agencies that have seen the unmarried mother only in terms of her being the means by which the agency can place a child for adoption must change their concept of the unwed mother and their responsibility to her. Whether she keeps her baby or places him for adoption, she *is* the agency's client. The increasing number of mothers keeping their children makes it necessary for agencies to extend their services. In addition to individual casework and group counseling, assistance is needed by many in housing (for mothers and babies), day care, schooling, and employment.

Some Jewish agencies are not doing enough to inform the community of the availability of help for unwed mothers. They prefer to create the illusion that "this does not happen to Jewish girls," or if it does, it is best not to let the community know about it. As a result, the Jewish unmarried mother feels that she must leave the community, arrange for a private adoption or an illegal and unsafe abortion.

Jewish agencies need to reach out to the Jewish unwed mother and her family. They must show their readiness to be of help with all essential prenatal and postnatal services.

There are some unmarried mothers who prefer to plan for themselves and who will not be interested in agency help. It is likely that the majority of Jewish young women, pregnant out of wedlock, will accept help that is geared to their individual needs.

Agency services should also be available to the father of the baby and to the parents of the unmarried mother and father. Involving the father in planning for the child is recognition that the child has two parents. This is especially important if the child is not surrendered for adoption. The child has a right to his father's interest in him, if this is in accord with the wishes of his mother and father.

## Responsibility Toward the Entire Community

Many Jewish children's agencies pride themselves in the fact that they provide care for all Jewish children in need of help. At the same time, in many communities there are hundreds, or even thousands of children who are uncared for. Some Jewish agencies believe that they are responsible only for the Jewish community. They will accept non-Jewish unmarried mothers and their children if the children can be placed for adoption with Jewish families. The sole interest is in the couple wishing to adopt and not in the unmarried mother.

The attitude differs in other communities where help is given to non-Jewish children because of the agencies' desire to expand service and to assist in meeting the growing need of all children. Such agencies see provision of services to Jewish children as their primary responsibility, but also feel an obligation to serve non-Jewish children. They believe that it is within the tradition of the Jewish faith to help all people regardless of religion or race.

The writer firmly believes that Jewish agencies should not feel satisfied with their accomplishments when so many children in every community throughout the country are in desperate need. Of course, Jewish agencies have a responsibility to the Jewish community. They also have a responsibility to the total community.

The changing attitudes by some Jewish children's agencies are reflected in a number of Jewish federations. In his annual report, presented in May, 1968, the president of the Federation of Jewish Philanthropies of New York City, stated: "Here in New York, our Jewish community, through Federation, has done a superb job in community organization for over 50 years. We have organized ourselves to provide services primarily for our Jewish community . . . but we have also accepted our role in and responsibility to the total community and over the years have moved forward to make services available to our neighbors of all races and religions. The welfare of our Jewish community is indivisible from the whole city in which we live."[4]

Many other Jewish Federations across the country have taken action on the urban crisis. The May, 1968, issue of the *Jewish Community Newsletter* referred specifically to the Federations in Boston, Philadelphia, Cleveland, Pittsburgh, and Detroit. The *Newsletter* stated that a number of other federations are in the planning stages of programs dealing with actions to help strengthen the local urban coalitions.[5]

---

[4] Annual Report by Samuel J. Silberman, President, Federation of Jewish Philanthropies, New York City, May 6, 1968.
[5] Monthly Publication of the Council of Jewish Federations and Welfare Funds, New York City, May, 1968.

A recent publication of the Child Welfare League of America dealt with the question of commitment to ensure the well-being of every child. The article states: "In the last four years, individuals in the child welfare field, along with others in social work, have become gravely concerned that major social policies in our country still show a lack of commitment to the well-being of children. . . . Those who are responding to the agitation are saying that every child welfare agency should be the advocate of every child in its community and that agencies have no choice but to awaken our society to the fact that countless numbers of children are in jeopardy and that our country's future policies must truly support and protect child life."[6]

Not only do Jewish agencies have a responsibility to be the advocate of all children; they must be ready to give direct help. As Jews and as social workers, we have no alternative. Children cannot wait. Tomorrow is too late!

---

[6] Rebecca Smith, "Developments in Child Welfare, 1962–1967," *Child Welfare*, March, 1968.

## 3

# LEISURE TIME AND THE JEWISH FAMILY

## Bernard Warach

*Introduction*

Shall we really look forward to the "brave new world" of Aldous Huxley, in which the few Alphas may enjoy the privilege of work and responsibility, and the multitudes are destined to a life of empty pleasure?

When does work end and leisure begin? With the increase in leisure time, leisure has become a matter of public concern, and a social problem. We retain a sense of misgiving with the increase in leisure time. The Calvinist feeling in American culture that work is good and idleness is sinful retains a compelling force. In Jewish literature, the Sages reflect their moral objection to the misuse of leisure in *Sehok,* useless degenerate play, or in idleness and boredom.

There is confusion and dispute over the meaning of the word "leisure." Is leisure recreation, play, free time, fun or amusement? The meanings of particular leisure activities differ for individuals, occupations, and social classes. Gardening may be hard work, yet a weekend pleasure for some suburbanites.

*Leisure Defined*

Leisure has been defined as the free time available to the individual after the practical necessities of life have

63

been attended to, as the time not occupied by making a living, as discretionary time.[1] Our concepts of leisure are rooted in historic religious beliefs and social practice. In Western society leisure was, up until recent times, available to the upper classes, but not to the masses. In 1912, Veblen defined leisure as "primarily non-productive consumption of time, from a sense of the unworthiness of labor."[2]

In very recent times, progressive social and educational movements have espoused the cause of leisure and the provision of facilities, programs, and leadership for its pursuit. The need for constructive recreation and play has been justified as a basic human requirement. The American recreation movement has succeeded in gaining universal acceptance of the notion that all people require leisure and opportunities for recreation.

The increase in leisure time in American society has quite obviously affected the lives of Jewish people, as individuals and as families. The need for rest and refreshment, for the body as well as the soul, had long been recognized in Jewish religious law. Significant resources have been devoted to leisure time institutions by the Jewish community in America. The early development of the Jewish settlement house, of the YM-YWHA movement, of Jewish youth and adult organizations, and of secular activities of synagogues all represent a Jewish communal response to the need to provide opportunities for constructive leisure time activities.

As the pursuit of leisure becomes a way of American life, a number of major problems related to its significance and meaning have been of deep concern to the Jewish community. These have included: the need to

---

1. Esther S. Neumeyer and Martin H. Neumeyer, *Leisure and Recreation.* New York: A. S. Barnes & Co., rev. 1949, Chapter 1.
2. Thorstein Veblen, *The Theory of the Leisure Class.* New York: Macmillan, 1912, p. 43.

strengthen programs of Jewish education and leisure time activities for youth; enlisting Jewish college students in Jewish social organizations; increasing intermarriage; the quality of Jewish family life; and the provision of leisure time activities for the elderly. The resolution of these complex problems will require considerable study of the varied facets of the leisure phenomenon.

## The Increase in Leisure Time

American technological achievement has made possible a reduction in the six-day, 60-hour week of the turn of the century, to the five-day, 40-hour work week prevailing today. The two-week paid vacation for office, sales, professional, and industrial workers has become universal. In addition, the majority of American workers receive seven or more paid holidays.[3] Most Jewish families also observe the High Holidays, adding to the cycle of leisure days.

The life cycle in work patterns has changed. The years of childhood now continue considerably beyond high school. Eighty percent or more of Jewish youth go to college. With the increasing life span, more years are spent at work; in 1900 an average of 32.1 years, to 45.1 years today.[4] Upon reaching 65, we can now anticipate another 14 years of leisure time in retirement.[5] Still, not all people retire. At ages 65 to 69 half remain at work; for men 70 and over, approximately one fourth are working or seeking work. Relatively fewer working women remain at work after 65: 33 percent of the single women,

3. Peter Henle, "Recent Growth of Paid Leisure for U.S. Workers." *Monthly Labor Review*, March, 1962, U.S. Department of Labor, Washington, D.C.
4. Seymour L. Wolfbein, "The Changing Length of Working Life," in Eric Larrabee and Rolf Meyersohn, eds., *Mass Leisure*. Glencoe, Ill.: The Free Press, 1958, p. 158.
5. Ben J. Wattenberg and Richard M. Scammon, *This U.S.A.*. Garden City: Doubleday, 1965, p. 24.

7 percent of the married women, and 20 percent of the widowed, divorced, or separated.[6]

The Southern California Research Council, in a study completed in 1968, concluded that by 1985 Americans will be able to enjoy six-month vacations and still maintain the present standard of living.[7]

The new leisure was made possible by technologic achievement. Trade unions have been the compelling force in securing the gains of increased productivity in added leisure for the blue collar worker, and now the white collar worker as well. In the New York Metropolitan area, the electrical unions have negotiated a basic work week of 32 hours, after which overtime pay begins.

And yet, for many, the "soaring sixties" were years of greater pressure, harder work, and longer hours than prior decades. As reported by Wilensky, large numbers of professionals, sales people, executives, and small business men continued to work extraordinarily long hours; 45 to 60 hours a week were not unusual. These, of course, are precisely the occupations in which a great number of Jews are found. Even at higher income levels the propensity to work longer and harder continues to be characteristic.[8] The Protestant ethic, rooted in the Biblical precept, "By the sweat of your brow shall you get bread to eat. . ." (Genesis 3:19), has obviously been adopted as a pervasive value in the life style of many Jewish men.

Moreover, the shortened work week and increase in vacation time have produced the phenomenon of the

6. Margaret S. Gordon, "Work and Patterns of Retirement," in Robert W. Kleemeier, ed., *Aging and Leisure*. New York: Oxford University Press, 1961, pp. 15–49.
7. "An Age of Leisure Expected by 1985," dateline Los Angeles, April 6, 1968, *The New York Times*, p. 28.
8. Harold L. Wilensky, "The Uneven Distribution of Leisure: The Impact of Economic Growth on 'Free Time,'" in Erwin O. Smigel, ed., *Work and Leisure*. New Haven: College & University Press, 1963, pp. 107–37.

second job—moonlighting.[9] In New York substantial numbers of school teachers, particularly men, many of whom are Jewish, have secured part-time employment after school hours and full-time jobs during the summer recess to supplement their income.

Women have chosen to return to work, as the trend toward smaller families and mechanism and simplification of household chores has continued. There has been a striking change in the participation of women in the labor force. In 1960, 41 percent of all women between the ages of 18 and 64 worked, compared with 31 percent in 1940.[10] The return of women to work at ages 45 to 54 has been the major factor contributing to this increase. As a consequence, women may enjoy no more leisure time than heretofore.

## The Pursuit of Leisure

How has this new leisure time been used? Despite the limited number of studies of the use of leisure time, some broad conclusions can be drawn. Studies of leisure have included inquiries into expenditures for leisure and recreation, the frequency of participation in activities and their importance, and the length of time devoted to specific pursuits.

## Expenditure Studies

National expenditures for leisure and recreation have become a major element in the economy.

A study completed by *Fortune* Magazine in 1955 estimated these expenditures to be $306 billion per annum.

9. Harvey Swados, "Less Work—Less Leisure," in *Mass Leisure*. Eric Larrabee and Rolf Meyersohn, eds., Glencoe, Ill.: The Free Press, 1958, pp. 353–363.
10. Ben J. Wattenberg and Richard M. Scammon, *This U.S.A.* Garden City: Doubleday, 1965, p. 182.

These expenditures have continued to rise during the past fourteen years. Expenditures on amusements, athletics, pleasure travel, boating, and games amounted to $18 billion. The second group of expenditures, totalling over $12.6 billion, included purchases of alcohol ($8.9 billion), television, radios, records, and eating out for pleasure.[11]

In a survey of consumer expenditures for recreational goods and services completed in 1956 by the U.S. Department of Commerce, which defined a more limited number of activities as recreational, expenditures were estimated at $12.4 billion. Major elements of expenditure were:

*Consumer Expenditures for Recreational Goods and Services, by Type, 1956*[12]

| | Amount (Billions of Dollars) | Per Cent |
|---|---|---|
| Theaters and Entertainment | 1.5 | 12.4 |
| Spectator Sports | .241 | 1.9 |
| Club and Fraternal Organizations | .633 | 5.1 |
| Participant Recreation | 1.097 | 8.8 |
| Reading | 1.015 | 8.2 |
| Gardening | .794 | 6.4 |
| Radios, Television, Music | 3.198 | 25.7 |
| Sports Equipment | 3.020 | 24.3 |
| Other Goods and Services | .895 | 7.2 |

Studies of consumer expenditures indicate the use of 5 to 6 percent of family income for recreation services and equipment. Expenditures rise modestly with increasing income levels, and fall proportionately after age 65. Inclusion of alcohol and dining out for pleasure as leisure expenditures would increase estimates of consumption to 12 percent of disposable income. The Community Council of Greater New York, in establishing a "modest but ade-

11. The Editors of *Fortune,* "30 Billion for Fun," Chapter X, in *The Changing American Market.* New York: Time, Inc., 1955.
12. Derived from U.S. Department of Commerce, *Survey of Current Business,* July, 1957, Table 30, p. 21.

quate" Family Budget Standard in October 1966 suggested the allocation of 8 percent ($9.25) of a net weekly income of $115 for a family of four for recreation, education, and tobacco.[13]

*Activity Studies*

Watching television at home ranks as the single most popular leisure activity for most Americans. Other leisure-time activities, in order of preference, appear to be: visiting with friends and relatives, working around yard or garden, reading magazines and books, pleasure driving, listening to records, going to meetings and organization activities, hobbies, going out to dinner, participating in sports, playing cards and table games, going to sports events, the movies, and to plays, concerts, and lectures.[14]

On the average weekday, the average male adult between 20 and 49 spends 3½ hours per day in leisure pursuits; at 50 years of age, 5 hours of leisure are available. Women of the same ages may have an extra hour a day of free time. Many activities have multiple character and significance. People can work and listen to the radio. Television is the most exclusive and demanding of leisure activities. The most significant change in the daily time budget occurs for men upon their retirement. Work time and commuting time, together amounting to nine to ten hours per day in the metropolitan areas, is eliminated, and new leisure patterns must be established.

In 1955, Alfred C. Clarke conducted a study in Columbus, Ohio, which confirmed the relationship between social status and leisure styles, and between occupational structure and the use of leisure time. The highest prestige-

---

13. *How to Measure Ability to Pay for Social and Health Services*. New York: Community Council of Greater New York, 1967, p. 25.
14. Sebastian and De Grazia, "The Uses of Time," in Robert W. Kleemeier, ed., *Aging and Leisure*. New York: Oxford University Press, 1961.

level individuals were most inclined to participate in attending theatrical plays, concerts, lectures, visiting museums, attending fraternal organizations and conventions, doing community service work, reading for pleasure, studying, and entertaining at home. These leisure-time activities are typical of Jewish men and women in all communities. By contrast, individuals of lower-prestige levels watched more television, spent more time fishing, playing poker, driving for pleasure, socializing in a tavern, visiting the zoo, and attending baseball games. Commercial recreation consumed relatively little time for all classes. Craftsmanlike activities interest varied inversely with the prestige level. Given added leisure time, the study respondents would, at the upper-class level, spend more time at reading and study, and, at the lower-class level, would rest, loaf, and relax.[15]

## Voluntary Association Membership and the Use of Leisure Time

Despite De Toqueville's early observations, large numbers of Americans are not joiners, and only a minority belong to more than one voluntary organization. In a national study completed in 1955, Wright and Hyman found 64 percent of American adults were members of *no* voluntary association, exclusive of union membership, and only 20 percent members of one, 9 percent members of two, 4 percent members of three, and 3 percent members of four or more organizations.

Differences in rates of membership distinguish the major religious subgroups of the population. The highest rate of membership is found among the Jews, next highest among Catholics, followed by the Protestants. Further studies have demonstrated that membership in formal

15. Alfred C. Clarke, "Leisure and Occupational Prestige." *American Sociological Review,* vol. 21, no. 3, June, 1956, pp. 301–7.

associations increases with higher social status. However social status is measured—by family income, education, occupation, or home ownership—this correlation is maintained.[16]

## The Calendar

At the turn of the century, in communities throughout the country, there was no doubt that the United States was a Christian country on Sunday. Public Sabbath day laws enjoined the citizens from visiting the saloon or attending commercial recreations. Sunday was celebrated quietly. The Sunday "blue laws" have been generally repealed and amended to permit citizens to enjoy the holiday at their pleasure. The mass exodus of Americans from their cities to weekend resorts, parks, and beaches is commonplace.

The weekly calendar marks the two-day weekend and some five to seven legal holidays as discretionary time. Regular weekly attendance at churches and synagogues has diminished. American public celebration of the holidays—Memorial Day, July 4, Lincoln's and Washington's Birthdays—has diminished and become insignificant. In a rationalized industrial society, there remains little sense of individual or family participation in communally sanctioned holidays.

The character of work will affect the quality, choice, and significance of leisure time activities of the individual and his family. In Wilensky's judgment, work has grown more disciplined in sequence and training, more inflexible in daily and weekly routines, and subject to more formal constraints than ever. The professionals, engineers, doctors, lawyers, teachers, professors, social workers, scientists, technicians, and salespeople are becoming more

16. Charles R. Wright and Herbert H. Hyman, "Voluntary Association Memberships of American Adults." *American Sociological Review,* vol. 23, no. 3, June, 1958, pp. 284–94.

bureaucratized. The accelerated pace of social and economic change increases the pressures upon the service vocations. The growing shortage of manpower in all of the services will maintain the pressure for higher productivity and a longer work week and a continued invasion of "leisure time" with work-related pursuits.

We are deeply impressed with the complexity of the leisure phenomenon in American society. By imperceptible increments, year after year, more time away from work— more paid vacations—have become available to millions of Americans. With continued full employment and rising income levels, the life of every American family has been affected by the new leisure. Even for those families whose gain in leisure time has been limited, the widespread enjoyment of leisure activities and their general acceptance have affected their outlook and their way of life. The Jewish family, so sensitive to social change, has been significantly affected by the new leisure.

*The Transformation of the Jewish Family in America*

The new leisure has been only one of many social forces affecting the transformation of the Jewish family. The impact of the new leisure cannot be understood without a brief appreciation of the history and culture of a people.

Amongst countless young Jewish immigrants, an older prophetic Judaism commingled with idealistic secular philosophies of the nineteenth century. Many immigrants identified with the idealism of the Social Democrats of the German States of 1848, of the Russian Narodniks of the 1880's, with the varied strains of socialism and nihilism of Eastern Europe. Plainly, the seeds of social change were carried across the oceans, and germinated in the teeming ghettos of the cities.

Great masses of Jewish youth shed their religious orthodoxy, even before disembarking in America. The poor immigrant had to work long hours, and six days a week or more, to make a living. The cruel demands of the American market place completed the destruction of the values of the traditional religion of a people, and of the way of life of the small Old World village. But this destruction was by no means complete. There remain significant numbers of the Chasidim and of the Orthodox who still maintain traditional practices. For the larger body of American Jews, members of Conservative and Reform congregations, or none at all, elements of historic Judaism remain—above all, profound attitudes and beliefs governing family life.

The impoverished Jewish immigrant, however buffeted by the vicissitudes of life, could find love, warmth and sustenance in the bosom of his family. Judaism placed the highest value on the family.

## The Sabbath

Jewish family life was governed by the weekly cycle of six days of work and the celebration of the Sabbath. The adjuration of Exodus 20: 8-11 states, "Remember the Sabbath day and keep it holy. Six days shall you labor and do your work, but the seventh day is a Sabbath of the Lord your God." In Jewish tradition, the Sabbath was not merely an enlightened act of social legislation to provide for a day of rest. As one of the Ten Commandments, observance of the Sabbath remains a fundamental tenet of religious law. The Sabbath was an "eternal covenant" between God and Israel. Rabbinical authorities have held the Sabbath to be "the single institution most directly responsible for the survival of the Jewish people."[17] In traditional Judaism, the Sabbath day of leisure

---

17. Rabbi Norman Lamm, *The Sabbath as Law, as Philosophy, and as Model for a Theory of Leisure,* presentation to the Jewish Education Committee, April 2, 1968.

is pervaded by religious significance. In its celebration, the Jewish family acknowledges God as Creator, and the Creation itself. Work is forbidden, and the Sabbath is actively celebrated and enjoyed. The study of the Torah is traditional Judaism's classical prescription for securing spiritual refreshment on the Sabbath.[18]

Rabbinical advisers have provided varied interpretations of appropriate activity and behavior on the Sabbath. There continues to be great debate and conflict within the Jewish community over the issue of appropriate observance of the Sabbath in communal institutions. There is no doubt, however, that most Jewish families in America no longer celebrate the Sabbath in traditional fashion. Synagogue attendance on the Sabbath has sharply diminished.

Despite the obstacles—tenement overcrowding, large families, and the unremitting anxieties of life in America —life improved materially. The restlessness, energy, and capacity of the Jewish immigrant for change and adaptation was noted. A heavy price was paid for this achievement. The single-minded devotion, long hours of work and study, the discarding of traditional ethics, the fierce competition and pace of the Jewish trades, all took a heavy toll in the physical and psychological well-being of the immigrant. The price of the success of the American Jew, in so short a time, is still being paid.

## The Acculturation of the Jewish Family

The American Jewish family of today has acquired many of the characteristics of typical American families. Indeed, it has been observed that American Jewish families have become most like upper middle-class Protestants, the dominant Anglo-Saxon group in the United States.

18. *Ibid.,* p. 23.

Nevertheless, we can discern the distinctive character and elan of the Jewish family.

The social findings of the very modest number of studies in Jewish sociology provide some useful data in understanding the Jewish family. Demographers suggest a national population of over 5,700,000 Jews in 1969, with over 1,500,000 family units of 3.1 persons per family in cities, and 3.5 persons in suburbia.[19] Jews, saving only the very pious Chasidim, have completely planned families, with fewer children than most other strata of American society.

The Jewish population appears to be older and more mature than the general population. There are estimated to be fewer children under 14, fewer youth 14-19, fewer young adults 20-24, and a greater proportion of people 25-64, and 65 years of age and older. The Jewish population has maintained its numbers and increased moderately by maintaining significantly lower rates of infant mortality and the higher longevity rates up to middle age, typical of a highly urbanized group.

The Jews have continued to be the most highly urbanized of the religious groups in America. In 1957, 96.1 percent of the Jewish population was estimated to live in urban areas. Some 87.4 percent were resident in cities of 250,000 or more.[20] Forty percent of the Jewish population lived in Metropolitan New York, and 75 percent lived in fourteen large cities. Jews have joined the march to the suburbs, and at a faster pace than the country as a whole.

Jews have become a predominantly middle-class group, heavily represented in the clerical, sales, management, professional, and business proprietorship occupations.

19. Alvin Chenkin, "Jewish Population in the United States, 1963." *American Jewish Yearbook, 1964*, vol. 65. New York: American Jewish Committee and Jewish Publication Society of America, 1965, p. 3.
20. *Ibid.*, p. 6.

Not all New York Jews, though, have become middle class; in 1957 in New York City 28 percent of the Jews were skilled and unskilled manual workers.[21]

The median income of Jewish families has risen significantly. Jewish family income is estimated to exceed the median income levels of $6,548 per annum reported for all white families in 1964.[22]

During a significant period in the life cycle of the American Jewish family, its youth are at college, and, more frequently than ever, away from home.

The increase in rates of intermarriage, with the continuing acculturation of the American Jew, has aroused great concern throughout the community and among Jewish parents. Erich Rosenthal, in 1963, reported intermarriage rates of 7.2 percent to 17.9 percent of all Jewish marriages in various American communities.[23]

Intermarriage, strongly discouraged by Jewish religious tradition, is seen by Rosenthal to reflect the increasing assimilation and acculturation of Jews. The walls of discrimination have been shattered, and the physical propinquity of Jewish and non-Jewish young adults, at college and at work, during the crucial premarital years, provides increasing opportunity for intermarriage to occur. Rosenthal's studies of intermarriage lead him to conclude that the ultimate fate of the Jewish population, barring an unanticipated large-scale immigration, will be assimilation.

The provision of leisure-time programs, adult leadership, and facilities under Jewish communal auspices, in the Jewish community centers and YM-YWHA's, in so-

---

21. C. Bezalel Sherman, *The Jew Within American Society*. Detroit: Wayne University Press, 1961, p. 98.
22. Ben J. Wattenberg and Richard M. Scammon, *This U.S.A.* Garden City: Doubleday, 1965, p. 126.
23. Erich Rosenthal, "Studies of Jewish Intermarriage in the United States." *American Jewish Yearbook, 1963*, Volume 64. New York: American Jewish Committee and Jewish Publication Society of America, 1964.

cial organizations for young people such as the B'nai B'rith Hillel Centers on college campuses, and in synagogue centers, has constituted one element of a major effort to strengthen leisure time associations of Jewish youth and young adults. In my judgment, this effort has met with only modest success up to this point.

The leisure time of Jewish children is limited by their attendance at religious school. In 1969, of an estimated school-age population of 1,375,000 from 5 to 17, over 550,000 children of all ages were enrolled in Jewish schools. Approximately 42 percent attended one-day-a-week Sunday schools, 45 percent attended two or more weekday afternoons, and 13 percent attended all-day schools. During the ten-year period 1952 to 1962, a 75 percent increase in enrollment was noted.[24] The renewed determination of a second-generation group of parents to ensure some Jewish education for *their* children, despite their own poor experience and Jewish illiteracy, is impressive. The sharp increase in Jewish school enrollment in the post-World War II years was undoubtedly a reaction to the years of Nazi oppression and the creation of Israel. Obviously, any accounting for the use of leisure time by Jewish children must include consideration of their obligation to pursue Jewish education.

Some observers have reacted to the evolution of the Jewish family with a deep sense of pessimism and concern for the future. The loss of authentic involvement in the Jewish community, the weakening of extended family ties, the isolation of the two-generation family, the acceptance of materialistic values, are viewed with dismay. The stress on consumption of material goods, hedonistic self-fulfillment, individualism, and privacy are matters of concern.[25]

---

24. Uriah Z. Engelman, "Jewish Education," *American Jewish Yearbook, 1963,* Volume 64. New York: American Jewish Committee and Jewish Publication Society of America, 1964.
25. Morton I. Teicher, "How Should Jewish Communal Agencies Relate

Despite the continued acculturation of the Jewish population, Jewish rates of divorce and separation appear to be lower than those of the general population.[26] Rates of crime and juvenile delinquency may even be declining. Studies of mental illness suggest a high correlation of the Jewish population and the incidence of neurosis, by comparison with Protestants and Catholics. The incidence of alcoholism, drug addiction, functional disorders, and severely disabling mental illness are lower for the Jewish population.[27]

Despite the stress of rapid social change and the impact of the relativism of Freudian theory on child-rearing practices and family relationships, the Jewish family demonstrates continuing strength and vitality. It has learned to use the complex structure of social institutions needed to sustain families in the conduct of their functions at a high level of well-being. Securing needed health, welfare, education, and leisure-time services has become a considerable task, and the Jewish family has become a very skilled consumer. The Jewish family has sustained significant Jewish communal institutions, such as the synagogue schools and community centers, to support its own essential developmental functions.

The Jewish family has, then, in common with most American families, become a nuclear group. Many Jewish women and wives begin their young adult lives at work, continue employment until their first child arrives, and, in maturity, when the children are grown, return to work. The raising of children continues to be the major concern of the American Jewish family, even as it was in the

to the Jewish Family Now and in the Future?" *Journal of Jewish Communal Service* 44, no. 4, Summer, 1968, pp. 320–29.

26. Ben Seligman and Aaron Antonovsky, "Some Aspects of Jewish Demography," in *The Jews, Social Patterns of an American Group*, ed. by Marshall Sklare, Glencoe, Ill.: The Free Press, 1958, pp. 66–68.

27. Jerome K. Myers and Bertram H. Roberts, "Some Relationships Between Religion, Ethnic Origin and Mental Illness," in *The Jews, Social Patterns of an American Group, ibid.*, pp. 551–59.

*shtetl* generations ago. Parents set the highest value upon the well-being and development of their children. Achieving a better milieu for the raising of children and a better education in a settled Jewish community remains a prime determinant in choice of a neighborhood of residence, and is a major factor in stimulating Jewish resettlement in suburban areas. Some mature families, with children grown, are moving back to apartment living in the cities. A few—perhaps a growing trend among the more affluent —are resettling in Florida and Arizona upon retirement.

## Leisure and the Jewish Family

In the absence of more extensive social data, we are left to our own impressionistic observation of the use of leisure by Jewish families in metropolitan New York over these last several decades. Certainly studies of leisure for the general American population have considerable validity for the Jewish family as well.

The gain in leisure time for the average man and woman—and the Jewish family—during the normal week has been modest. Jewish men have moved into the middle occupations and professions, which are demanding of the energy and time of the employee or entrepreneur. The need and desire to maintain a secure and better environment for the family and children has stimulated the rapid movement to the outer limits of the boroughs and the suburban counties. Travel time to work averages no less than 10 hours per week, and as much as 15 hours, portal to portal. The growth in home ownership by Jewish families, including many families of modest means, adds to the time spent on "obligatory" functions: home maintenance and repairs, gardening, and the like.

For the Jewish women returning to work, the burden of maintaining a home and a job adds considerably to the tensions of family life.

There is no doubt that Jewish families spend much time at home. Jews do attend theatre, concerts, cultural affairs, read, and buy books in greater proportion than other people.

For the children, the continued expectation of the Jewish family has been achievement. Scholastic achievement and extracurricular activities, needed to "round out the man," are assumed. Add a Hebrew school schedule and a music lesson or ballet class, and the Jewish child is scheduled as tightly as his or her parents.

The longer vacation has been enjoyed by the Jewish family. More family travel vacations appear to be taken. Proportionately more Jewish children attend camp and day camp. More Jewish adults travel abroad during their vacations. The mid-winter vacation to Florida has become a ritual of the Jewish upper middle class. The vacation is justified by the need to "relax and unwind."

The present generation of Jewish older adults face the most difficult dilemmas of all, in their retirement. The poorer the older adult, the crueler his situation. The Jewish older adult has been left behind by his grown children, to remain in older, changing neighborhoods. Many older adults had long ago forsaken the religious beliefs and practices of their fathers. They retired without leisure-time skills or hobbies. The long hours of enforced leisure are a more difficult burden for the retired man than the woman, who must fulfill continuing household responsibilities.

Only 8 to 10 percent of the Jewish elderly are participants in leisure-time facilities under public and Jewish communal auspices.

What, then, remains of Jewish family life at leisure that is distinctive? Does the Jewish family still possess a culture which governs its activity?

While the fundamental Jewish mores and customs remain, the observance of Jewish religious tradition and law has been abandoned by the vast majority of the Jewish population. Synagogue membership has been estimated at 60 percent.[28] Only during the High Holidays do the majority of Jews attend services. Jewish traditional observance in the home has diminished.

Celebrations of the now major American festivals—Chanukah and Passover—have become significant family rituals. Members of the extended family still attend the rites of circumcision, Bar Mitzvah, weddings, funerals, and mourning, even if they see little or nothing of each other between times.

Jewish families continue to spend the greater part of their leisure time at home. The advent of television and longer weekends and vacations have probably increased the amount of time spent by the primary Jewish families with each other.

Jewish families have continued to support and participate in a wide variety of Jewish organizations and institutions in their leisure time. These have included the Jewish Community Centers and YM-YWHA's, the Synagogue centers, communally sponsored camps, B'nai B'rith, Zionist and religious youth organizations, and myriad adult associations. The strength of the institutions often seems sorely tested by the apparent disinterest of the adults. The response of the people, who flocked into every Jewish institution during the June War in Israel in 1967, was surprising. The strength of the ties of the people was evident. No one can prophesy the turning of history in the future and the new crises yet to come.

*Strengthening Jewish Family Life Through the Leisure-Time Organizations of the Jewish Community*

The social and cultural life of the early Jewish com-

---

28. Albert I. Gordon, *Jews in Suburbia*. Boston: Beacon Hill Press, 1959, p. 85.

munity of New York was conducted under family and synagogue auspices. The swelling immigration compelled the establishment of a great variety of organizations and institutions to satisfy the needs of a heterogeneous population. The present-day Jewish Community Centers and YM-YWHA's owe their origins to the young people's literary societies of the late 1850's.

After more than one hundred years of evolution, the Jewish Community Center and YM-YWHA has become a major national institution. In Greater New York, including Nassau and Westchester counties, thirty-two YM-YWHA's and Jewish Community Centers are supported by the Federation of Jewish Philanthropies. These Centers serve a membership of over 117,000 young people, adults, and older adults. The Center is based upon a concept of service to a community—a neighborhood of a big city, or a suburban area.

The Jewish Community Center provides an extensive range of services to individuals to assist the family in vital family developmental tasks. These include:

1. Provision of clubs, classes, hobby groups, and physical education activities to provide constructive leisure-time opportunities;
2. Teaching crucial social skills in personal adjustment;
3. Fostering Jewish values and ideals and teaching Jewish traditions and customs;
4. Providing constructive social opportunities for young adults and other unmarried persons to meet.

While Jewish Center services have largely been based upon individual participation, the last several decades have seen a modest increase in family programming. Holiday party events, picnics, meetings, athletic events, parent-child discussion meetings, suppers, teas, and luncheons have been noted as family activity. It is apparent that much more can be done in stimulating family-centered activity.

The summer camps and day camps sponsored by Federation agencies serve more than 25,000 children every summer. These institutions provide another important resource for the Jewish family of metropolitan New York. Graenum Berger has urged a major reorganization of Jewish Community Centers to emphasize the primary function of the Center as an agency for the education of the Jewish family in Judaism. The Center would provide programs in family life education, cultural arts education, and Jewish education.[29]

The Jewish community continues to sponsor and support many social organizations and religious institutions for which satisfaction of the leisure-time needs of their membership may only be a secondary consideration, however important the leisure-time activities are intrinsically. Their primary concerns are fulfillment of religious functions, Jewish education, Zionist aspirations, and community service or philanthropic goals. Given the historic tradition of the Jewish people of living righteously and performing mitzvoth, the highest order of use of leisure time for the traditionally minded Jewish people is indeed in the performance of such righteous deeds. These may begin with the study of the Torah, for the religious, and include the obligatory participation of adults in U.J.A. fund-raising dinners.

The national associations of synagogues, the B'nai B'rith, the B'nai B'rith Hillel Foundations, the National Council of Jewish Women, and the American Zionist organizations all sponsor activities which engage young and old in constructive leisure-time activity of great importance to the Jewish community. With the YM-YWHA's, these organizations share concern for the continued well-being of the Jewish family and community.

---

29. Graenum Berger, "The Center as a Jewish Educational Institution," in *The Jewish Community Center, a Fourth Force in American Life*. New York: Jewish Education Committee Press, 1966.

The very success of the American experience confronts Jewish parents and the Jewish community with some profound problems and dilemmas. The wall of separation between ghetto and city, between *shtetl* and feudal domain, between integrated work and school life and enforced segregated leisure time pursuits, has largely been demolished. The Jewish family has become a nuclear unit, losing its children in early youth to the university, often far removed from home. Many second- and third-generation Jewish families, acculturated and lacking in Jewish education, expect the Jewish school, the synagogue, and the YM-YWHA to provide a Jewish education for their children. Jewish parents seek to protect their children from the terrifying influences of a youth culture infected with drug addiction, amorality, and outright rejection of the values of their families.

The elderly must resolve some of the most difficult problems of all: securing the resources to overcome the infirmities of aging, and, especially, finding new friendships and opportunities for constructive use of leisure time.

A concerted effort by all Jewish communal organizations must be made to strengthen leisure-time services under communal auspices in the following areas:

1. To engage Jewish college youth and unaffiliated young adults in the metropolitan area in participation in Jewish organizational life.
2. To organize extensive programs of Jewish Family Life Education in community centers, synagogues, adult associations, and philanthropic organizations for parents and adults.
3. To stimulate family activity programs for parents, children, and grandparents on a regular, recurrent basis in all Jewish community institutions and societies.
4. To encourage the large-scale organization of lei-

sure-time social, educational, and recreational programs for older adults.

5. To undertake a collective effort to re-establish the
Sabbath Day and the cycle of Jewish holidays for
the contemporary Jewish family.

During this restless time, Jewish families have had to
create new patterns of living, in a complex, explosive urban society. Added leisure time, new affluence, new burdens and responsibilities have tested the strength of the
Jewish family.

In response to the changing circumstances, the Jewish
family and community have refashioned one historic institution—the synagogue—and created a uniquely American development: the Jewish Community Center—YM-
YWHA.

We can look forward to an increase in leisure time for
all, in the future. When it comes, it can be an opportunity
to engage in activities which reflect a continued dedication
to righteous living. Jewish families, however acculturated,
do believe in the pursuit of the higher life, and the more
ethical life. Our institutions will need to reshape their
programs, their facilities, and, indeed, the direction of
their leadership to serve the Jewish family in an age of
leisure. Our culture and tradition give us some guidelines
to the future. And, somewhere along the way in the new
era, we must find time to pause and refresh our body,
mind, and soul in some unhurried place, and find surcease
from the never-ending cares we carry.

## 4

# THE USE AND MISUSE OF ALCOHOL
# AND OTHER DRUGS

Stanley Einstein

Diana Gecht, *Resource Consultant*

David Millman, Barbara Malarskey
*Research Assistants*

*"Who hath woe and who hath
sorrow? They that tarry
too long at the wine."*
Proverbs 23:30

Long before alcoholism was conceptualized as a disease,
the Jews knew what alcohol could do to a person: *Wine is
one of the things useful in small quantities. While one cup
of wine is recommended for a man, two are disgraceful,
three are demoralizing, four brutalizing.*

The ancient Jews were aware of, and in their awareness
they had developed an antidote for drunkenness and alcoholism: *Wine should be taken with meals—in between
meals it intoxicates.*

Both of these quotations are derived from the Talmud,
the compendium of Jewish civil and canonical law—a
guideline for daily living. There was a time when commitment to these daily guidelines may indeed have been
the significant factor preventing the misuse of alcohol and
perhaps even other drugs by Jews. But the time when
Immanuel Kant could say "women, ministers and Jews do
not get drunk" is long since gone.

86

The thesis posited by Snyder (1958) that the Jew has identified with a set of habits and attitudes about drinking which are fundamental to Jewish life and culture, and which intervene in his drinking to excess, is of little value today. Not long ago the words in the folk song "Shikker Is a Goy" might have given solace to some. But that time is also long since past.

Part of the mythology about drug misuse is the comfortable assumption that only people we don't know misuse drugs. Not long ago drug abuse was associated with slum life, economic and social poverty, and with a number of ethnic groups. Unconsciously, and for some of us consciously, we felt secure about our children, friends, and relatives when we read about Negroes, Puerto Ricans or Mexican Americans being arrested for drug use or sale of drugs.

Drug misuse was not a Jewish problem! In the 1950's an attempt was made to organize a committee to be concerned with drug misuse in New York's Federation of Jewish Philanthropies. The attempt failed. Drug misuse was not a Jewish problem.

But in the last few years, the mass media and various scientific studies have confronted us with the fact that drug misuse knows no boundaries.

This fact is really not new—white middle-class drug use was well known at the beginning of this century, and was documented by Terry & Pellins (1928). Jewish drug misuse is certainly not a new fact of life in America. The few studies that have reported upon the religious affiliation of addicts noted that Jews ranged from 3 percent to 20 percent of the visible drug addicts. These studies include those reported by:

1. Lambert (1930)—Twenty percent of 318 drug addicts voluntarily committed to Bellevue Hospital from May 28, 1928, to May 16, 1929.
2. Dai (1937)—Five percent of one group of 801

drug addicts, and a little over 3 percent of 118 female addicts in the Chicago area.

3. Jandy & Floch (1937)—Nearly 4 percent of 343 male addicts sentenced to the Detroit House of Detention between 1931 and 1936.

4. Pescor (1943)—Four percent of 1,036 addict patients admitted to the United States Public Health Service Hospital at Lexington, Kentucky, between July, 1936, and June, 1937.

5. Knight & Prout (1951)—Twelve percent of 75 addicts who voluntarily committed themselves to New York Hospital between 1930 and 1950.

6. Alksne (1959)—Approximately 5 percent of voluntary admissions of adolescent addicts to Riverside Hospital in New York during 1957.

Jews continue to be part of the group of drug users that come to the attention of the public—the visible drug user. (For a variety of sociological reasons they are not often likely to be arrested, incarcerated, or hospitalized in public institutions.) There are a few recent findings that note the presence of these *visible* Jewish addicts.

Jaffe & Brill (1966) began their pilot project with cyclazocine, a new drug to treat addicts, with an initial sample made up entirely of middle-class male Jews between the ages of 20 and 38.

Over 4 percent (118) of the addicts certified to the New York State Narcotic Addiction Control Commission during its first year, April, 1967, to March, 1968, were Jews (Glaser, 1969).

During the years 1964 to 1968 Jewish admissions to the United States Public Health Service Hospital at Lexington, Kentucky, decreased annually from New York City as well as from all other locations. During these years the annual admissions averaged 2,000, while the Jewish admissions were 93, 75, 74, 59, and 55 (O'Donnell, 1969).

Lastly, approximately 19 percent of addicts being maintained on methadone in New York City, since the inception of such a program, were listed as being Jewish.

The obvious conclusion to be drawn from this 30-year span of available data is that Jewish drug misuse has been, is, and in all likelihood will continue to be a problem.

Meetings in the Jewish community, particularly the 1968 conference sponsored by the Commission on Synagogue Relations of the New York Federation of Jewish Philanthropies, have come up with overwhelming findings: not only are Jewish religious youth involved in drug misuse—but Chasidic youth are involved as well.

The present study was undertaken because of these two facts:

1. Drug misuse is felt not to be a Jewish problem and thus does not merit effort and/or concern from the organized Jewish world;

2. Drug misuse is on the increase among Jews generally, and some religious Jews specifically.

The purpose of the study was to explore the extent to which the rabbinical community was aware of drug problems among their congregants, and to learn what they had done or what they were planning to do about this.

The study was requested by the Commission on Synagogue Relations, Federation of Jewish Philanthropies, and was carried out by the New York Council on Alcoholism-ACCEPT.

## Procedure

Two questionnaires were developed; each was sent to 400 rabbis in the metropolitan New York area. One questionnaire was a one-page form asking the respondents to note: the incidence of the misuse of alcohol and various drugs among Jewish adolescents and adults in their synagogues; whether their synagogues were interested in a preventive program; and what other services were needed.

The longer questionnaire covered these areas and others in greater depth. It was hoped that even those rabbis who felt they did not have the time to answer the longer form would answer the shorter one.

The respondents were rabbis of congregations in all five metropolitan New York boroughs, and various Long Island and Westchester communities. Background characteristics were only available for the 41 who completed the long form, and not for the 26 who completed the short form. The average age of the responding rabbi was 41, the age range being 30 to 59. They had been rabbis for an average of 17 years (range 3 ½ to 40 years) and were at their present synagogue an average of 10 years (range 6 months to 40 years).

The older, the younger, the experienced, and the relatively inexperienced were included in this sample.

## The Extent of the Problem

The misuse of alcohol and other drugs by members of New York congregations is not easily comprehended, based on data available in this survey. One immediate conclusion that can be drawn before analyzing the data is quite significant: only 16 percent of 400 rabbis felt that the use and misuse of drugs and alcohol was sufficiently important and relevant to their work to participate in this study. This lack of interest in no way detracts from the existing problem. It may, however, mean that an important resource for prevention, education, referral and counseling is not available for the Jewish community. Four rabbis reported an awareness of the misuse of alcohol, and 18 the misuse of drugs among their congregants. Fifteen rabbis did not know the extent of alcohol misuse, and 11 did not know about the extent of drug misuse. Table I shows respondents' awareness of the extent of these problems in their congregations.

TABLE I Awareness of the Problem of Alcohol and Drug Misuse
in the Respondent's Congregation

(A)
Alcohol Misuse

|  | Total Respondents | | Respondents (39) | |
|---|---|---|---|---|
|  | (n) | (%) | (n) | (%) |
| Yes | 4 | 10 | 4 | 10 |
| No | 20 | 48 | 20 | 51 |
| Don't Know | 15 | 37 | 15 | 38 |
| No Answer | 2 | 5 |  |  |
|  | 41 | | | |

(B)
Drug Misuse

|  | Total Respondents | | Respondents (39) | |
|---|---|---|---|---|
|  | (n) | (%) | (n) | (%) |
| Yes | 18 | 44 | 18 | 46 |
| No | 10 | 24 | 10 | 26 |
| Don't Know | 11 | 27 | 11 | 28 |
| No Answer | 2 | 5 |  |  |
|  | 41 | | | |

Many of the rabbis were unaware as to whether their congregations had such problems. Of those that were aware, the obvious conclusion was that they were more sensitive to the existence of drug problems than alcohol problems.

The extent of alcohol misuse is generally reported as being quite small. One rabbi reported that 5 to 10 percent of his congregants may have this problem; the other respondents indicated it was 1 percent or less. Regarding the misuse of other drugs, one rabbi commented *"enough to be concerned";* the others reported that this problem ranged between .1 and 5 percent.

The conclusion from such data is obvious: although some congregants misuse alcohol and drugs, as far as the rabbis were concerned it was an insignificant problem. Unfortunately this was not further substantiated by the 26 rabbis who completed the shorter one-page version of the survey. Their responses are presented in Table II.

TABLE II The Incidence of Drug Use Among Jewish Adolescents and
Young Adults in Synagogues in New York*

| | Hard Drugs (Heroin, Cocaine) | | Other Drugs (LSD, Amphetamines) | | Marijuana | |
|---|---|---|---|---|---|---|
| | (n) | (%) | (n) | (%) | (n) | (%) |
| Some | 3 | 12 | 7 | 27 | 10 | 40 |
| None | 19 | 72 | 17 | 65 | 14 | 52 |
| Don't Know | 3 | 12 | 1 | 4 | 2 | 8 |
| No Answer | 1 | 4 | 1 | 4 | | |
| | 26 | | 26 | | 26 | |

* Data derived from the one-page questionnaire.

Depending upon which drugs were involved, less than half of the rabbis reported an awareness of drug use, while at most three rabbis were unaware of this behavior. Marijuana was apparently the drug of choice among the users in their communities. One rabbi reported that its use was *"extensive,"* another that its use reached "30 percent of the high school students."

These data create a dilemma. Why are some rabbis aware of the existence of the problem of substance misuse—which from federal, state and municipal reports is taking on epidemic proportions—and others are not aware? Whose problem is this? A number of the responses give us clues to both questions.

"I am pleased to note that no case of drug addiction by a Jewish child in our community has come before my desk. Rumor has it that some children are on pot. I have no personal verification of this."

"The problem hardly ever comes to my attention, or the families affiliated with this synagogue."

The answers to the two questions that were raised are quite simple. Drug misuse, by definition and selective attention, is not a Jewish problem.

*Concern about the Problem*

Table III shows data relevant to the rabbis' evaluation

of the importance of alcohol and drug misuse in their daily responsibilities. With all of the rabbis responding, 9 percent felt that alcoholism was of some importance in their daily responsibilities, and 41 percent felt that drug use was.

TABLE III Estimation of Importance of the Issue of Alcoholism and Drug Abuse with Regard to the Rabbi's Daily Responsibilities

(A)

|  | Alcoholism (n) | (%) |
|---|---|---|
| Very unimportant | 29 | 71 |
| Unimportant | 8 | 20 |
| Moderately important | 2 | 5 |
| Important | 1 | 2 |
| Very important | 1 | 2 |
|  | 41 |  |

(B)

|  | Drug Abuse (n) | (%) |
|---|---|---|
| Very unimportant | 16 | 39 |
| Unimportant | 8 | 20 |
| Moderately important | 6 | 14 |
| Important | 2 | 5 |
| Very important | 9 | 22 |
|  | 41 |  |

Concern about these problems is present among the rabbi's congregants. Table IV presents these data.

TABLE IV Concerns Manifested by Congregants about Alcohol and Drug Misuse During 1968

(A)

Alcohol Misuse

|  | Total Respondents (n) | (%) | Respondents (38) (n) | (%) |
|---|---|---|---|---|
| Concern manifested | 4 | 10 | 4 | 11 |
| No Concern manifested | 34 | 83 | 34 | 89 |
| No answer | 3 | 7 |  |  |
|  | 41 |  |  |  |

(B)
Drug Misuse

|  | Total Respondents | | Respondents (40) | |
|---|---|---|---|---|
|  | (n) | (%) | (n) | (%) |
| Concern manifested | 26 | 63 | 26 | 65 |
| No concern manifested | 14 | 34 | 14 | 35 |
| No answer | 1 | 3 | | |
|  | 41 | | | |

Whereas both the rabbi and his congregants are in agreement about the problem of alcohol misuse—viewing it as a relatively minor problem—the congregants are more concerned than their rabbis are about drug misuse (65 and 46 percent, respectively). This difference is apparently due to less awareness on the rabbi's part about drug misuse among his congregants and in his community.

Not only are the congregants concerned about these problems, and have gone to their spiritual leader, but others in the community have come to him as well.

TABLE V  Non-Congregational Concern About Substance Misuse

| During 1968 | Total Respondents | | Respondents (39) | |
|---|---|---|---|---|
|  | (n) | (%) | (n) | (%) |
| Concern manifested | 26 | 63 | 26 | 67 |
| No concern manifested | 13 | 32 | 13 | 33 |
| No answer | 2 | 5 | | |
|  | 41 | | | |

Such concern which has come to the attention of two-thirds of the responding rabbis has generally come from community residents, friends, visitors to the community, from other synagogues and police officials.

TABLE VI  Congregants and Non-Congregants Concerned About Alcohol and Drug Misuse by Categories

|  | (n) | (%) |
|---|---|---|
| Parents | 25 | 83 |
| Young marrieds | 2 | 7 |
| Young single adults | 6 | 20 |
| Adolescents | 9 | 30 |
| Others | 2 | 7 |

The most concerned group is easily predictable; it is the parents. Twenty-five of the rabbis (83 percent) report this. Adolescents and young single adults are reported to have sufficient rapport with the rabbis to come to them with their concerns as well. Police, other rabbis and neighbors, as well as young marrieds make up the smallest group. It is interesting to note that among the different groups of people who come to the rabbis for help, only one person was reported requesting help in regard to *religious attitudes toward narcotics.*

What is startling is that while no more than 18 (46 percent) rabbis reported being aware of these problems among their congregants, and 17 (41 percent) considered it to be of some importance in their daily responsibilities, 26 reported that both their congregants and noncongregants were sufficiently concerned to come to them with their concerns.

The focus of these concerns include requests for: general information, counseling, information about treatment services, development of synagogue programs, as well as requesting help *"to stir up pressure so that something could be done about drugs in the school."* Table VII presents the various categories of requests.

TABLE VII Categories of Requests Made to Forty-One Rabbis
About Alcohol and Drug Misuse

|  | (n) | (%) |
|---|---|---|
| General information | 20 | 49 |
| Counseling | 18 | 44 |
| Information about treatment services | 10 | 24 |
| Initiation or sponsorship of synagogue programs | 6 | 15 |
| Other | 6 | 15 |

## Facets of Drug Misuse That Do Concern Rabbis

Given the fact that the rabbis in this survey have been made amply aware by their congregants and noncongregants about the problem of drug misuse, the data in Table VIII are most interesting. Only one rabbi ("other") noted any concern about "ethical and moral"

TABLE VIII Aspects of Alcohol and Drug Misuse That Rabbis are Most Concerned With*

| | Alcohol Misuse | | | | Drug Misuse | | | |
| | Tot. Respondents | | Respondents (10) | | Tot. Respondents | | Respondents (26) | |
| | (n) | (%) | (n) | (%) | (n) | (%) | (n) | (%) |
|---|---|---|---|---|---|---|---|---|
| Psychological | 7 | 17 | 7 | 70 | 19 | 46 | 19 | 73 |
| Sociological | 6 | 15 | 6 | 60 | 17 | 41 | 17 | 66 |
| Legal | 2 | 5 | 2 | 20 | 10 | 24 | 10 | 38 |
| Medical | 2 | 5 | 2 | 20 | 7 | 17 | 7 | 27 |
| Pharmacological | | | | | 1 | 2 | 1 | 4 |
| Other | | | | | 2 | 5 | 2 | 8 |
| None | 1 | 2 | 1 | 10 | | | | |
| No Answer | 31 | 76 | | | 15 | 37 | | |

* All answers and no answers are tabulated, but each respondent may have noted multiple responses.

aspects of drug misuse. Thirty-one (76 percent) didn't indicate what aspects of alcohol misuse they were concerned about, and 15 (37 percent) did the same for drug misuse. It is, of course, obvious that whether we are or are not interested in certain aspects of these problems, these multifaceted behaviors continue to be a daily reality for the rabbis. Many different people in the community have been communicating this to them.

The aspects of both alcohol and drug misuse that do interest the responding rabbis are the psychological, sociological, legal, medical, and pharmacological ones. One rabbi took the time to note he was uninterested in any aspects of alcohol misuse. Paralleling this is the fact that no rabbis manifested any concern for the pharmacological aspects of alcohol misuse. Given that alcohol remains the most dangerous drug known to man, at the same time that it is an integral component of Jewish ritual, it is somewhat of a mystery why no interest in this area is manifested.

It would appear that our rabbis have identified with the prevalent theories that alcohol and drug misuse are symptomatic of individual and societal illness. They are, however, asked because of their training and position to be diagnosticians and healers of the spirit—and only one rabbi indicated a concern for this aspect of the problem. That rabbi phrased his concern most succinctly: "A synagogue is or should be primarily concerned with the ethical. In addition, development of the *yetzer tov* is the only effective internal control over the *yetzer ha-ra*."

The majority of the responding rabbis stated that their concerns were related to various effects upon the actual alcohol and drug misuser; only five rabbis noted that their concern embraced the various effects of substance abuse upon the community as a whole—the nonusers.

*Responses to the Misuse of Alcohol and Other Drugs*

One synagogue reported carrying out a program concerned with alcohol misuse; 11 with drug misuse.

TABLE IX   Alcohol and Drug Programs Developed and Carried out by Synagogues

| | Alcohol | | | | Drugs | | | |
|---|---|---|---|---|---|---|---|---|
| | Total Respondents | | Respondents | | Total Respondents | | Respondents | |
| | (n) | (%) | (n) | (%) | (n) | (%) | (n) | (%) |
| Have had programs | 1 | 2 | 1 | 3 | 11 | 27 | 11 | 30 |
| Have not had programs | 31 | 76 | 31 | 97 | 26 | 63 | 26 | 70 |
| No answer | 9 | 22 | | | 4 | 10 | | |
| | 41 | | 32 | | 41 | | 37 | |

It once again becomes apparent that alcohol misuse is considered to be a sufficiently insignificant problem that it does not merit special programs given or sponsored by the synagogues. The ancient myth of there being no Jewish alcoholics prevails again. Although eleven rabbis reported the development of drug programs, this must be evaluated against the knowledge that 26 of the rabbis have been told by congregants and non-congregants that there is concern about this problem (Table IV-B).

The kinds of programs that were developed for both teen-agers and adults included:

1. Single lectures
2. Film presentations
3. Adult education institutes
4. Panel discussions, and
5. Oneg Shabbat programs.

The survey explored whether the rabbis had *considered* developing any kind of program focusing on drugs or alcoholism. The majority of the rabbis (63 percent) reported that they had not.

Those rabbis that had thought about developing such a program considered the use of open forums, films, lectures, discussions, rallies and counseling. Their plan was to utilize the resources of law enforcement agencies, staff of the local YMHA, family agencies and other mental health services, and members of the congregation. One respondent did not know whom he would turn to. The Federation of Jewish Philanthropies, the comprehensive umbrella for Jewish agencies in the Metropolitan area, was not considered to be a resource.

## Knowledge about Drugs, Their Use and Misuse

The rabbis in this survey, were they to develop any synagogue programs relevant to drug misuse, would have to turn to others for help. Only one rabbi reported receiving any specialized training in alcoholism, and three reported specialized training in drug misuse. The training resulted from courses in pastoral counseling, experience as an army chaplain, lectures, and involvement with and proximity to addicts. Ninety-two percent of the sample noted that they had not received any training in these two areas. Table X presents the data relevant to whether the rabbis feel that their present daily responsibilities require special training.

TABLE X Need for Special Training in Alcoholism and Drug Misuse for Daily Rabbinical Responsibilities

|  | Total Respondents | | Respondents (36) | |
|---|---|---|---|---|
|  | (n) | (%) | (n) | (%) |
| Need special training | 12 | 29 | 12 | 33 |
| Do not need special training | 24 | 59 | 24 | 67 |
| No answer | 5 | 12 | | |
|  | 41 | | | |

One-third of the responding rabbis felt that they had need for special training, 67 percent felt it was not necessary for them. Two major factors may contribute to such a position: the individual feels that the problem doesn't merit special training or he feels that he already has sufficient knowledge about the area.

Earlier parts of this paper focused on the state of rabbinical concern. This section focuses on perception of the problem of drug and alcohol misuse.

## Etiology of Drug Misuse

The rabbis were asked to give their ideas about why "people misuse drugs." Table XI presents their views about this.

TABLE XI Why People Misuse Drugs*

|  | Total Respondents | | Respondents (19) | |
|---|---|---|---|---|
|  | (n) | (%) | (n) | (%) |
| No answer | 22 | 54 |  |  |
| Don't know | 1 | 2 | 1 | 5 |
| Psychological problems | 15 | 37 | 15 | 79 |
| Becoming addicted medically as a patient | 2 | 5 | 2 | 11 |
| Person's need for stimulation | 3 | 7 | 3 | 16 |
| Function on higher level | 1 | 2 | 1 | 5 |
| Environmental & social factors | 2 | 5 | 2 | 11 |
|  | 41* | | | |

Although more than 50 percent of the sample did not answer this question, the great majority of those that did felt that psychological problems were the major cause of drug misuse. These problems included the desire to escape from reality, insecurity, instability, loneliness, self-dissatisfaction, and boredom. These reasons, and the many variations of them, are the ones most often given to account for drug misuse. It is interesting to note that only one rabbi reported "social conditioning" as a factor leading to drug misuse. Given that we all live in an era in which we are bombarded with the message that there is a chemical solution available for all of our problems, the fact that only one rabbi is apparently aware of this is startling.

## Who Uses Drugs?

The survey included a section devised to explore the rabbis' perception of a typical drug addict. More than 50 percent of the sample answered the question. Seven (32 percent) did not know what this typical addict was like; 4 (18 percent) indicated that there was no such person as a typical addict. For the remaining 50 percent of

* Multiple answers were categorized separately.

TABLE XII The Typical Drug Addict as Perceived by a Sample
of New York Rabbis in 1969

| Age | Years of Drug Use | Family Background | Ethnic Background | Religion | Years Completed Schooling | Number Hospitalizations | Number Arrests |
|---|---|---|---|---|---|---|---|
| Teen-ager | 6 years | Any | Any | Not Jewish | H.S. Drop-out | 2–3 | 2–3 |
| **Range** | | | | | | | |
| Teen-ager (2) | DK 1 | Any (1) | Any (4) | DK (1) | DK (1) | DK (1) | DK (2) |
| 14 (1) | 3 (1) | Large (1) | Negro (5) | Any (2) | 8 (3) | 0 (2) | 0 (1) |
| 15 (3) | 4 (2) | Broken (2) | White (1) | Non Jewish (6) | 10 (2) | 2 (2) | 2 (2) |
| 16 (3) | 5 (3) | Disadvantaged (3) | | Little Religious Training (1) | 12 (2) | 3 (1) | 3 (2) |
| 17 (2) | 6 (2) | Middle Class (4) | | | | 4 (1) | 5 (2) |
| 18 (2) | 7 (2) | Affluent (1) | | | | 5 (2) | |
| 19 (1) | 10 (3) | | | | | | |
| 20 (1) | | | | | | | |

THE USE AND MISUSE OF DRUGS 103

the group, the typical addict was a teen-ager, who had been using drugs for approximately six years, who came from any kind of a family (spanning the "disadvantaged" to the "affluent"), any kind of ethnic background (although half of the group noted specifically that he was a Negro); was a high school dropout who had been arrested two or three times and hospitalized two or three times for his drug use. The majority of the respondents noted that the typical drug addict was not Jewish.

While this perception of *the addict* is not that of the off-white disadvantaged slum child, it nevertheless does lead one to conclude that drug misuse happens to many kinds of people, but not to Jews.

## General Attitudes about Drug Misuse

The survey attempted to assess some of the attitudes that the rabbis might have regarding drug misuse. They were asked to note their agreement or disagreement with four statements. These questions, the responses to which are noted in Table XIII, can empirically be answered in the following way:
1. No empirical evidence for this;
2. Empirical evidence is present to the extent that the misuse of any substance can have serious consequences;
3. Empirical evidence is available for this;
4. No empirical evidence for this.

The majority of the rabbis did not answer this section of the survey: the *no answers* ranging from 73 percent to 83 percent. Of those who did answer, the majority believed that marijuana led to other drug use; and that drugs can make healthy people sick.

What is apparent is that the rabbis generally have integrated the attitudes regarding drug use that the community at large has, whether these attitudes are valid or not.

TABLE XIII Attitudes Held by Rabbis Regarding Alcohol and Other Drugs

| | | Marijuana use invariably leads to the use of other more dangerous drugs | Drugs make sick people healthy and healthy people sick | Given the medical and psychological consequences resulting from the misuse of various drugs, alcohol is the most dangerous drug known to man presently | Drug misuse is generally associated with particular ethnic groups, of particular socio-economic backgrounds |
|---|---|---|---|---|---|
| Agree | (n) | 7 | 6 | 4 | 3 |
| | (%) | 64 | 67 | 50 | 43 |
| Disagree | (n) | 3 | 2 | 3 | 3 |
| | (%) | 27 | 22 | 38 | 43 |
| Don't know | (n) | 1 | 1 | 1 | 1 |
| | (%) | 9 | 11 | 12 | 14 |
| No answer | (n) | 30 | 32 | 33 | 34 |

## Specific Knowledge about Drugs and Drug Concepts

Part of the survey was devised to assess the knowledge that the respondents had about crucial concepts in the area of drug misuse. There were many reasons for doing this. The significant one for this particular sample was to learn whether the responding rabbis believed that any of these concepts were clearly and validly definable as indicators of danger to the person. Theoretically the rabbi could be in a position to voice Judaic tenets to dissuade their people from turning to things rather than to people. Fundamental to Judaism is the concept that behavior which is dangerous to the person is prohibited to him, that is, the sick need not fast.

## What Are Drugs?

Fourteen rabbis (34 percent) did not respond to this; four of them indicated that they didn't know how to define drugs.

TABLE XIV What Drugs Are to 27 Rabbis

|  | (n) | (%)* | |
|---|---|---|---|
| Chemicals | 11 | 41 | |
| Affectors: | 16 | 59 | |
| of mind & body | 10 | | 37 |
| of body | 3 | | 11 |
| of mind | 1 | | 4 |
| of pleasure | 1 | | 4 |
| of habit formation | 1 | | 4 |
| Medicines | 5 | 19 | |
| Specific types of drugs | 4 | 15 | |
| Don't know | 4 | 15 | |
| No answer | 14 | 34 | |

* Percentage of those responding. No answer is of the total 41.

For the remaining 23 rabbis, drugs were defined as

chemicals, affectors of the mind and/or body, medicines, and as specific types of drugs. The predominant theme was that drugs affected the person and were chemicals. Dangers were not implicit in the definition.

## General Dangers Caused by Misusing Drugs

Once again 14 rabbis (34 percent) did not respond to this; two who did respond did not know what the dangers could be.

TABLE XV General Dangers Caused by Misusing Drugs
as Perceived by 27 Rabbis

|  | (n) |  | (%)* |
|---|---|---|---|
| Physical and psychological consequences | 17 |  | 62 |
| Physical & psychological |  | 12 | 44 |
| Destruction of body & mind |  | 2 | 7 |
| Death |  | 3 | 11 |
| Physical consequences | 6 |  | 23 |
| Physical |  | 1 | 4 |
| Genetic |  | 4 | 15 |
| Brain damage |  | 1 | 4 |
| Psychological consequences | 5 |  | 19 |
| Moral consequences | 1 |  | 4 |
| Social consequences | 6 |  | 23 |
| Effects on non-users |  | 4 | 15 |
| Criminality |  | 2 | 7 |
| Type of drug use | 16 |  | 59 |
| Addiction |  | 8 | 30 |
| Dependence |  | 7 | 26 |
| Further drug involvement |  | 1 | 4 |
| Don't know | 2 |  | 7 |
| No answer | 14 |  | 34 |

* Percentage of those responding. No answer is of the total 41.

The most prevalent dangers noted by the rabbis had to do with physical and psychological consequences, and the results of specific types of drug abuse (that is, addiction, dependence, and further drug use). One rabbi noted that there might be residual effects, effects occurring long after the drug experience. What is interesting to note is that social consequences, such as criminal behavior or the effects upon members of the non-drug-using community, were mentioned by less than 25 percent of the respondents. What is mystifying for a sample such as this one is that only one rabbi noted that there may be moral consequences—"moral degradation."

We must keep in mind that the issue is not necessarily the validity of the response, since we all recognize that how we perceive something or define it will significantly determine our relationship to it. When a spiritual leader defines a particular behavioral consequence as being physical and/or psychological in its essence, he is beginning to define himself out of the situation.

When rabbis were asked to rate whether medical, psychological, genetic, or other problems may result from the misuse of specific drugs, a number of patterns became clear:

1. Medical problems were felt to predominate over psychological problems in relation to addicting drugs, whereas for 3 of the 4 non-addicting drugs the reverse was true.

2. Excluding LSD, genetic effects were not perceived to be a major consequence of drug misuse.

3. The responding rabbis were able to discriminate between various drugs.

This last point is a most significant one. If indeed one can perceive shadings of a problem, then one would expect shadings in the responses to the problem. By and large the present survey notes that the respondents are fairly sophisticated to many facets of the drug misuse problem, and certainly no less so than the average religious, political, or community leader—yet they are almost uniformly consistent in their avoidance of the problem.

TABLE XVI Consequences of the Misuse of Various Drugs as Perceived by 41 Rabbis

| | No Answer (n) | Don't Know (n) | Don't Know (%R) | Medical Problems (n) | Medical Problems (%R) | Psychological Problems (n) | Psychological Problems (%R) | Genetic Problems (n) | Genetic Problems (%R) | Other Problems (n) | Other Problems (%R) |
|---|---|---|---|---|---|---|---|---|---|---|---|
| *Addicting Drugs* | | | | | | | | | | | |
| Alcohol | 13 | 4 | 14% | 22 | 79% | 17 | 61% | 2 | 7% | 4 | 14% |
| Heroin | 14 | 3 | 11% | 19 | 70% | 18 | 67% | 5 | 19% | 3 | 11% |
| Barbiturates | 14 | 5 | 19% | 16 | 60% | 11 | 41% | 1 | 4% | 1 | 4% |
| *Non-Addicting Drugs* | | | | | | | | | | | |
| Tranquilizers | 15 | 7 | 27% | 13 | 50% | 14 | 54% | | | 1 | 4% |
| Amphetamines | 14 | 7 | 26% | 14 | 52% | 12 | 44% | 2 | 7% | 2 | 7% |
| LSD | 15 | 4 | 15% | 11 | 42% | 14 | 54% | 13 | 50% | 1 | 4% |
| Marijuana | 15 | 7 | 27% | 5 | 20% | 17 | 65% | | | 4 | 15% |

## *What Is Addiction?*

Addiction is a term used to define what happens to a person after he uses addicting drugs such as opiates, barbiturates, and alcohol over a period of time. The general situation is for the person to need increased amounts of the same drug in order to experience today what was experienced yesterday (tolerance), and when deprived of the drug the person can experince mild discomfort, comas, or may even die as his body adjusts to a non-drug state (withdrawal symptoms).

TABLE XVII What *Addiction* Means to 26 Rabbis

|  | (n) |  | (%)* |
|---|---|---|---|
| *Behavior Related* | 9 |  | 35 |
| Inability to function without drugs |  | 9 | 35 |
| *Drug Related* | 7 |  | 26 |
| Inability to stop using drugs |  | 4 | 15 |
| Physical reactions |  | 3 | 11 |
| *Concept Related* | 11 |  | 43 |
| Dependency |  | 7 | 27 |
| Habituation |  | 2 | 8 |
| Compulsion |  | 1 | 4 |
| A Crutch |  | 1 | 4 |
| Don't know | 2 |  | 8 |
| No answer | 15 |  | 37 |

* Percentage of those responding. No answer is of the total 41.

For the 26 responding rabbis, two did not know what the term addiction meant; the majority eleven (43 percent) defined this concept in terms of other concepts (that is, dependency, habituation, compulsion, crutch); nine (35 percent) felt that addiction connoted an inability to function without drugs; and seven (26 percent) noted that addiction was drug-related.

When asked to categorize whether three addicting and four non-addicting drugs were addicting or habituating, the response pattern was the following:

1. Many more rabbis felt that they knew about addicting drugs than they did about non-addicting ones.
2. Heroin was easily categorized by the vast majority of the respondents as being addicting, whereas alcohol and barbiturates were almost equally seen as being addicting and habituating.
3. Amphetamines, the base for most diet pills taken by female congregants, posed problems for the rabbis.
4. Marijuana and tranquilizers were readily defined as being non-addicting.

TABLE XVIII The Addiction Status of Various Drugs
as Perceived by 41 Rabbis

|  | No Answer | Don't Know | | Addicting | | Habituating | |
|---|---|---|---|---|---|---|---|
| Addicting Drugs | n | (n) | (%R) | (n) | (%R) | (n) | (%R) |
| Alcohol | 15 | 1 | 4% | 14 | 54% | 15 | 58% |
| Heroin | 14 | 1 | 4% | 25 | 93% | 2 | 7% |
| Barbiturates | 13 | 2 | 7% | 13 | 46% | 14 | 50% |
| Non-Addicting Drugs |  |  |  |  |  |  |  |
| Tranquilizers | 14 | 5 | 19% | 5 | 19% | 17 | 63% |
| Amphetamines | 12 | 10 | 34% | 5 | 17% | 14 | 48% |
| LSD | 14 | 7 | 26% | 6 | 22% | 14 | 52% |
| Marijuana | 15 | 4 | 15% | 4 | 15% | 18 | 70% |

One fairly obvious conclusion that could be drawn from comparing the results in Tables XVII, XVIII, XIX and XX, which is to be discussed, is that notwithstanding the knowledge that is actually present the respondents could make more use of informational resources.

## What Is Drug Dependency?

Dependency upon drugs is a way of saying the person needs the drug psychologically and not physically. It is a neutral word whose meaning we have so distorted that one could almost write it as graffiti. We are all dependent on many people and many things in different ways. The diabetic is dependent upon insulin; the newly marrieds are dependent upon one another—and if they are not part of the 33 percent that divorce, they may live out their lives together in a state of satisfying dependency.

When it comes to drugs, however, dependency is a word generally used to frighten with, rather than to explain about.

TABLE XIX What *Dependency* Means to 26 Rabbis

|  | (n) | (%)* |
|---|---|---|
| *Behavior Related* | 18 | 69 |
| A psychological need | 12 | 46 |
| Inability to function without drugs | 4 | 15 |
| Reliance | 1 | 4 |
| Strong need | 1 | 4 |
| *Concept Related* | 5 | 19 |
| Habit-forming | 1 | 4 |
| Addiction | 1 | 4 |
| Less than Addiction | 3 | 11 |
| Don't know | 4 | 15 |
| No answer | 15 | 37 |

Fifteen rabbis (37 percent) did not define dependency; four did not know how to define it. The remaining 22 categorized *dependency* into being *behavior-related* and *concept-related*. Nearly half of the respondents noted that dependency was a psychological need.

## What Is Habituation?

Habituation is really identical to dependency minus the moral overtones imputed to dependency.

Sixteen rabbis (39 percent) did not define habituating; seven did not know how to define it. Approximately one-third of the responding Rabbis defined habituating in terms of other concepts. Six (24 percent) noted that it was related to patterns of drug-taking, and four (16 percent) defined it in terms of it being a psychological need.

---

* Percentage of those responding. No answer is of the total 41.

TABLE XX What *Habituating* Means to 25 Rabbis

|  | (n) |  | (%)* |
|---|---|---|---|
| *Related to Pattern of Drug Taking* | 6 |  | 24 |
| Established drug-taking pattern |  | 3 | 12 |
| Repeated use |  | 1 | 4 |
| Using increased doses |  | 1 | 4 |
| Automatic use |  | 1 | 4 |
| *Behavior Related* | 4 |  | 16 |
| Psychological need |  | 4 | 16 |
| *Concept Related* | 8 |  | 32 |
| Habit-forming |  | 3 | 12 |
| Addicting |  | 1 | 4 |
| Leads to addiction |  | 1 | 4 |
| Leads to dependency |  | 1 | 4 |
| Not as strong as dependency |  | 1 | 4 |
| Similar to dependency |  | 1 | 4 |
| Don't know | 7 |  | 28 |
| No answer | 16 |  | 39 |

In summary, the issues that are often raised about drug misuse, the specific concepts that are often used as weapons or total answers, are apparently understood by many of the rabbis, but are of little use to them when they are confronted by the problem of drug misuse.

## Judaism and Drug Misuse

One might expect that if scientific knowledge is not the source for the rabbinical community to depend on in order to cope with drug misuse, then perhaps the concepts and traditions of Judaism might be.

Assessing this was a particular goal of this survey, since a rabbi, Zalman M. Schacter, has in recent years been proselytizing that there are "many parallels between LSD and Hasidic experiences," and that LSD can have specific religious usefulness and meaning for Orthodox Jews (Metzner, 1968).

Approximately half of the sample noted that they were

---

* Percentage of those responding. No answer is of the total 41.

aware of Rabbi Schacter's position and his writings. A number of the respondents questioned his sanity; one went as far as to say he was not a rabbi.

The vast majority noted that there was no religious or cultural basis for the misuse of drugs by Jews.

TABLE XXI The Religious or Cultural Basis for Drug Misuse by Jews as Perceived by 29 Rabbis

|  | Total | | Respondents (29) | |
| --- | --- | --- | --- | --- |
|  | (n) | (%) | (n) | (%) |
| There is none | 26 | 63 | 26 | 90 |
| There is | 3 | 7 | 3 | 10 |
| No answer | 12 | 29 | | |
|  | 41 | | | |

The majority of the rabbis in this survey agreed that Judaism could be turned to either to prevent or terminate the misuse of drugs. They noted that:

"Religion does not encourage experimentation with items that may prove dangerous to one's being."

"Judaism provides plenty of opportunities for *getting high and turning on* without resort to harmful artificial stimulants."

"Any misuse of God's gifts—and drugs are in that category—is a violation of religion."

"Drug abuse is contrary to the basic Jewish concept of the sanctity of life."

"No one may misuse what God has created; no one may abuse his body."

"Misuse of drugs is destructive. Judaism is thoroughly humanistic and life-oriented."

When asked to consider "what factors in contemporary Judaism do you feel are reinforcing the misuse of drugs?" the initial response was to deny that there were any relevant factors operating. The answer which perhaps best expressed the rabbis' views was: "Contemporary Jews share the major culture. As it is permissive, so are contemporary Jews tending to permissiveness."

Many of the respondents actively blamed drug misuse among Jews upon the breakdown of the traditionally close Jewish family, materialism, and the increase in secularism. The feeling tone of many of the responses was: there is little that we can do, and little that our role has to do with this problem. It was as if, at the end of the questionaire, the respondent was reaffirming for himself that this problem was not his.

Two of the rabbis differed quite significantly in regard to this attitude: "Home is rarely religiously or morally supportive. Moreover, the average synagogue service is so boring and ethically and psychologically unsatisfying that I am not surprised that some Jews look in more exotic areas for satisfying a basic human need, for a warm authentic community and a sense of identity."

"The diluted and emasculated tenets of non-traditional preachments" were noted as re-enforcing the misuse of drugs.

Of the many conclusions that can be drawn from this, one of them is glaringly obvious. The rabbis by and large feel drug misuse is not a Jewish problem and doesn't merit their active concern. They know about many facets of this behavior. Congregants and noncongregants come to them with their concerns about the problem. The rabbis, as a group, do what the rest of the population generally does—they perceive the problem as being the result of socio-psychological factors. Obviously this has little relevance to Judaism. They do not attempt to use the strength of their heritage as a tool to prevent or combat a problem which has reached epidemic proportions.

One respondent typified the attempt to rationalize the rabbis' disinvolvement from the problem of drug misuse: "Assuming that drug misuse by Jews is primarily to be found among young people who are alienated, as most

American Jewish youth is, I also assume that there would be no responses on the part of the addict to Judaism."

Whatever merit this statement has, in all fairness one has to add to the concept of alienation of youth, the remoteness of adult leaders, as a factor creating and even reinforcing social problems.

## Conclusions

The most devastating conclusion that can be drawn from this study is not based upon what the respondents noted. Rather, it is based upon the fact that hundreds of rabbis failed to respond at all to a one-page questionnaire.

To be a community leader and not to take an active position—irrespective of the position—on a community problem as prevalent and as significant as the misuse of alcohol and other drugs is to stay on the outskirts of one's community.

A number of questions should be raised concerning the results of this pilot project:

1. Is anyone suffering as a result of the rabbis' attitudes regarding the misuse of alcohol and other drugs? Who? In what way?
2. What action, if any, should be taken by the rabbinical community?
3. What should be the rabbi's role regarding these problems?
4. Does the rabbi have something unique to contribute to a problem area that is presently being attacked by a variety of people in an uncoordinated manner?
5. To whom can the rabbi turn for education and training in order to be effective, if he so chooses.

These questions and others that come to the mind of the reader will be answerable only when the rabbinical community actively acknowledges drug misuse as a problem that concerns them and that they are willing to confront in a way meaningful to them and the people that they serve.

*Appendix I*

### Drug and Alcohol Misuse: A Synagogue Survey
#### I

Name _____ Position _____

Name of Center and/or Synagogue _____

Age _____

Address _____

_____

Number of years at *present* institution _____

Number of years as Rabbi or in Community Center work _____

Have you ever been called upon to serve in your professional capacity in any program related to alcoholism or drug misuse? Yes _____ No _____

Are you now participating in such a program? (Please specify)

#### II

1. Please estimate the importance of the issue of alcoholism with regard to your daily responsibilities:
   1.1 Very Unimportant _____ 1.2 Unimportant _____
   1.3 Moderately Important _____ 1.4 Important _____
   1.5 Very Important _____
2. Please estimate the importance of the issue of drug abuse with regard to your daily responsibilities:
   2.1 Very Unimportant _____ 2.2 Unimportant _____
   2.3 Moderately Important _____ 2.4 Important _____
   2.5 Very Important _____
3. Since January 1968 have members of your synagogue or community center indicated any concerns about these problems?

*3.1 Alcohol*                  *3.2 Drugs*

Yes _____ No _____          Yes _____ No _____

   *3.3* Have individuals other than members indicated concerns about these problems during 1968? Yes _____ No _____ (please specify)

4. What has been the focus of these concerns?

   4.1 a General information _____ b Counseling _____ c Information about treatment services _____

   4.2 Requests for program to be initiated or sponsored by your institution _____

   4.3 Other (please specify)

5. Have these people generally been:

   5.1 Parents _____ 5.2 Young single adults _____

   5.3 Young marrieds _____ 5.4 Adolescents _____

   5.5 Other (please specify)

6. To the best of your knowledge, are there members of your institution that are currently *misusing:*

   *6.1 Alcohol*

Yes _____ No _____ Don't know _____

   *6.2 Drugs*

Yes _____ No _____ Don't know _____

7. What approximate percentage of the membership does this involve:

   7.1 Alcohol _____% 7.2 Drugs _____%

   7.3 Don't know _____ 7.4 Don't know _____

8. Have you considered the need for developing any kind of program focusing on drugs or alcoholism for your institution? Yes _____ No _____

9. What kind of program? (please specify)

10. Whom, if anyone, do you plan to turn to for help in developing such a program? (please specify)

11. Has your institution already developed and carried out such programs?

   *11.1 Alcohol*                  *11.2 Drugs*

Yes _____ No _____          Yes _____ No _____

12. What kinds of programs were they? (please specify)

13. Which aspects of these problems are you concerned with:

*13.1 Alcohol*
Sociological \_\_\_\_
Psychological \_\_\_\_
Pharmacological \_\_\_\_
Medical \_\_\_\_
Legal \_\_\_\_
Other (explain) _____

*13.2 Drugs*
Sociological \_\_\_\_
Psychological \_\_\_\_
Pharmacological \_\_\_\_
Medical \_\_\_\_
Legal \_\_\_\_
Other (explain) _____

14. Which aspects of these problems are you *most concerned* with:

*14.1 Alcohol*
Sociological \_\_\_\_
Psychological \_\_\_\_
Pharmacological \_\_\_\_
Medical \_\_\_\_
Legal \_\_\_\_
Other (explain) _____

*14.2 Drugs*
Sociological \_\_\_\_
Psychological \_\_\_\_
Pharmacological \_\_\_\_
Medical \_\_\_\_
Legal \_\_\_\_
Other (explain) _____

15. Why are you concerned about this aspect of the problem (explain)?

16. Have you received any special training in the field of:

*16.1 Alcoholism*
Yes \_\_\_\_ No \_\_\_\_

*16.2 Drugs*
Yes \_\_\_\_ No \_\_\_\_

17. If *Yes*—please specify *where;* what *kind* of training and what was the *specific focus:*

18. If *No*—do you feel your present daily responsibilities require special training in these areas: Yes \_\_\_\_ No \_\_\_\_

## III

Listed below are a series of questions which are designed to indicate your knowledge about alcoholism and drug addiction. Your answers will enable us to assess what the present state of knowledge is for rabbis and community center personnel.

If you are unable to answer the question, write in DK. (Don't know)

1. Drugs are best defined as:
2. The general dangers caused by *misusing* drugs are:
3. Addiction is best defined as:
4. Dependency is best defined as:
5. Habituating is best defined as:
6. The following drugs are addicting (A); habituating (H): Please fill in (DK) if you don't know.
   Alcohol _____ Heroin _____ Barbiturates _____
   Tranquilizers _____ Amphetamines _____ LSD _____
   Marijuana _____
7. The *misuse* of the following drugs may lead to medical problems (M), psychological problems (P), genetic problems (G), other problems (O); (please specify): Please fill in (DK) if you don't know.
   Alcohol _____ Heroin _____ Barbiturates _____
   Tranquilizers _____ Amphetamines _____ LSD _____
   Marijuana _____
8. People misuse drugs because:
9. *The typical drug addict* is a person who began using drugs at age _____, has been using drugs for _____ years, comes from a _____ family, of (ethnic) _____ background, is a _____ (religion), has completed _____ years of schooling, has been hospitalized _____ times for his drug use, and arrested _____ times.
   (You may add or delete from question 9 in order to state your views concerning the *typical* drug addict.)
10. Given our present state of knowledge about various drugs and alcohol, one can safely state that (check one only):
    10.1 Marijuana use invariably leads to the use of other more dangerous drugs _____.
    10.2 Drugs make sick people healthy and healthy people sick _____.

    10.3 Given the medical and psychological conse-
quences resulting from the misuse of various
drugs, alcohol is the most dangerous drug
known to man presently _____.

    10.4 Drug misuse is generally associated with par-
ticular ethnic groups of particular socio-economic backgrounds _____.

## IV

Recently, Rabbi Zalman M. Schacter, a Lubavitcher
Chasid, has indicated that LSD can have specific religious
usefulness and meaning for Orthodox Jews. He indicated
that:

(a) He found "many parallels between LSD and Hasidic
experiences."

(b) LSD "is less expensive to the body than fasting, and
less expensive to society than withdrawal, and easier
on the economy than holy-man mendicancy."

  1. Are you aware of Rabbi Schacter's position and his
writings? Yes _____ No _____

  2. Do you feel that there is a religious or cultural basis
for the misuse of drugs by Jews? Yes _____ No _____
(Please explain)

  3. Do you feel there is a religious or cultural basis that
can be turned to in order to prevent the misuse of
drugs by Jews, or its cessation once the process has
begun? Yes _____ No _____ (Please explain)

  4. What factors in contemporary Judaism do you feel
are: Reinforcing the misuse of drugs (Please explain):
Preventing the misuse of drugs (Please explain):

## Appendix II

If you cannot answer the longer questionnaire, could you
give us the following information:

1) What is the incidence of the narcotics and alcohol problems among Jewish adolescents and young adults in your Synagogue:
   A. Hard Drugs? (Heroin, Cocaine)
   B. Other drugs? (LSD, Methadrine, Amphetamines)
   C. Marijuana?
2) Is your Synagogue interested in a program of drug and alcohol prevention? Yes _____ No _____
3) What services for this group do you believe are needed?

*5*

# THE JEWISH DRUG ADDICT —
# A CHALLENGE TO THE JEWISH
# COMMUNITY

## Meyer H. Diskind

*Jewish Attitudes Toward Drug Addiction*

Before going into a discussion of the treatment aspects, I would like to make some general comments about the Jewish community attitude toward drug abuse.

In 1962, I was asked to serve as community organizer for the Long Island City Health Center Drug Addiction Program. At that time, there was a sharp upsurge of drug experimentation among the youth of the area, and the local Health Center organized a treatment and referral program. In order to insure continued community concern and involvement in the program, I organized a series of six narcotic seminars for community leaders, and established contact with all the civic, religious, business and social groups in the area, in an endeavor to achieve complete community planning and participation in a vexing problem that has caused such wide concern. It was at that time that I first met Father Pitcaithly, who was Chairman of the Narcotics Committee of the Long Island City-Astoria Community Council. Community interest was so great, that practically every group in the area was represented at the seminars, with one exception—the Jewish community.

At the conclusion of the highly successful seminar program, I contacted several of the local rabbis and the leaders of some of the local Jewish organizations to inquire about their failure to participate. The universal answer was that this was not a Jewish problem and did not concern them directly, although each of the respondents admitted that he had heard about an occasional Jewish addict in the area.

The Jewish response was unsatisfactory for two reasons. A community problem is everybody's problem. Jewish businessmen and home owners are victimized by drug-dependent persons to the same extent as non-Jews. But more important, the contention that there were very few Jewish addicts was completely false. The local health center's records revealed that numerous Jewish parents had contacted it for advice about their drug-dependent or drug-experimenting children. Being sensitive and embarrassed over their children's affliction, they avoided discussing the problem with their rabbi and friends, and even kept it a secret from other family members.

About a year later, one of the local rabbis told me in confidence that he was fully aware of the existence of the problem among Jewish youths in Astoria. However, he deliberately did not wish to become involved on a community basis lest his presence be tantamount to an acknowledgment of a Jewish problem, as if such acknowledgment would stigmatize the entire Jewish community.

This ostrich attitude has characterized the Jewish approach to the drug problem for the past two decades, and only recently has the Jewish community begun to acknowledge some concern—due largely to publicity concerning drug experimentation on campuses and the listing of Jewish names among persons arrested for drug violations. Jewish social agencies have known for some time about the impact of drug addiction upon family life.

*Magnitude of the Problem*

Before any consideration can be given toward the Federation's involvement in this area, it is essential that we have some knowledge about the magnitude of the problem insofar as Jews are concerned. It should be emphasized at the outset that nothing approximating accuracy of figures can be achieved, for several reasons.

1) In conducting a drug addiction census, addicts do not come forward to volunteer the information. Most available figures on the incidence of drug addiction are culled from arrest records.

2) While a doctor would not normally hesitate to report to the local Health Department cases of venereal disease, typhoid, measles and T.B., and other diseases with a public health component, the same situation does not pertain to the reporting of drug addicts. In the first place, most doctors would not undertake to treat a drug addict, for reasons we need not enter into here. In those instances, where a doctor does become involved with such patients, he frequently will not report for fear that disclosure would come to the attention of law enforcement authorities despite the Health Department's assurance of confidentiality.

3) With regard to Jewish drug addicts, the facts become even more obscure. Unlike the ghetto addict in lower socio-economic groups who must resort to illegal activity to maintain the habit, the average Jewish addict comes from a middle-class background, and generally has a higher educational achievement record. Bcause of a lesser degree of illegal involvement, they are less prone to become an arrest statistic. Many Jewish parents, particularly mothers, subsidize the financial cost of their children's habit for fear that otherwise they would indulge in criminal activity. The parents' sense of shame and guilt im-

mobilizes them to such an extent that they fail to utilize existing community treatment resources lest the condition become known to the outside world.

With these considerations in mind, let us examine some of the available statistics on Jewish addicts. To the best of my knowledge, the only study ever made on this subject was by Rabbi Joseph R. Rosenbloom, formerly chaplain at the U.S. Public Health Service Hospital in Lexington, Ky. In an article, "Notes on Jewish Drug Addicts," published in 1959 in *Psychological Reports,* he revealed that out of 2,709 patients admitted to the hospital in 1959, 203 or 7.5 percent were Jews. Ninety percent of the Jewish patients were from New York City. A detailed study of 32 of the Jewish patients revealed that 30 had arrest records, that 70 percent were either the youngest sibling in the family or the only child, and that there was a weak or absent father figure in the patient's formative years.

Although the statistics quoted above are rather limited, they do give us some indication about the size of the problems. The number of heroin addicts in New York has been variously estimated as between 50,000 and 100,000. Assuming the lower figure as the actual addiction incidence, and assuming a 7 percent Jewish addiction rate in line with Rabbi Rosenbloom's study, then there are 3,500 Jewish addicts in New York City.

As of the middle of April of 1968, 3,793 opiate addicts were certified to the New York State Narcotic Addiction Control Commission. Of this number, 136 or 3.6 percent were Jewish. Projecting the same rate to the 50,000 narcotic addicts in New York City, there are 1,850 Jewish narcotic addicts.

My feeling is that 3.6 percent figure is an underestimation of the actual situation. Most voluntary petitions for certification to the Narcotic Commission are made by parents. For the reasons outlined before, namely, the reluctance of Jewish parents to involve outside agencies, particularly public agencies, the Commission is probably not getting a true ethnic representation. I receive numerous telephone calls from Jewish parents and friends of drug addicts for advice usually with prefaced remarks about their reluctance to appear in court for certification purposes.

The figures cited above refer to the hard-core addict, usually heroin addict. It does not include the users of such drugs as barbiturates, amphetamines, LSD and other dangerous drugs who represent even higher drug-abuse rates. It therefore appears that we are dealing with substantial numbers, and from that standpoint, the Jewish community is morally bound to take definitive action.

### Why a Federation-Sponsored Treatment Agency?

If we recognize that a Jewish problem does exist, the next question is why the necessity for a Jewish-sponsored agency? There are numerous public and private agencies in the city which are geared to meet the problem, my agency being the largest. Why ghettoize the treatment of drug addiction?

1) I suppose the primary answer is that, traditionally, the Jewish community always supported its underprivileged, sick, poor, aged, and troubled. It is precisely for that reason that we have a Federation which supports Jewish-sponsored agencies.

2) For reasons mentioned above, Jewish families with a drug problem are reluctant to seek outside help. They believe that their affliction is unique and singular, and consequently they try to suppress the knowledge that a drug-dependent person is part of their family unit. However, the creation of a Jewish agency will bring the family closer to the realization that other co-religionists are plagued by the same problem, and that help can be made

available to people with similar spiritual, cultural, or religious values.

3) What would be unique in a Jewish-sponsored treatment agency is the introduction of spiritual and cultural values. The introduction of the chaplain in the correctional institutional treatment program is an indication of the efficacy of the spiritual approach. In our materialistic society there is frequently a tendency to negate or underestimate spiritual and cultural values. Our Jewish identity has been preserved for so many years because of the ethical concepts that we have incorporated into our daily existence. It is only when we have become acculturated at the expense of our own heritage that society's ills have begun to plague us. This accounts for the increase among Jews within the past several decades of alcoholism (a rare phenomenon in older days), divorce, suicide, and other social maladjustive phenomena. And perhaps to some extent, this is also responsible for the rise in Jewish drug abuse.

As a criminologist and trained social worker, I can report to you an extremely low rate of criminality in drug addiction and alcoholism among persons who received a well-rounded Jewish education. I do not for one moment wish to convey the impression that Jewish education alone is responsible for successful social adjustment. The cohesive Jewish family structure and the resultant emotional security no doubt is a pervasive factor. But perhaps the family cohesion is also an outgrowth of the Jew's ethical and spiritual standards.

I believe, therefore, that the antisocial manifestations of drug abuse can be remedied to some extent by filling in the void in the lives of persons who have been deprived of their rightful ancestral heritage. Any Federation-sponsored treatment program should include instruction in such areas as Jewish history, Bible and moral concepts. This component can be better structured by the rabbis and educators. Of course, this service would be in addition to the psychiatric, psychological and social work support.

4) Drug-dependent persons frequently are what they are because of pathological family relationships. An effective treatment program must therefore involve the parent as well as the patient. In other treatment settings, I observed that very few Jewish parents are involved in parent groups which meet weekly, undoubtedly for the reasons mentioned previously. Such parents would undoubtedly be more comfortable in a group of peers with similar backgrounds and who share a similar problem.

5) From time to time I receive telephone calls and visits from rabbis for advice after a parishoner confided in them about their son's or daughter's drug problem. Like the drug abuser's parents, the rabbi is frequently reluctant to suggest that outside agencies be utilized. However, the rabbi would be more comfortable in suggesting referral to a Jewish agency.

6) Having been engaged in the field of addiction treatment since 1957, I have observed two general types of addicts: the Sociological Addict, and the Psychological Addict.

Sociological Addict

He is a product of environmental forces. The same factors responsible for delinquency are essentially the same which spawn addiction, e.g., slums, poverty, cultural and economic deprivation, lack of employment skills, poor recreational opportunities, etc. In a milieu of this sort, addiction is more or less tolerated and drugs are readily available. Youngsters reared in such ghettos experiment with various types of drugs and it almost becomes part of the growing-up process. Most treatment agencies concentrate on filling in these voids by providing such services as vocational and academic training, economic assistance, and housing, and by providing recreational facilities.

Most Negroes and Puerto Ricans fall into the category of Sociological Addicts, and the highest rate of success was achieved with them during the ten years that I headed the State Parole Narcotic Treatment Program.

Psychological Addict

This type of addict has deep-seated personality conflicts and has a poor emotional equilibrium. He may come from a middle-class family with economic and educational opportunities and achievements. Rabbi Rosenbloom's study, previously referred to, reveals that in a significant number of cases there was an absent and weak father figure with a domineering and extremely overprotective mother. While this situation characterizes the lives of most addicts, it assumes more pathological proportions with families of Jewish addicts. Consequently, the psychological addict—and most Jewish addicts fall into that category— uses drugs as an adjustive mechanism to resolve inner conflicts and ease tension. Drugs to him serve as a true adjustive and adaptive value. To help a psychological addict, psychotherapy of some depth is essential to get at the underlying causes that precipitate addiction.

Again going back to my Parole experience, we encountered relatively little success with Jewish addicts, probably because we could not provide the intensive psychotherapy that they required. Furthermore, effective psychotherapy requires long periods of treatment. With the Sociological Addict, environmental manipulation proved to be effective. When he acquired a vocational skill, or got some additional schooling, or received financial or medical assistance, the feeling of frustration which impelled him to drugs in the first place was dissipated. Obviously, this type of treatment would not be responsive to the needs of the Psychological Addict.

I do not wish to convey the impression that all addiction falls so neatly into the two categories I just described.

There is a good deal of overlapping—the Sociological Addict, for example, may also have been bruised psychologically and emotionally by early childhood experiences, and he too could benefit from therapy. Indeed, most treatment programs provide this type of service as well as other social services. But as a working concept and as a blueprint for further planning, the classification is a practical one.

If the Jewish drug user is of the psychological nature that I have just described, it follows that the emphasis would be somewhat different than that of most existing treatment modalities.

7) In addition, and this is something I cannot document, I believe that there are a number of Jewish addicts who would volunteer for a Jewish agency treatment program who would otherwise not become involved in treatment. The affinity of interests, the similarity of cultural and ethnic backgrounds, and the common problem might prove attractive to Jewish addicts because of an important therapeutic element—mutual identification. Most addicts lack a feeling of self-worth, and Jewish drug addicts, in particular, display a sense of guilt because of the worry they cause their families. They would, therefore, be more responsive to suggestions regarding the availability of a sectarian sponsored treatment program. It is generally recognized that the group therapy and encounter programs which have been developed by Synanon and Daytop are effective. Group encounters can be meaningful only when there is group identification and a community of interests. The establishment of groups with similar racial and cultural characteristics would tend to enhance the cohesiveness of the group.

8) Finally, there are in existence several religiously oriented treatment programs. I refer specifically to the Teen Challenge and programs with which Father Pit-

caithly has been identified and which have proven to be fairly effective.

## Integration vs. Segregation of Addiction Treatment

At a recent meeting of the Commission on Synagogue Relations Narcotics Committee, the question was raised whether a separate agency or a separate entity within an agency need be created to meet the drug problem. Could not the adolescent addict, for example, be treated by a Jewish agency dealing with disturbed or pre-delinquent youths? Is there a danger that by segregating drug-dependent persons we might be reinforcing the pathology since the only element in common would be the fact of drug depndency? Since the underlying cause of addiction is an emotional disturbance, would we not be treating the symptom rather than the basic cause if addicts were segregated? Or to put it differently, if emotional disturbance is the cause of addiction and delinquency, why not integrate both types of patients in one treatment setting?

The issue of integration vs. segregation of addiction treatment has been explored at great depth by professionals in the field for some time. Although no definitive conclusions have been arrived at, there appears to be general consensus that a degree of specialization is needed in dealing with the addict because of the unique problems that he presents.

1) In the first place, social agencies have long ago abdicated their responsibility in this area. Treatment of an addict is a most frustrating and unrewarding experience because of the high rate of recidivism. Despite the therapist's best efforts, traditional approaches have proven ineffective. Social agencies therefore shied away from the problem, and with their limited staff and facilities, preferred to invest their time and energy with clients with a

better prognosis. As a result, a number of private agencies were established during the past ten years devoted exclusively to addiction. The only general private agency that has established a program for addicts is the Salvation Army, but the program itself is segregated from the overall agency program. Similarly, the medical profession and the hospitals concluded that addiction treatment programs in a medical setting warrant specialization. Consequently, the Bernstein Institute of the Beth Israel Medical Center is a separate entity. Similarly, state hospital drug programs are apart from the general program.

2) While it is true that emotional aberration might be the basis for addiction as well as other symptoms of social dysfunction such as alcoholism, delinquency, truancy and sexual promiscuity, it does not necessarily follow that generic treatment approaches are equally effective for all maladjustive manifestations. Faulty diet habits may be responsible for dental cavities as well as stomach disorders. It does not follow that both symptoms can or should be treated by the same practitioner or even by the same discipline.

3) We live in an area of specialization, whether it be in the legal, medical or social work professions. Treating the drug addict presents such unique problems that specialization is a *sine qua non*. In an intramural setting, for example, it is important to adopt security measures in order to avoid the smuggling in of contraband, chemical testing procedures are established, visitors are screened. In-patient and out-patient psychiatrists agree that traditional therapeutic approaches are ineffective. In a social agency as well as medically oriented settings, we think in terms of short-term rather than long-term goals. We are dealing here with a notoriously unmotivated patient or client with hedonistic impulses, who has low frustration tolerance, is manipulative, has low feelings of self-worth and experiences a sense of social alienation. The worker

must have a high frustration tolerance, be able to recognize manipulative patterns, be firm, be adept at individual as well as group counseling. Group therapy sessions, in contrast to traditional approaches, must emphasize the reality concept, namely, the necessity to assume responsibility for one's actions rather than the probing for unconscious motivations and causations. In short, the therapist, whether he be a social worker, psychiatrist or psychologist, must be equipped with specialized skills and training.

In the New York State Division of Parole, parolees with a history of narcotic addiction were included in generalized caseloads of all types of offenders. But the rate of recidivism was so great that, in 1957, specialized caseloads were established as an experimental measure. The rate of success jumped to such a degree that the specialized program became a permanent feature of State Parole operations.

4) There is always the danger that drug-dependent clients might infect clients with other symptomatic maladjustive behavior. Community centers, for example, generally are reluctant to accept such clients into their programs for that reason.

Young adolescents who have begun to experiment with drugs and who present such self-destructive tendencies as delinquency, truancy and irresponsibility can and should be treated in existing Jewish agencies geared to meet these problems. However, having become fully addicted, the patient should be handled in a specialized setting.

*Should a New Agency Be Created?*

I do not think that this is necessary. Existing resources might be utilized with the proviso that a separate unit be established within the existing agency for addiction treatment. While I referred to the need for specialization, the value of generic skills is not to be underrated. Consequently, agency workers might be transferred to the specialized program with additional training. The use of existing agency administrative structure, professional and office staff and research personnel would probably result in more economical operations than would be the establishment of a brand-new agency.

## Treatment Modality

Our prime purpose in this paper is to explore the advisability of establishing a treatment program for Jewish drug addicts under Federation sponsorship. The details of the program need not be discussed at this time and perhaps should best be left to the professionals.

In a general way, however, I would like to present my concept of the broad outline of a realistic and effective program. I would like to emphasize from the outset that a variety of programs with different types of approaches are currently on the scene. There are programs whose basic underpinning is the judicious use of ex-addicts (Synanon and Daytop), Maintenance Programs (Bernstein Institute), the Multidisciplinary approach, Authoritative approach (Parole) and the religious approach (Teen-Challenge). The best features of each should be incorporated in the Federation-sponsored program with the exception of maintenance dosages. The latter type of program can best be initiated in an in-patient hospital setting under medical supervision.

The proposed treatment program should consist of a halfway house where detoxification, psychiatric, medical and social services would be available as well as the Jewish cultural and spiritual components I previously referred to. Similar services would be provided to patients after they leave the structured halfway house setting. Aggressive casework requires that the worker go into the home frequently to try to modify faulty family attitudes as they might impinge upon the client's adjustment. It is vitally important that the parents, particularly mothers, also be involved in treatment. This calls not only for individual but group counseling as well. The judicious use of the rehabilitated ex-addict should not be overlooked, but I would rely heavily upon professionals—psychiatrists, psychologists, group and case workers. While a variety of social services should be made available in accordance with the individual client's needs, I think that a rather heavy emphasis should be placed upon psychotherapy for the reason I mentioned previously—the fact that we are dealing mainly with the psychological as opposed to the sociological addict. The rabbi should be a member of the treatment team.

Jewish agencies must be prepared to modify their objectives and functions in the light of changing conditions in a rapidly changing society. The plague of addiction has unfortunately begun to affect the lives of a significant number of our people and I think that it is time for the Jewish community to abandon the ostrich posture and involve itself more directly in a solution of the problem.

## 6

# THE RABBI AND THE ADDICT

### Richard I. Schachet

Many people ask, "How is it that a rabbi gets involved in the field of drug addiction?" After all, they say, there aren't any Jewish addicts. In my case, my involvement began one night about five years ago when I had parked my car quite illegally on West 44th Street. (That's something rabbis tend to do—park their cars illegally, put down the clergy sign, and pray.) When I approached my car at about 1:00 A.M., a girl with bleached red hair, a flower print blouse and tiger-striped pants was waiting for me. She asked me if I was a clergyman. When I answered in the affirmative, she told me she wanted to speak with me. Barbara (that was her name) turned out to be a thirty-one-year-old, typical run-of-the-mill Jewish drug addict prostitute. As Barbara's story unfolded, a whole new world began for me. Barbara had been using drugs for some sixteen years. She came from Far Rockaway, where her father, a pharmacist, had his store. She at this time had no friends . . . her family had disowned her . . . no job skills outside of being a prostitute. No home except for the hotels she stayed in with her "johns" —the men she picked up. No clothing except the barest of necessities. In short, Barbara had nothing.

I sat with her all that night, and when I went home I decided to see if there was anything I could do to assist Barbara. After making numerous phone calls I discovered the almost unbelievable fact that in the entire city of New York there was a total of 50 beds available for detoxifi-

136

cation of female addicts. This, in a city where estimates run as high as 100,000 addicts of which 20,000 are female. This means, assuming that these figures are near correct, that one in every eighty are addicted to some type of narcotic.

I went back to see Barbara the next night and the next and the next. While seeing her I met many other addicts, both male and female, and became involved in their plight; and so a whole new life began for me. The life as "The Junky Rabbi."

Since this paper is especially for the Jewish drug addict, I am limiting myself to that area. I will not touch at all upon other socio-economic groups and their particular problems.

In our society today there is a new type of status symbol. Many years ago the status symbol was the exodus of families from Brooklyn or the Bronx into a town like Laurelton or Valley Stream. In later years the status symbol became the moving even farther out to Long Island to to towns like Merrick, Hicksville, Huntington. Today we witness a new status symbol, the return to the fancy apartment houses in New York City. Today's other status symbols are the mink coat, the annual trip to Miami Beach (which has since become the trip to Europe), then the trip to Israel (which is not so bad), and two cars. However, with our affluent society as it is, we are in a position where most people can afford (through perhaps extra work and extra savings) most of these things: so yet a new status symbol had to be found. The new status symbol became our children . . . and our children's grades. How many A's do they get on their report cards? Do they have early acceptance into college? Do they get a New York State Regents Scholarship? How do they do on their College Boards? How do they do compared to their cousins? For some reason or other we all like to compare with something or someone; cousins are, in many cases, handy. And so our children became a status symbol scholastically. Were they accepted to a *good* college: Columbia, Brandeis, Harvard? God forbid that our children should not go to college! Nobody questions whether the youngster is ready for college, either educationally or emotionally. Might not the pressures be a little bit too hard for them? You've all heard the story of the grandmother wheeling her two grandchildren in a carriage when someone remarked, "How cute. How old are they?" At which time the grandmother replied, "The doctor is two, and the dentist is four!" This really does happen. There is nothing wrong with wanting a good education for our children. I'm positive we all want that. However, what *is* wrong is pushing our children to far exceed their educational or emotional abilities. So this is cause number one: the great deal of educational stress and pressure.

The second cause is a great deal of social stress which begins at a very early age—even as early, for instance, as seven, eight, or nine, when the young boys are starting to attend Little League. The other night I spent the evening with the father of an eight-year-old who was playing Little League baseball and he was telling us how angry and upset he was with his son who was just not inclined toward athletics. The boy did not know how to play third base. The boy did not know how to catch a ball. And the father really got very angry at his son. He couldn't comprehend that his son was not yet athletically inclined. The father himself was a good ballplayer, so why wasn't the son? I have seen parents hit their children because they missed a ground ball that lost the ball game.

The stress is present with girls as well. Parents are having pajama parties for their seven- or eight-year-old daughters. We want our children to grow up socially. I think one of the best ways of bringing this home is to describe something I saw very recently in Alexander's Department Store. While shopping one day, I saw a large sign that was beyond my comprehension. In big letters the sign said, "Sale training bras." Now I assume that a training bra is for a girl ten years of age. If you could tell me what a ten-year-old girl is training for, I would like to know. It sounds funny . . . it sounds strange, but these are the additional pressures we're putting on our children. We push our children (and I'm not saying this is bad in all cases) and we should cut down and let our children feel their own way. We want our children to go to the synagogue dance. This is fine! When I was a youngster (and I don't think it was that many years ago) at the age of twelve, thirteen, fourteen, we had dances at the synagogue with our youth group. We had records. It was a record hop then, and we danced. Not today. Today they have live bands. We are paying out $50 and $60 and $70 and even $100 in some cases for this live band. Senior proms which were already out of hand in my day, when the high school seniors went out to night clubs and stayed out all night, are now being held in junior high schools where the youngsters are staying out all night. We do have this new morality. How many mothers are buying their fifteen-year-old daughters diaphragms or contraceptive pills . . . "just in case"? It's amazing the number of abortions that are performed on teen-age Jewish girls. So you see the social pressure of modern parents sometimes is too much.

Thirdly, of course, there is the keen awareness of the world's problems. Martin Luther King's assassination . . . Vietnam . . . the lack of knowledge whether or not our country will be in a state of war right here on our own shores within a few days, is quite disrupting to the children of our society. The modern parents have said, "Be liberal, all men are created equal." However, when the child is liberal, when the child does have Negro friends, the parents say, "Not you—the next generation should do it!" They thereby cause another problem for the children. So all these additional pressures are being forced on the middle-class teen-ager of today.

Fourthly, there is the problem of the overdominant Jewish mother. It seems in our society that suddenly the woman has taken over most roles. The woman gets the father's pay check, the father gets his allowance. The woman pays most of the bills at home from the father's pay check. The dominant Jewish female is many cases is not content with what she has and is always striving for more. This is not so terrible except that is means that the father of the household, in many instances, must work long hours, two jobs, and overtime, and he's just not home enough for the children. The parents are not as interested in this case in the children as they are in the luxuries that money can buy. Of course, conversely, the father has given up his male dominant position.

Let me give you a typical case of the fifteen-year-old Jewish boy.

The boy is pressured into going to a Temple dance on a Saturday night. Now if any of you have ever been to dances or chaperoned a teen-age dance, you know that when you walk in you see the boys on one side and the girls on the other side. Now what has happened? No one has asked if this fifteen-year-old boy is ready or not to go to a dance. No one asked if this boy is too shy, not ready yet to socialize with the opposite sex, but he is pressured into going. On his way there, he meets a friend of his who says to him, "Hey, you going to the dance? Wanna have a real good time? Why don't you sniff some of this white powder?" And the boy does sniff the white powder—almost like snuff. It burns, but he feels good, he feels relaxed after sniffing the white powder. Now he doesn't care about school, he doesn't care about the pressures. He doesn't worry about meeting the girls. He wants to meet the girls. He is completely and truly relaxed, in a state of euphoria, and he goes to the dance and has a tremendous time because he's so relaxed and at ease. In fact he is the hit of the dance. He does the monkey, the twist, the watusi, and the other modern dances of today. He might even be courageous enough to ask a girl if he could take her home and she might agree . . . he might even kiss her good night, maybe for the first time in his life. He has such a good time at this dance that next week he seeks out this friend of his for some more white powder, and he gets it. Either he buys it or it's given to him for nothing. After a while, the boy starts using the white powder both in school and on Saturday night if he goes out. Finally, one night he sniffs in the white powder and it doesn't do too much . . . he gets very little kick out of it. Then his friend says, "Listen, inject it into your arm, that ought to do you some good." He injects it into his arm; sure enough, he gets a good kick out of it. This might happen on Friday night, Saturday night, and even on Wednesday night, because on Wednesday night he may have had a big fight with his parents because of all the pressure, and the boy wants to escape somehow. Now one day he finds that he's not getting as big a kick or as quick a kick by just injecting into his arm, and his friend says, "Why don't you inject it into your vein; it really feels good then." The boy does inject this white powder, mixed with a couple of drops of water, into his vein and he really feels good.

One morning, he wakes up and he is sick. He has diarrhea, he is vomiting, he is sweating, stomach cramps— what we would consider a very bad "virus" or "grippe"— and he finds that when he takes this white powder, which of course is heroin, and injects it into his arm all the pain goes away. The euphoria comes back, the boy feels good. This is the morning that the young man has become physically addicted to heroin. However, the first time he sniffed in the heroin, that very first time, he found a solution to his problem, he became mentally addicted to heroin. It is this mental addiction that is our problem. The physical

addiction can be dealt with easily. A man can be detoxi-
fied in three days, maybe four days, tops, but the mental
addiction, this craving for the escape, is our biggest problem. And so we see that a new life starts for this boy. His
lying, conning, stealing, and doing everything antisocial
are in order to gain the money to obtain his heroin. If it is
a girl—and the story can be the same with a girl—she
now must also begin a life of lying and stealing, but for
her it's a little bit easier to make money because she can
be a prostitute. If she's young and pretty she can make as
much as $80 to $100 on any given evening. But this new
life begins.

Let me carry you one step further . . . to the youngster
who has been through high school, graduated, and is now
attending college. Now we come to another problem in the
field of narcotics abuse. I say narcotics abuse because it is
a known fact that both marijuana and LSD are not physically addicting. Again, note the word "physical" addiction
as opposed to "mental" addiction. The college student of
today is faced with many problems, many pressures. The
pressure of belonging to a group is one. There is a strong
desire to belong to and be a part of something or someone.
He finds that he wants to get high, he wants to escape
from these pressures. So this college student is able to
make contact with someone and he starts to smoke pot,
grass, mary jane, marijuana (it's all the same). If he
really wants to go way out, go on a trip, really see God,
so they say, really smell music, taste music, taste art and
get a great deal of insight into his senses, he goes on a
trip. LSD is one of the most potent things known to men.
One gallon—four quarts of LSD put into the New York
City water system—will render this entire city completely
helpless. It's not very much; a couple of drops is all that's
necessary for an overdose of LSD. Fortunately for us,
the use of LSD, STP and other hallucinatory drugs is on
the decline. The use of pot, however, because of fallacious

advertising, so to speak, is on the increase. The use of pills, both barbiturate and amphetamine, is also on the increase. College students try and stay awake all night, and so take the diet spansule-type pills or "speed balls," and they make the student want to go, go, go.

I think it is interesting to note that in all my experience in the field of addiction, I have never met a Yeshiva *bocher* or *bachurah* who has been addicted. This does not mean that if your child attends Yeshivah he or she will not become addicted . . . but I feel that there is something that we must look into here. I further found that there is little addiction in a practicing Jewish home, whether that practice be Reform, Conservative, or Orthodox. The old adage, "The family that prays together, stays together," may just have something to it.

Although this is highly unscientific, my experience has shown that there are approximately six male addicts to every female addict; however, among the Jewish population there are approximately three male Jewish addicts to every female Jewish addict. Further (and this is also unscientific, but comes from personal observation and discussions), if one were to analyze all the white female drug addicts, I believe that about half are Jewish.

One common element in all addicts is immaturity. The addict's emotional maturity might range from age three or four on up to pre-teen, although the chronological age may be late teen through late twenties.

To summarize, it appears that there are a number of causative factors toward which we can attribute the increase of drug addiction and drug abuse in the Jewish home. Briefly they are:

1. Educational pressure—on one who is not able to cope with that pressure.
2. Social pressure—on one who is forced to grow up sooner than he is ready to do so.

3. Female dominance in the home as well as male passivity.
4. The need by most people to belong and to be a follower in the "in" group.
5. Lack of togetherness in the home as well as a lack of religious practice.
6. Emotional immaturity and failure on the part of many parents to cut the umbilical cord.

## 7

# ON THE PREVENTION OF DRUG ADDICTION

## Adolph E. Wasser

The Jewish students among those who were recently picked up for narcotics violation at the campuses at Stony Brook, Harpur, Cornell, and Syracuse universities, and the Jewish students among the protesters at Columbia and other universities seem to have two things in common:

1) Their number among both groups seem disproportionate to the number of Jewish students on the respective campuses. *Time* Magazine of May 3, 1968, citing recent studies, states that "almost half of the protest-prone students are Jewish." Another study revealed that "one out of five 'hippies' in San Francisco's Haight-Ashbury District is Jewish." I have been assured that the percentage of Jewish youths in New York's East Village is considerably larger.

2) Most of them come from families which reflect the general tendency for Jews to be liberal and permissive. As a result, there is less assertion of parental authority among Jews than among the same socio-economic Protestant or Catholic groups.

Prevention of drug abuse among Jews, in my opinion, could best be assured if Jewish social agencies, synagogues and other Jewish communal institutions made a concerted, cooperative effort to teach Jewish parents how to use "parent power" and to strengthen the Jewish family.

The Jewish family of today is, by and large, child-centered and proudly so. That is part of being a permissive parent and a liberal. We are up on the latest psychological theories. In such a family the child is protected against reality unless it be a "fun and happiness"-oriented reality. I am sure that many of you will be able to corroborate my experience of being reprimanded by parents—really by mothers, and that's part of the problem, because the father is, at best, a shadowy figure— for having exposed their offspring to the reality of the Holocaust. Many Jewish youngsters know nothing about the Hitler years, and in my institution some even thought that Hitler had been "a good man." Yet the Jewish mother feels that there is no need to expose her child to such "horror" stories for fear that it may be a traumatic experience and may affect the psyche of her child.

Few demands are made on the Jewish child unless it be to excel scholastically. But *then* the pressure is *fierce*. The child's ability to "produce" is, however, secondary to the glory reflected on the parents; and if a child should be unable or unwilling to "produce," then the blame, in many cases, is projected on the teacher or on the school.

I was confronted with such parents the other day. A father and mother came to complain that their child had not been accepted to the Usdan Music and Art Camp. The mother explained that the child plays beautifully and that, as a matter of fact, many people thought, and had so told her, that the child was a prodigy. This was confirmed by the father who told me that he had taped the child's playing and that everybody who heard it marveled at the child's musical genius. Upon receipt of the rejection by the camp, the mother had cried all day and so had the child. To make a long story short, when I supported the camp and questioned whether the child was really as good a musician as the parents seemed to think, and when I pointed out that perhaps in their desire to encourage the child they were really giving her an unrealistic picture of herself, the father seemed shaken because that's what his child had told him. "You lied to me, Daddy," and she cried that she had known all along that she really could not play well. The outcome of this, however, was that the parents still refused to accept this situation and are now projecting blame on me and on the camp.

Children need strong limits. They need standards after which they can pattern themselves. They need guidelines which they can follow and against which they can test themselves. They need to be told "you shall and you shall not." The Midrash teaches us that "he who does not rebuke his son leads him into delinquency." Children must know what is permitted and what is prohibited.

Jewish tradition teaches that within every person there is an "inclination toward evil" and the "inclination toward good" and that these are in constant struggle with each other. It is the role of Jewish parents to feed and support the "inclination toward good" so that it may overcome the "inclination toward evil." Parental failure to set strong limits, to exercise their "parent power," will result in children whose "super-ego"—"the inclination toward good"—is weak or nonexistent.

Dr. Bruno Bettelheim, in a speech at the Annual Convention of the American Ortho-Psychiatric Association, was quoted by *The New York Times* to have said the following: "There is no doubt about the underlying violence with which we are born. Whether we are going to have violence depends to a very large degree how we develop the super-ego and the controls of the coming generation . . . What we have got to develop is trust in the institutions of society, from police and teachers all the way up to the President, whatever you may think of him personally . . ." Dr. Bettelheim said that "liberals, the press and teachers who fail to assert their authority all shared some blame for denying super-ego models to the young . . ."

Some children are unable to accept authority; they reject and deny their fathers and are alienated not only from society but particularly from Judaism and from the Jewish community. They are unable to face reality. For many of them their main escape lies in withdrawal into the unreality of a hallucinogenic Nirvana induced by opium and drugs.

The educational approach to prevention, of course, has to be continued and stressed. We must continue to bring to our youth and to their parents scientific and objective evidence of the potential danger inherent in the abuse of these drugs. To quote Dr. Stanley Yolles, Director of the National Institute of Mental Health (*New York Times,* March 7, 1968): "Scare techniques are not only ineffectual but are even detrimental to conveying needed information about the hazards of drug abuse. With the present incidence of marijuana use, many students have either experienced or observed, firsthand, the effects of this drug. They know that psychoses or other grave consequences are not an inevitable concomitant of smoking one marijuana cigarette. It is clear that to be effective a preventive educational effort must be carefully tailored to specific population groups and must be based on the best educational and scientific footing. The decrease in LSD use is at least in part, I would suggest, a function of the degree to which users will respond to scientific evidence of potential danger."

Because we as Jews, however, have special reason to be concerned with this rising scourge of drug addiction among some of our young people, we must work for preventive measures beyond science and education. Long-range prevention for us can best be accomplished if the organized Jewish community were to give primary concern to ways and means of teaching parents how to use their "parent power" and of strengthening the Jewish family according to Jewish insights and religious values which have, over thousands of years, contributed toward the spiritual and physical well-being of each Jew.

## 8
# ON THE PREVENTION OF ADDICTION—
# A FAMILY AGENCY VIEW
## Arnold Mendelson

Family agencies are continually confronted by a variety of social ills from the most exaggerated character deviations or psychoses to more benign adjustment reactions, particularly in children. With the proliferation of drug use by teen-agers and the obvious increase in the number of youngsters using barbiturates, amphetamines and other psychedelic drugs, the incidence of such cases coming to our attention is definitely on the rise. Use of marijuana, LSD, and other so called mind-expanding drugs are clearly affecting a broad spectrum of the Jewish community. Increasingly, we see younger and younger drug users. As a result, more and more families are affected, a factor reflected in the increase in the number of applications we have received in which the presenting complaint involves some suspicion or knowledge on the part of the family regarding drug use. Today, the unmistakable truth is that middle-class suburban communities suffer as much as lower-class urban areas from a high incidence of drug use and abuse. Addiction is no longer just a problem of the ghetto. Drugs are not only part of the college scene, but readily available in almost any high school in this city, to say nothing of its growing use in our suburbs. The ready availability of drugs in our communities and the general acceptance of the use of hallucinogens by large numbers of youth are significant factors in the widespread use of drugs that is now taking place. The problem is here, it is growing, and it needs to be faced squarely, realistically and constructively.

If we talk about prevention, we must inevitably talk about family and its capacity to foster the healthy development of all its members. Prevention is as much a family affair as it is a problem for the sociologists, psychologists, clinics, or social agencies. It is everybody's problem, for everybody pays the price. The cost to the individual, his family and society is enormous. One need only take note of the massive programs treating the addict, specialized probation and parole projects, the increasing number of Halfway Houses serving addicts, and the centers, both private and public, attempting to deal with this most serious situation. Despite our best efforts, we are only beginning to scratch the surface of this most complex but pressing issue. There yet remains enormous, serious gaps in the specific knowledge of addiction as well as its treatment.

Any consideration of the problem of drug abuse must take into account the transformation of family patterns brought about by rapid social and technological change and the resulting effects on family stability and health. We are in the midst of revolutionary changes in our educational, scientific and social systems unparalled in history. The impact on family organization and family functioning is pervasive. The alienating and disintegrative forces of family life seem to tear at the fabric of the family and threaten its very existence. Runaways have multiplied alarmingly. Youngsters today are leaving home at earlier and earlier ages and in ever greater numbers. Under these conditions the vulnerability of individual members to mental and emotional breakdown or panaceas that temporarily bring relief from everyday conflicts and pain is not so surprising. The family as a stabilizing force in a rapidly changing world is itself in crisis as it seeks to adapt to present conditions. Family relations are out of balance. There is less intimacy, less closeness and sharing, a trend toward alienation; not separateness but separation, not a strengthening of self but a sense of selflessness, a lack of identity. The emotional climate within the home has become one of individualism and self-interest, mistrust and distance. The roles of father, mother and child have become blurred. Symbols of authority and standards of behavior are confused. Parental attitudes reflect this confusion and the uncertainty about the values they wish to instill in their children. The consequence of this is a generation gap where parents are isolated from children and one family member becomes alienated from another. The capacity of the family to withstand the pressures on it and to maintain its own equilibrium is being challenged. The consequences of these disturbances in the balance of family functions is an impairment in that family's potential for growth. What we may then observe is a trend toward recurring crisis in family life, a movement toward disorganization in the family group, or the isolation or alienation of one of its members.

It is the family which transmits values that make for positive mental health or the conflicts that lead to unhappiness and deviant behavior. Prevention, if it is to be effective then, must to my way of thinking bring about a strengthening of the family. There can be no such development where communication is impossible, where mutual respect is nonexistent, or where parental excesses either punitively or permissively color the atmosphere in the home. Lack of discipline or failure to set limits, reflected in an earlier vogue of permissive child-rearing, can contribute to drug use in youngsters who feel unable to tolerate frustrations and who by virtue of being overindulged, fixated on a level of early omnipotent narcissism, are poorly equipped to deal with the pressures and responsibilities of life. The domineering, frequently seductive mother, and passive father not uncommonly seen with addiction-prone youngsters, create poor role models for children struggling with basic conflicts concerning their own identities. Parental failure to set standards of behavior and the trend toward self-gratification and instant satisfaction of impulses highly publicized by the news and advertising media, cannot help but promote drug use in offering the illusion of having what one feels is lacking.

While it is true that kids "play it cool" with drugs, any close examination with parents of such youngsters usually reveals their long-buried suspicions that something was wrong, that their child was behaving strangely at times, seemed unusually secretive, was listless, cut classes, just wasn't himself. It is increasingly evident that the parents live through a period in which they minimize observed behavior that strongly suggests something is wrong. Their complacency not infrequently exists in the face of unconscious attempts on the part of some youngsters to make known their wish for parental intervention. In their denial of what is occurring, parents passively and unwittingly encourage continuation and acting out. Seen early, or educated to the signs of drug abuse, many families could avail themselves of help before drug use has taken hold or a crisis situation has developed. Our most effective means of dealing with addiction is its prevention. To be effective, however, parents need to take their heads out of the sand and not pretend all is well when what they see, feel, and sense tells them otherwise. They cannot afford to join their teen-age children (our young people) in denying the seriousness of what is occurring, for in doing so they abdicate (their) responsibility as parents and give a clear signal of their lack of readiness to confront the problem.

In marked contrast to their parents, the youngsters we have seen do not generally consider their use of marijuana or other hallucinogenic drugs a problem. Rather, they either blandly deny there is any reason for concern or otherwise identify the problem in terms of the parents' overdetermined response. Our observations of the young people we have seen lead us to believe that not only are they alienated from their families and society, but equally detached from their own feelings and from other people. Their blandness and at times promotion of drugs can and has been quite misleading to parents who find the controversy surrounding the use of marijuana, in particular, quite confusing. Controversy or not, where we see youngsters who increasingly find themselves unable to cope with the pressures of everyday life, who are truants, are unable to keep up with their studies, are moody, tense and generally feel "up tight," there is reason enough to feel that young person is in need of help. Drug abuse and/or addiction does not occur overnight. Like other manifestations of emotional instability it can often be traced to influences brought upon the child in his formative years. Unfortunately incipient behavior indicative of personality disturbance is not always recognized early enough nor can we expect that less aware parents can take the family temperature and have a ready-made barometer of its state of health. It is, however, an idea that has merit and I will come back to this point a bit later on.

A brief word, if I may, about family agencies and family therapy as one approach to the prevention and treatment of drug abuse, particularly where adolescents or young adults are involved. Experience has shown us that interaction within a family and the functions of each member have decisive and significant reciprocal influences. A symptom or illness in one member is frequently linked to conflicts and forces within the network of family relationships. Conflict in the family and conflict in an individual child are interrelated. Phenomenological studies of schizophrenics and their families bear this out in clearly demonstrating that behavior regarded clinically as symptomatic of an illness is the intelligible outcome of what has been going on in the family. To state it more simply, many kids are turning on as a way of coping with situations they are otherwise unable to face. Drugs then may be the individual's unique adaptational efforts to deal with the demands of his environment. For some it is a means of survival, for others part of the struggle for identity or a way of handling unacceptable sexual feeling or confusions.

Processes of interaction within a family frequently have and do lead to the selection of one or another individual as a repository for family pathology. It is precisely for this reason that a family approach is at times particularly desirable as a way of more fully assessing the roles of certain key figures whose actions can be destructive to a child's adjustment or development. Problems of drug abuse by youngsters seem to me better understood when viewed within the context of the family and its total functioning.

I do not wish to suggest that family agencies have the answer to the drug problem. It is clear where fragmentation and disintegration of the family seem irreversible or where there are rigid, unbending patterns of alienation, a family-centered approach is really not possible. It is my belief, however, that family agencies can make a contribution in seeing drug-prone youngsters before they have reached the point of dependence or have become so alienated from society and family as to render them inaccessible to a family-centered approach to the problem. In essence, I see our current efforts as directed to the early, beginning user. In this regard, our service can be considered preventive in that it deals with beginning dislocations, conflicts, and the variety of other ills afflicting families.

Earlier I make reference to the desirability of a yardstick by which we could measure the general social health of the family. We have long seen advocated a medical and dental checkup to determine an individual's physical health, and in the process have helped countless thousands to secure necessary medical care. Perhaps a *family* checkup, as suggested by Frances L. Beatman, might equally reveal potentially destructive forces within a family system requiring intervention and psychological assistance. If, as Mrs. Beatman states, we believe "that cultural and social change contain the seeds for the development of difficulties in all families, we shall not be bound by a narrow psychological concern and deal only with families that have experienced actual impairment. Rather, we shall be concerned with broad issues and endeavor to build immunity and resistance in all families to the germs of disturbances that are endemic in our society. The need for preventive work by social institutions, and particularly those that are committed to serving the family, is becoming increasingly clear."

It is perhaps, then, through the implementation of such a far-reaching program that we can help families avoid difficulties and provide better ways for them to deal with their confusions. The complexities in establishing such a program are admittedly considerable. But the concept of a "family health maintenance program" deserves active consideration by all of us interested in the emotional well-being of the family.

## 9

# THE ROLE OF THE SYNAGOGUE IN SEX EDUCATION

### Norman Lamm

The topic assigned to me is "The Role of the Synagogue in Sex Education." However, my concern in this paper shall be not with the synagogue as a specific institution within the community, but with the view and role of the whole Jewish tradition, as represented and symbolized by the synagogue, in sex education.

The sources for sex education in Jewish literature are almost nonexistent. Why? A number of factors come to mind. For one thing, the whole idea of the need for sex education is probably not much older than a century, when special impetus was given to it by Freudian analysis and its emphasis on childhood sexuality. Then, most Jews in time past were raised in a rural environment where sex was a part of life on the farm, and where a child accepted it quite naturally when he noticed the processes of reproduction among barnyard animals and poultry. In our technopolitan society we cannot appreciate that as much as we ought to. Furthermore, in those days earlier marriages meant the minimization of sexual frustration as well as celibate adolescence that complicate contemporary sex education and introduce a number of troubling factors that were not present in pre-modern times (see Kiddushin 29b, 30a).

There is only one learned article that I have found that treats the problems of sex education from a strictly Jewish

THE SYNAGOGUE IN SEX EDUCATION

point of view. It deserves to be translated into English.
It was written by Rabbi Mosheh Munk of Israel and appeared in *Ha-Me'ayan* of September (Tishri), 1966.
Much of what I shall say is based on information and
ideas presented in this article.

I hope to discuss in this paper four primary questions:
Should we, from a Jewish point of view, undertake sex
education? What should be taught, conceptually? Who
should do the teaching? How shall it be transmitted?

Let us begin with the second, the conception problem—
what should be taught? The question of content will necessarily determine all the other questions, even the question
of whether or not we ought to involve ourselves at all in
sex education.

Let me begin way back. One of the major influences on
the world of antiquity and, therefore, also to an extent on
the modern world, was that arcane philosophy called
Gnosticism. It predicated a very strict dualism of body
and soul, of this-world and the other-world. The object
of man is to flee from this world and all its trappings, its
evil, its degradation, its sin, in an attempt to achieve entry
to the other world, the world of purity, and nobility and
sublimity. There are many sinister means which the physical world uses in order to ensnare the soul in the net of
material existence. The mightiest of these weapons is
sexual love. The problem of the Gnostic is how to liber-
ate himself from this great seduction of sexuality. Two
answers were offered that were apparently in utter con-
tradiction; yet both were fundamentally antisexual. One
of them is asceticism, the denial to oneself of any of the
pleasures of this world, especially the sexual. The other
is libertinism—the idea of overindulging in the pleasures
of this world, especially the sexual; in both asceticism and
libertinism, the theories of the non-use and abuse of the
sex drive, sex is an episode rather than a relationship. It
is something I do rather than something I become. The

result, whether of non-use or abuse of sex, is in both cases identical, the depersonalization of sexuality and its attenuation into mere sex. Sexuality has disappeared as a way of communicating with another human being who has become a thing, an object which one can accept, embrace, and abuse, or which one can reject and banish from the area of one's intimate personal concern.

Historically, paganism and its libertine attitude toward sex, indeed its inclusion of sex in cultic worship, engendered a reaction in the ancient world by Christianity, especially in its Pauline and Augustine forms. There arose a movement in the opposite direction—the denial of sex and the idea that sex was invented by the devil in order to keep man from communion with God. That is why Paul said that "it is better to marry than to burn" (by which he mean to burn with passion, not in hell). Marriage was regarded as a concession, a dispensation by the church to man in acknowledgment of his frailty in the face of temptation. If you are going to indulge, you might as well be married.

The pagan attitude of which we spoke has experienced a renaissance, and today we are confronted with a neopaganism, a religion whose high priest is Hugh Hefner, whose bible is *Playboy,* whose *kedeshot* are called "bunnies," and whose central dogma or doctrine is "play it cool." Essentially, this whole attitude is antisexual, as antisexual as the old monasticism. Hefner's bunnies are not people but objects, and they are treated as such. The man who frequents this kind of establishment nowadays knows that his first rule is, "don't get involved." Carry out your sexual role, but don't commit your emotions to it. This means that your partner is not to be considered a human being but an object to be used and enjoyed—and discarded when this function can no longer be discharged efficiently. This articulates beautifully with the prevailing philosophy of our times, namely, hedonism—the idea that pleasure is the ultimate goal worth striving for. The pursuit of happiness is not only a privilege of freeborn Americans, but is transformed into a duty. It is sometimes a duty which we pursue with the same kind of dogged determination and devotion that the Puritans brought to their joyless duties. This "pursuit of happiness" determines the whole moral structure of contemporary American society in its attitude toward sex, abortion, and euthanasia. The major theme of today is how will my actions affect me; will it produce misery in my life or will it increase my peace of mind and happiness? This pragmatic American hedonism has a certain moral dimension to it, but it breaks down in the area of sex.

*Enjoy, Enjoy* is not only the name of a book by some cracker-barrel philosopher who happened to grow up on the East Side, but the clarion call of hedonism. If I reproach my congregants some Saturday, I normally expect them to be very angry with me or embarrassed at my rebuke. Instead, they sometimes tell me, "I enjoyed it very much"—as if enjoying and pleasure are the ultimate goal and, therefore, the greatest encomium is "I enjoyed it." I actually had a case in which I left a funeral where I had delivered a eulogy, and one of the mourners said, "Rabbi, I really enjoyed it." This is the caricature of an awesome reality with which we must learn to live. I recall an incident I witnessed in a summer camp several years ago. A boy, celebrating his fifteenth birthday, received a telegram from his father who was traveling through Europe. The contents of the telegram was: "Congratulations, today you are a playboy"—an index of the kind of hedonistic values which prevail in our society.

The Jewish view is neither that of asceticism nor that of paganism; it rejects Gnosticism and both its paradoxical consequences. It clearly and firmly sets itself against hedonism. Rather than transgress *giluy arayot*—unchastity, a term which comprehends adultery, incest, and other forms of immorality—*yehareg v'al yaavor,* one should allow himself to be done to death; one must rather submit to martyrdom than commit these immoral acts. Judaism maintains, as we say in our pre-Rosh Hashanah prayers, "Both the soul and the body are Thine." We do not subscribe to the absolute bifurcation of body and the soul as two truly separate entities. The Bible's first commandment is "be fruitful and multiply," that of reproduction. We are told in one verse in Genesis, "In the image of God did He create him, man and woman created He them," as if to tell us that there is no fundamental conflict between man's God-resemblance (the "image of God") and his sexuality. Man is made in the image of God, yet he is either male or female—a sexual being.

Indeed, in the two accounts of creation in the first chapters of Genesis there are given two views of Judaism on marriage and the conjugal relationship. In one of them (Genesis 1:27, 28) we are told that man and woman were created and told to be fruitful and multiply; the object of marriage is procreation. Man is here seen as part of the panorama of nature. In the other (Genesis 2:20-24), man alone among all creatures of God, has no mate. The divine judgment on his celibate condition is, "it is not good that man should be alone," and so he receives a wife. Here, obviously, having a mate is meant to fill the need for comradeship rather than for procreation.

To be seen in perspective, the problem of sexuality must be considered in the larger context of Judaism's view of man. The purpose of man is to achieve holiness or self-transcendence. We are to strive for holiness because God is holy. As He is beyond the world, so must we strive to rise beyond our physical and biological limitations. How can this God-imitating holiness be achieved? Primarily through the moral disciplines imposed on us by Torah and tradition, through control of our sexual drives and the proper channeling of our libidinal impulses. That is why on Yom Kippur, just before the climax of the Holy Day's service, we read the Scriptural portion from Leviticus containing the list of prohibited sexual liaisons. When we have learned to control our sexual impulses, we have already taken the first step in that self-discipline that ultimately results in a state of holiness. The first blessing under the wedding canopy confirms the relationship of the avoidance of illicit sexual unions—and its corollary, the acceptability of legitimate sexual congress—to *kedushah,* the purpose of all life. Thus when we bless God who has commanded us concerning sexual morality, who has forbidden us to have marital relations with those to whom we are betrothed but has permitted to us those to whom we are married, we bless God, our Lord, *asher Kideshanu,* who sanctifies us, who gives us holiness. By the act of marriage, sex becomes an integral aspect of a life striving for *kedushah.*

Judaism, thus, by no means denies the legitimate pleasurability of sex, but the pleasure aspect is not the exclusive goal of sex. Marital love is the response to a divinely acknowledged existential quest. Sexuality is a vehicle for personal communication among individuals, the attempt to abolish human loneliness which is *lo tov*—"not good" (Genesis 2:18).

The founder of Hasidism, Rabbi Israel Baal Shem Tov, said that whenever you witness or experience human love, it should inspire a sense of religious wonder and cause you to contemplate the source of such love, called *hesed*—and remember that its origin is in the divine attribute of *hesed.* Even incestuous love is referred to by the Torah as *hesed,* for it is the corruption of what is in essence a supernal divine love.

Hedonism, which is contemporary man's unofficial but real doctrine of sexual behavior, and the striving for *kedushah* or holiness in Judaism, must inevitably clash. Such divergence necessarily affects the problem of sex education.

From a basically secularist point of view, such education is necessary, it is said, in order to help the individual achieve a happy, healthy sex life and thus assure him or her of a normal, stable family life.

The Jewish view of sex education has no objection to happiness, to health, to normality or stability, but its primary aim is to help the individual achieve holiness and purity, to learn how to realize in his or her life the divine norms contained in the Torah. It is not puritanical, but it is also not hedonistic and completely anthropocentric. To put is more precisely, a secularist-hedonist approach may approve of a certain continence as an aid in the attainment of mental health happiness. Judaism turns it the other way around; it considers a healthy and stable mind as a necessary step in the quest for *kedushah*. But Judaism cannot agree to the use of its normal norms as mental health devices, as another item in the psychologist's and social worker's medicine bag. *Kedushah* requires the submission of the ego to the demands of One higher and infinitely more valuable than it. A god *used* for man is but an idol— even if it be one and invisible. *Kedushah* may and should avail itself of the categories and contributions of mental health and emotional happiness, but the reverse spells the corruption of genuine religion.

As an example of this conflict, consider the problem of condoning extramarital relationships under certain trying and extenuating conditions. Is there really a good reason to decry adultery if it injures no one and does not offend against mental health? Would you counsel a young man against premarital relations, considering all the modern facilities for avoiding unwanted pregnancies or disease, if it would help develop his confidence and personality? There simply is no really good reason that is psychologically persuasive and personally convincing for not indulging in certain sexual liaisons. The hedonistic ethos cannot say a thing against it as long as it is psychologically healthy and makes one happy. No wonder that unmarried sexual activity, even itineracy, is becoming more and more normal, or if not "normal" then "average." But the Jewish ethos would reject this as being the antithesis of holiness and purity, no matter what its social and psychological benefits, no matter that "it hurts no one," and no matter that it can be justified by "situational ethics." Our main concern must always refer back to the metaphysical fundaments: is our primary goal health or holiness? The very fact that these issues can be drawn so sharply affects all other items on our agenda.

Let us now turn to the question of whether we should enter into this area at all. Obviously, there is a tremendous need to prepare the youngster with a *Jewish* sex education. The adolescent lives in a society where discussions on sex take place daily, sometimes hourly, and perhaps with even more frequent regularity. Questions of contraception and abortion are now front-page material in our most respected newspapers. Our "new morality" is discussed from podium and pulpit. If we do not raise these matters, we sin against the Jewish tradition which we have silenced with our cowardice, against these youngsters to whom we have denied the guidance of Judaism, and against the community as a whole.

However, in order to present sex education in a Jewish manner, we cannot merely repeat what has already been attempted—a kind of antiseptic instruction in reproductive anatomy and physiology plus a few pious clichés about love and maturity. What we must do is to weave sex education into the whole texture of Jewish education in general, even as in our view sex itself is not restricted to the genital apparatus or the act of coitus, but is an integral part of the total personality. Sex education must therefore be considered in the arena of the over-all values by which and for which we live.

Having drawn the basic outline of the conceptual problem, and having determined that sex education unquestionably should be a prerequisite in Jewish education, the question then is: Who shall do the teaching? Who will be the sex educators?

I would like to make it clear that in my discussion of who should take the responsibility for such sex education, I wish to avoid adjudicating between rival institutional claims. If the value-climate is right and the instructor is qualified, then the locale is irrelevant. A spirit of holiness can permeate a "Y," although it usually does not. The spirit of uncleanliness, of moral degradation, can dominate in the synagogue, and too often it does. The question of centers or synagogues, of both or none, with respect to who should accept this responsibility, will depend on the much more serious problems that remain to be solved in the theoretical structure of a Jewish view on sex education.

Nevertheless, a few comments on the alternatives are in order. One agency that I would disqualify is the public school. I have long been disabused by the myth of its so-called ideological neutrality. The public schools are not neutral. They are really the brokers of contemporary morality in all its aspects, although always just a bit behind the times in terms of the applications of the values that they wittingly or unwittingly foster. (One wag suggested that sex education by the public schools may be the answer to a very painful dilemma faced by the world today. Considering the questionable success of the public schools in teaching reading and writing, if we now give them the responsibility for teaching sex education, that might help solve the problem of the population explosion. . . .) Yet if we do not bestir ourselves to provide a sex education in a Jewish context, we will be left with no alternative. Public school instruction would still be preferable to the misinformation usually obtained from the traditional children's underground where the "facts of life" are acquired by mysterious whispers and nervous giggles.

Should, then, the Jewish Centers and "Y's" serve as the sources for Jewish sex education? Frankly, I am skeptical as to their ability to execute the task successfully. Jewish values cannot be dispensed like so many aspirin tablets—a Jewish value here and a Jewish value there in the context of a group discussion. In order to be meaningful and effective, individual values must issue out of a total value-system which I do not believe exists in most Centers or "Y's." Nor do I believe that most group workers or social workers, who would be assigned the task of sex education, are the kind of people who either personify or are acquainted with this totality of Jewish values and so represent, in their persons, the values which we wish to transmit. The very atmosphere of most Centers, perforce dictated by the nature of their constituencies, does not harmonize with a religious sexological view. The Centers are built on a broad communal base, and hence must accommodate themselves to contemporary mores, whereas religion must be highly critical of much of modern life. A Jewish view will never confuse mores with morality, the average with the normal. What is average may very well be subnormal and what is normal may be very rare indeed.

I am not a partisan of the synagogue as the proper agency of sex instruction. A synagogue is a place for prayer. When it teaches, it is Torah that it teaches, and this must be in a form that lends itself to public exposition. The nature of our subject therefore precludes the synagogue as the locale for sex education, no matter what other faults the synagogue possesses in this regard.

Parents are probably the least equipped to undertake the sex education of their children, and yet should have the greatest responsibility of all. I know that as a child my own great problem—and I did not receive my information in the way I am prescribing it for others—was, "How can I keep my father from knowing that I know?" Now, my great problem as a parent is, "How shall I tell my children?" There is a mutual reluctance by parents and children to engage in this kind of conversation. I think I have a good relationship with my children; I know that I had and have a splendid relationship with my father and mother. Yet the intimate aspects were never discussed, especially— and perhaps I may be accused of being regressive—with regard to the anatomical aspects of sex. I believe that a good, healthy Jewish modesty would preclude parents as the instructors. Thus, the Talmud (Pesahim 51) discusses the morality of bathing. In those days, one did not have his private bath, and had to avail himself of a public bath. Jewish morality, as formulated by the Talmud, dictated that a man should not go to bathe, and therefore see in the nude, his father, his father-in-law, his mother's husband (if he was not his father), and the husband of his sister. Rashi explains that upon seeing the other person disrobed and his private parts exposed, the sudden shock of recognition that "that is where I come from" or "might have come from," leads one to illicit thoughts. It means that this kind of encounter arouses latent incestuous feelings. By the same token I believe that the reluctance of both parents and children to discuss sexual matters relating to anatomy and the like should be respected, and one should not make demands upon parents or upon children that cannot be met forthrightly.

Furthermore, I should like to refer to an idea propounded by a great German Christian theologian, Helmut Thielicke (in his *The Ethics of Sex*). The existential aspects of sex, its role in the very life patterns of a person, its "mystery," cannot be imparted merely by instruction in biological processes; it cannot be transmitted just by talking about it. It can only be given in a sense of trust.

Children must trust parents to the extent that they will accept that there is a dimension of sexuality which, because of many reasons, they cannot know now but later will comprehend. They must have faith in their parents regarding matters of sexual understanding, and this faith must be undergirded and reinforced by parental example in their domestic relations.

Let us illustrate this point by way of an experience in traditional Jewish life. According to normative Jewish practice, sexual relations are not conducted during the period of the menses and for one week thereafter. At the end of this week, the wife is required by Jewish law to immerse in a body of natural water, a *mikvah,* and recite the proper blessing before resuming cohabitation with her husband. Now, Jewish law prohibits the woman from immersing in the daytime. The explanation is given in the Talmud: the daughter, seeing her mother immerse during the day, will not realize that this is the eighth day (from the cessation of her menses) but may think it is the seventh day. In that case the daughter will be misled, and when she is later married, she will perform the *tevillah,* the immersion, before the seventh night and thereby violate the law. Obviously then, Jewish daughters knew when their mothers went to the *mikvah!* This is of great psychological and sociological interest. Jewish girls were sufficiently intimate with their mothers, so that when the latter went to the *mikvah,* their daughters had an inkling of what it meant. The mother, for her part, was not prudish or excessively shy. Although, as is apparent from the Talmud, they did not have intimate discussions (otherwise they would have told them explicitly that this was the eighth day), yet there was between them an understanding that this is a normal part of the life of a Jew. There existed, then, this sense of trust.

So in the matter of sex education, the responsibility of the parents in transmitting not factual information but the existential and axiological dimensions of sexuality depends upon the parents—their relationships with each other and with their children, their own outlook, their *Weltan-schauung*. Too often, however, the parents have their own unresolved problems, especially in the complex and tense times in which we live. Life is not as simple as it used to be. Therefore, unfortunately, parents are usually not the adequate answer to our question of who shall teach. They are disqualified from providing the purely descriptive biological information (from the point of view of psychology and morality, as I said above, not because of ignorance of the facts), and too often are ill prepared for the far greater responsibility which requires the sense of trust, and which in turn brings into play all the profound personal nuances that are part of sexuality rather than merely sex. The sense of trust between parents and children in our very confused and complicated age is all too infrequent.

The optimum locality as the source of sex education, therefore, is the religious school—where sex education can be transmitted as whole cloth, as part of total, integrated world-view. It is here, therefore, that sex education ought to be presented in its proper Jewish setting.

I must emphasize again that were such a total Jewish environment available in the Center or synagogue or any other place, I would just as well have it done there. Our problem is educational, not institutional. Moreover, my further comments, based upon an over-all Jewish educational milieu for sex instruction, presume an ideal environment. Yet, I confess that the situation in Jewish education is very far from ideal. In fact, it is close to scandalous. Some schools, unfortunately, are no less secularistic in accepting uncritically the operative values of society today than are other Jewish institutions. They are outrageously ineffective in substantially imparting any Jewish values of significance. The lack of professionally

THE SYNAGOGUE IN SEX EDUCATION 169

trained personnel is something so painful that I would rather not speak about it. Nevertheless, the Jewish school is the most appropriate agency for what I believe is an authentic Jewish education in sex and sexuality.

Our last problem is methodology. A Jewish sex education should at all times consider with respect and reverence man's natural sense of *bushah* or shame, and should protect the privacy of the individual from unauthorized intrusion by anyone else, adult, parent or peer. Jewish tradition recognizes *bushah,* together with compassion and social ethics, as a special Jewish characteristic. Shame, as Helen Merrell Lynd has pointed out, is a healthy and normal aspect of life and one which (and it is different from guilt in this respect) touches the very sense of identity as a human being, as a particular individual (*On Shame and the Search for Identity,* 1958). A Jewish sex education will neither exaggerate nor deny the feelings of guilt that are usually associated with sex. To negate all guilt regarding sex is an extravagant abuse of pop-psychoanalysis. It is obviously un-Jewish. It leaves a human being totally unprepared to cope with new, powerful urges that come to the fore about the time of puberty, and for which normal guilt feelings act as inhibitors that protect society, enhance a young person's moral restraints and convictions, and develop him into a healthy, Jewish personality. Yet, certainly, a Jewish view will deny any of the extravagant guilt feelings that so often accompany the varied distortions of all kinds in sex information. How does Judaism manage to do this? By viewing sex as not qualitatively different from other areas of concern in Jewish law. Sexual guilt should be treated by us in our own minds as well as in relating to children, as no different from other healthy redemptive kinds of guilt that should come to a person when he violates a law such as honoring his parents, violating the *Shabbat,* or *Kashruth,* gossiping, or anything of this nature.

The element of *bushah,* shame, means that we must be sensitive to the psychological idiosyncrasies of individuals, so that matters of such delicacy and intimacy as sex should not be discussed in large groups. Nevertheless, individual instruction may not be the answer. The child may feel singled out, and may think that these tremendous urges that surge from within him are somehow not shared by anyone else and mark him therefore as a monster.

The Mishnah (Hagigah 2:1) teaches us that sex should not be discussed in groups of three or more. Of course that refers to sex law, the code of permitted and prohibited relationships (the reasons for that are irrelevant to us). Nevertheless, I believe that the principle applies to sex education as well. Therefore, small groups are preferable, especially if other such small groups are assembled in school for instruction in other subjects.

Furthermore, as one who tries to understand the Jewish tradition, I would not offer sex education to mixed groups of boys and girls, and I would insist that the instructor be of the same sex as the students. Girls and boys need different treatment, and develop at a different rate. *Bushah,* shame, should not be frustrated before it has a chance to grow and flourish. (Of course, I may be considered Neanderthal, but I believe that all instruction, in both the junior and high school levels, ought not to be coeducational.)

Were instruction in *musar,* ethics, done properly— were it done at all!—it would be wise to make the ethical aspects of sex education an integral part of such ethical instruction. To illustrate this point, the Talmud teaches us that the love of one's wife is a fulfillment of the commandment "Thou shalt love thy neighbor as thyself" (Kiddushin 41a). A man should marry only a woman whom he considers attractive, because if he will not love her, he will be in violation of this *mitzvah,* or commandment. "Thou shalt love thy neighbor as thyself" refers pre-eminently to one's wife.

Included in the Jewish ethics of sex should be the marvelous discourse by the late Jewish *musar* teacher, Rabbi Eliahu Dessler, of blessed memory, who describes the human propensity for giving as preceding and causing, rather than following and being the effect of, the state of love. Man is naturally acquisitive, but in addition to this, he also has a natural desire to give. This is understandable, given the premises of Judaism, for man is created in God's image, and God always gives. He is a giving personality. Man, therefore, has built into his personality a predisposition to give, and this is his noblest endowment. Now the function and purpose—and, yes, the protection—of marriage is not to demand but to give: to give pleasure, to give love, to give gifts, to give comfort, to give security, to give confidence, to give trust. In this manner, sex becomes not just self-expression—which makes it little more than masturbation *à deux*—but communication, an act which both actualizes and enhances an authentic love relationship. All this is terribly anti-hedonistic!

In this context sex is degenitalized and reintegrated into the personality as a whole. It is made independent of its sadomasochistic base, and makes for holier and happier conjugal existence in which courtesy and consideration will come naturally to the individual.

The kind of sex education of which we have been speaking must be integrated into the entire curriculum of the Jewish school, whether afternoon Hebrew or day school, including Bible, Talmud, and Jewish law. Sex education, and its ethics, should be related to *Chumash* studies, especially such topics—which many of us studied frequently before we became disingenuous—as the attempted seduction of Joseph, the almost illicit relationship of Judah and Tamar, the seduction and rape laws, the levitical problems of gonorrhea and so forth. There are many opportunities to integrate sex education in the study of the Talmud. As an example, tractate Kiddushin, relating to marriage, begins by establishing the three modes of betrothment: giving money for the value of money, writing a deed, and intercourse. It is good, of course, if students have the education in time to know the meaning of all three terms.

Sex education, to be Jewish, must be more than a sanctimonious gilding on the descriptive biology of reproduction. It must be taught together with the Jewish laws relating to Jewish sex morality. A few examples should suffice: unchastity as a major crime; the prohibition against promiscuity; the *mitzvah* of procreation; the laws of *niddah,* referred to before, which regulate conjugal relations based upon the menstrual cycle; the prohibition of certain forms of contraception; the obligation of a man to his wife or her conjugal rights (in Jewish law, coitus is the duty of the husband and the right of the wife—and it is a legal right, actionable in a court of law, an illustration of Judaism's regard for the woman's autonomous sexual rights in her marriage).

Sex education, as part of the curriculum, introduces the student into accepting as normal and welcome the differences between maleness and femaleness as qualities of personality rather than as strictly anatomical features. This follows from the distinction, in Jewish law and life, between the roles of the man and the woman. Far from being a case of sexual discrimination, this contributes to an avoidance of sexual ambiguity—so very prevalent nowadays.

In the traditional Jewish day schools, more explicit sexual education would hold additional advantage for a child. Without elementary sex education, a student is taught in Talmud about the many varieties of sexual experience, including a number of paranormal and even abnormal acts. These usually leave the child bewildered. What was I, as a student in the Yeshiva, to make of the legal speculations concerning *biah shelo ke'darkah* (anal intercourse) when I had not the vaguest notion of *biah ke-darkah,* normal vaginal intercourse? I am not so concerned about the psychological confusion; that eventually straightens out and, even more, it give a certain tolerance to the *Ben Torah* (the student of Torah) in matters of sexual behavior and its many varieties. But such study contributes to an academic sloppiness and intellectual fuzziness which do not always disappear later on. If I can study the legal problems of intercourse and not know what it is all about, I can study anything without an adequate understanding, and still be satisfied with it. In other words, I learn to talk without knowing what I'm talking about.

Nevertheless, learning about matters of sexual intercourse in Talmudic discourses has a remarkably therapeutic consequence. Paradoxically, although one may think naturally of a sexual object in a depersonalized manner, one cannot (especially as a youth) think about sex as such without involving all his emotions—and his distortions. These stand in the way of a healthy balance. The way to disentangle one from such intensively personal involvement is by a process of objectification of the condition which threatens to overwhelm him.

Let me cite two examples from other areas of experience. My revered teacher, Rabbi Joseph B. Soloveitchik, in his famous essay *Ish ha-Halakhah,* writes of his grandfather, a historically renowned Talmudic scholar, who was sitting and brooding. He was asked, "What is the matter, Rabbi?" "I am just contemplating death," he answered. (Incidentally, this is understandable for the *Halakhic* personality—death is a threat to one's existence in this world, and this world is the arena of *Halakhah.*)

He was then asked, "How do you get out of it?" He answered that when in this depressed mood, he opens up the *Code* of Maimonides and studies the laws relating to the impurity adhering to death. By looking upon death objectively, as an impersonal conceptual datum, he was able to disentangle himself from his personal, subjective involvements.

Dr. Viktor Frankl, in his *Man's Search for Meaning* (p. 117), writes that, when he was in a concentration camp, he felt that his very sanity was threatened by the indescribably inhuman conditions he faced. He managed to survive with his sanity intact by imagining that he was lecturing *about* these conditions and these helpless victims in the postwar period to a convention of psychiatrists describing the psychopathology of the concentration camp. His attitude toward what threatened him subjectively was that of objectivity, considering the various items of his personal experience impersonally and with detachment. By so doing he was able to achieve the psychological distance which allowed him to treat the problem with a sense of proportion.

This same process of objectification is at work in the young Talmud student learning the laws relating to matters sexual. I remember as a child studying the beginning of Tractate Ketubot. A man claimed that he found his bride was not a virgin. The discussion concerned itself with this problem: was her hymen ruptured by accident or was it caused by an illicit relationship, determining in the context, whether an adulterous liaison had taken place before the betrothal (a contractual form of marriage, unlike our "engagement,") and the consummation of the marriage? In mastering the legal concepts, the student is led not to sexual stimulation but—by objectifying the questions of sex, virginity, the fear of clumsiness, etc., and seeing them in this new context—to a certain serenity and tranquility.

To conclude, I hope that my delineation—which is only

a feeble preliminary attempt, for there are many more problems than solutions—of a Jewish view on sex education, has been sufficient to convince you of the differentness of a Jewish value-based sex education from that which expresses the working principles of contemporary hedonism.

It is because of these differences and this differentness that Jewish sex education will be highly critical of society's values imposed on the youngsters and upon their parents as well. The values transmitted will be those of *kedushah* (sanctity), not unrestrained concupiscence; of *taharah* (purity), not titillation; of reproduction—especially in our underpopulated Jewish community—as a *mitzvah* and not as an avoidable accident. It will emphasize modesty and oppose the mini-morality of our day. It will disapprove of pornography—whether in literature, screen, or television. It will discourage premature dating, which means forcing a child cruelly before he or she is ready, into an adult pattern, and, truth to tell, into a precocious going-steady which is not so much the result of an enlightened and liberated world view (for, as I said at the beginning, that is really a modern version of the ancient Gnostic anti-sexualism), as it is an opportunity for a frustrated parent to relive his or her youth through identifying with the child. That kind of parental psychological imperialism is intolerable, and contributes to making our problem so much more difficult.

Almost nothing worth reading has been written with respect to a Jewish view of sexology. The one thing we do have, the English translation of the *Kitzur Shulhan Arukh,* the abbreviated Code of Jewish Law, is a disaster —not that the translator failed in his technical ambitions, but that I do not believe that this volume represents the entirety of the Jewish view on sex and sexuality. It gives the reader the impression that Judaism is hopelessly outdated and antedeluvian. I recommend it to no one.

We are challenged to do something, and to do it well, to

fill the gap. Educators, rabbis, social workers and psychologists must, in mutual commitment to the Jewish tradition, take up this challenge and prepare a course of action which will include: a statement of the philosophy of Jewish sexology and a suggested curriculum for Jewish schools; the preparation of a manual for teachers and principals; a manual for parents; and, possibly, a manual for children.

I am frankly pessimistic about what can be done with the resources and willingness or unwillingness in our community at the present time. Until such time as a properly prepared program and personnel are available, the Jewish schools cannot solve the problem in its entirety. There should be some way in which all agencies, including the rabbis and Center workers, can be involved. But even at best, this is a bandaid, when we need surgery. We must issue a call to the community to be aware of the dimensions of the problem. Perhaps this, in turn, may lead some far-sighted philanthropist to contribute a sum of money to be used for interdisciplinary research teams to set up this kind of program.

Sex has been around for a long time and, unless the genetic engineers have their way, it will continue to be in vogue for a long time to come. But its exploitation in ways offensive to Judaism has been facilitated in our urban, technological, hedonistic culture as never before.

## 10
# SEX EDUCATION IN THE JEWISH COMMUNITY

### Rav A. Soloff

Sexual morals and mores are changing in all segments of our society these days, though at varying rates. It is obvious that American Jews are deeply affected by these changes. Concern for the healthful development of our children and the stability of our families during this revolutionary period has led to many proposals for "sex education" in synagogues, Jewish schools or YM-YWHA's. By and large the leadership of these institutions, both laymen and professionals, have favored some sort of programs to meet this need, but no one approach has been widely accepted. A number of pioneering efforts should be considered, and this chapter will deal at some length with the program in which the author participated.*

Among traditional Jews, sex education was never a separate subject, though the modesty of parents or teachers often obscured the implications of a text from the eyes of students. The principals of a number of Hebrew day schools located in the metropolitan New York area, however, report that their students are not shielded from discussions of sex in the course of studying classic Jewish sources, that is, Bible or Talmud. In a few cases, Yeshivot

---

* "A Temple Course on Some Socio-Sexual Aspects of Maturation," by Rabbi Rav A. Soloff, Dr. Howard M. Newburger, and Dr. Sidney Q. Coblan, *News and Views* Magazine, Volume 10, Number 3 (March-April, 1968), pp. 3ff.

have set up special courses for adolescents to help them come to a clearer understanding of sexual matters. One Yehiva offers a class each week for a full half year, on the seventh-grade level, with boys and girls meeting separately to learn about physiology, reproduction, homosexuality, masturbation, and, for girls, menstruation. Other Yeshivot integrate some basic information on these subjects in their deliberately scheduled discussions of appropriate sections of the *Code of Jewish Law* or the Book of Leviticus or the Talmud. Often the sex education efforts of the Yeshiva are not extensive, but serve rather to "break the ice" so that further discussions may take place between parents and children in the home.

The Jewish Community Center of Staten Island developed an extensive program of sex education for teen-agers on different levels. In each case several sessions were scheduled at weekly intervals, to permit social workers, cooperating physicians and rabbis to deal with diverse aspects of "sex education." The older boys and girls were grouped together, while the younger boys and girls met separately. Lectures, film presentations and discussions were included in these programs to convey physiological information on the level of the particular group, to present concepts of responsibility and to respond to all sorts of teen-age questions, such as, "How do you determine just what is appropriate? And even if it is not appropriate and you still want to—what then?"

East End Temple developed a psychology course for the tenth grade (Confirmation Class) which started from *Consecrated Unto Me: A Jewish View of Love and Marriage* by Roland B. Gittelsohn (Union of American Hebrew Congregations, 1965), but went on to encompass a great deal more than "sex education." The goals were threefold: 1) to advance the personal growth of the individual student in terms of maturity, personal integration, goal directedness and self-protection; 2) to demonstrate and reinforce the use of Judaism as an asset to the students in their growth and future careers; 3) to help students deal effectively and constructively with several specific situations, such as dating, bereavement, ambivalence in love relationships, evaluating money, confronting prejudice and authoritarian personalities, creating a home and raising secure, happy Jewish children. These goals were pursued by dividing the fifteen- to sixteen-year-olds into socio-metrically equal groups, including both sexes, and then using techniques of role playing, sociodrama and action-level training methods, as well as more traditional discussions or lectures. The sessions were held under the joint guidance of the rabbi and a psychologist (or, in the case of sessions which dealt with physiology, the rabbi and a pediatrician). Dual leadership proved extremely flexible and effective, both for the students and for the instructors. Each class (or in the case of very large classes which were broken down into sections, each section of a class) took on its own unique character. Yet, three years' experience with five different groups has validated both the use of two adult leaders per session, and primary reliance upon psychologically dynamic techniques, with relatively strong personal involvement on the part of the students, rather than upon the more passive participation of students in lecture or recitation classes. Psychological testing, before and after confirmation classes, supported expectations that such depth experiences might contribute to real growth and change, though no "proof" could be established by the questionnaires and projective tests without control groups having been set up.

While the initial structuring of the level of involvement was made with full awareness that many of these teen-agers dated each other, went to school together and lived near one another, nevertheless something more than intellectual participation was solicited. This raised the likelihood that material of potentially embarrassing or even damaging nature might be forthcoming, so it was always important to be prepared to handle such material if it could not be contained or circumvented by action beforehand. With proper safeguards, however, these risks seemed reasonable in the light of the vastly greater benefit accruing to students not limited to intellectual or very shallow emotional involvement. On a number of occasions "emergency action" by the psychologist was indicated. One young man had experienced pangs of unrequited love while working as a busboy during the preceding summer and unexpectedly poured out all the details of his unhappy affair in an exhibitionistic manner. Some other members of the class already knew the grosser aspects of the experience, but it was the task of the psychologist to protect the outspoken individual insofar as possible, and minimize the likelihood of further reactions outside the controlled setting of the classroom. This problem was more acute since the exhibitionistic boy had been developing some feelings of self-respect, so that a cruel response from his classmates would have exposed him to suffering or even self-destructive impulses. Fortunately, under the guidance of the psychologist, the group responded with support and sympathy so that the young man could accept their reassurance, and in the course of the semester's work he made further gains in self-respect as the exhibitionism diminished and his integration into the class improved.

On another occasion, before either the rabbi or psychologist could open the scheduled session, a student announced, "Last night I had a dream; can you tell me what it means when . . ." Then, in spite of the rabbi's interruption to explain the fallacies of "parlor analysis," and in spite of the psychologist's explanation of the functions of dreaming, the student insisted upon asking what his dream of a train "meant." The rabbi asked the psychologist to mention the case of a certain young woman who had a phobia regarding trains, to dramatize the fact that two individuals might have entirely different associations to the same symbol. Then the psychologist casually asked the student if he ever rode the subway. Since the boy did so every day, to and from school, his dream lost portentousness and appeared commonplace—naturally he would have a train figure in his dreams!

The psychologist was always kind and careful to make sure that no student was left in a vulnerable position, or subject to unresolved stress at the end of a session. In this case he did not rest with "defusing" the situation. Instead, he went on to speak of a train as a symbol of motion, and to assure the students that they were, and should be, in transition. "The question is, where is the train going and what are the stations along the way?" When that class ended, considerable information had been offered, attitudes of respect for the sanctity of each personality had been verbalized and demonstrated, growing adolescents had been affirmed in their processes of development, and some specific protection had been afforded one or more youngsters against unintentionally hostile "Freudian interpretations" by laymen. Discussion of dreams in the second class that day, introduced by the leaders rather than by the students, did offer the same information and did verbalize attitudes of respect for the sanctity of each personality, but the degree of student involvement and benefit was palpably lower.

Another situation spontaneously arose in a group that was discussing intermarriage. The difficulty students had in projecting themselves into a situation where they might fall in love with and want to marry a person of another religion was paralleled only by the boredom of the instructors at the thought of still another rehash of the same old stuff. However, instead of a discussion, a sociodrama was arranged. A student who appeared needful of the support was named as director. The situation was determined; a young couple (he Jewish, she not) and their parents were to meet with the rabbi. What was un-usual was the director's casting: one of the students was selected as rabbi and our rabbi was selected as the young man who wanted to enter the intermarriage. The turn-about in role sparked the group first with amusement, then with interest, and then finally with total involvement as the action and spontaneity built up. It is difficult to tell whether rabbi, psychologist, or students benefited the most as insight followed upon catharsis and spontaneity replaced inertia and passivity.

It might seem that the group process resulted too often in episodes like these just described. However, such things were sometimes allowed to occur whenever a matter of individual concern arose, simply because we were intent upon developing our adolescents into fine young Jewish men and women who would become useful members of the community. For the most part, our objectives were out-lined well in advance and were generally adhered to. Re-viewing the material covered in the course of one year, we find these topics, related in some cases to chapters of the textbook *Consecrated Unto Me*:

*September*: 1) Evaluation and/or testing; 2) Chapter I, rebellion, prejudice; 3) Chapter II, infatuation—why marry, some of the nonconstructive reasons.

*October*: 1) Chapter III, more reasons for marriage; 2) maturation, defenses and anxieties; 3) Chapter IV, child-rearing, LSD, rebellion; 4) Chapter V, maturation, responsibility.

*November*: 1) Chapter VI and Chapter IX, intermar-riage (socio-dramas); 2) Chapter VIII, physiology, first lecture by the physician; 3) Chapter VI and VII, the family, dominant and other roles in the family (socio-drama), contraception and family structure.

*December*: 1) Chapter VII, the family; money and time (socio-dramas); 2) Chapter VIII, the physician's second lecture; 3) dreams, psychopathology of promis-cuity, mythology of sex.

*January*: 1) Chapter X, sex and self-hatred, sex and total relationships; 2) Chapter XI, sex and marriage; 3) dating (psycho-drama); 4) more dating (psycho-dramas), hints and rules for dating, how to succeed in making the other party feel good.

*February*: 1) Group standards and expectations; 2) the family, influence by the teen-ager, what is family love, adult responsibility and real goals, what are the rewards; 3) personal standards, how to be a millionaire, independence, escape from freedom.

*March*: 1) Anti-Semitism, why men hate (psycho-drama), self-hate, martyrs; 2) anti-Semitism, group motives (socio-drama); 3) role of Jew in corporate structures, reaction to insults, variety of Jewish responses to anti-Semitism.

*April*: 1) Bereavement; 2) what makes for happiness without drugs, what makes for richness in life, inner experience, meaning of life; 3) work and leisure, extrapersonal patterns.

*May*: Summary sessions and testing.

Although the general response of students and parents was very favorable, it should not be imagined that these sessions were free of problems. Classical attitudes of rebellion, common to the age, were sometimes even more obvious in our students than in others. Side conversations, lateness, questions and statements of an inciteful nature, taking a habituated oppositional viewpoint, or even non-participation, can be construed as rebellion. Quantitatively, these tended to disappear following some discussion and acting out in situations involved with dependence, rebellion and independence. As might be anticipated, our most acting-out young rebel became the most impatient with diversions and distractions of others in areas in which he was most concerned on his own behalf, once he found that the best way to help himself was not necessarily in attempting to overthrow vested authority. Other students, however, remained resistant to some degree throughout the course, or "blew hot and cold" as the subjects affected them personally.

The physician's contribution to the course was devoted to an exposition of the anatomy and physiology of the reproductive system. It was presented in colloquial language, using a stylized format which described the genital tract of a representative newborn girl and boy, and then following their psysiological development to puberty and into adulthood. Accepted biologic terms were used, always followed by the commoner, more polite synonyms known to some teen-agers, and occasionally a not-so-polite synonym (but still in reasonable taste) known to all of them.

The anatomy and physiology of intercourse and pregnancy was then discussed, followed by an exposition of contraception and venereal disease.

The group attitude and response was typical except for the added adjustment of hearing these problems frankly discussed as part of their Sunday school training. At first there was a feeling of timidity and a peculiar cynicism that most adolescents exhibit when they anticipate being "lectured at" and "talked down to" by an adult. The style, intimacy, frankness and humor gradually changed this attitude in most of the children—but there is always a hard core with a "superior" attitude of "having been through all this before."

The question-and-answer period revealed a marked disparity in sophistication and understanding. As always, it is very difficult to evaluate the impressions and impact in this age group. However, through the attention paid, and the questions asked, it appeared evident that this was a needed and constructive exercise.

Subsequently, sporadic comments from some of the parents indicated that at least some of the children had achieved added knowledge and better understanding. A typical quote from child to parent was, "That was pretty good—I learned something." One parent said: "Coming from him that's something! He thinks he knows everything."

Our feeling of the general reaction at the Sisterhood Meeting after completion of the course was that, under the smiles and the laughter at some of the anecdotes related by the teachers, was a degree of relief that someone else had undertaken communication in an area in which some parents feel ineffective and otherwise embarrassed.

Provision was also made for individual conferences with the rabbi or psychologist at the confirmand's request. The confirmands generally limited themselves to casual exchanges with the instructors before and after the formal class. We have found, however, that long after these sessions were concluded, the ready availability of the instructors continues to be of value to former students. Both the rabbi and the psychologist have been consulted professionally by some of the young people and their families about personal matters that were touched upon in class.

In addition, perhaps because this course brought about more widespread community awareness that such services are available, a score of premarital, marriage, and family situations, unrelated to the confirmants or their parents, were brought to the rabbi and psychologist for joint counseling during these three years.

Experience with "sex education" programs indicates that in most cases the respective values and helping roles of the rabbi, the Jewish social worker, psychologist and physician are potentially harmonious and complementary. Full cooperation among these professionals can greatly benefit Jewish individuals, families and communities in many areas of life.

## 11

# A PROFILE OF JEWISH EDUCATION
# IN THE UNITED STATES

## Alvin Irwin Schiff

"May we and our children and our children's children know Thy Name and study Thy Torah for its own sake." (From the daily service of the traditional prayerbook.)

Jewish education occupies a unique position in Jewish life. The study of Torah (which includes the Pentateuch, Prophets, Sacred Writings, Talmud, the Rabbinic commentaries and other religious writings) is a cardinal principle of the Jewish faith. Knowledge and study are not only a means to religious and ethical behavior but are in themselves a mode of worship. Indeed, the Jewish liturgy reflects the fact that worship finds expression on the intellectual as well as the esthetic and the emotional planes as it combines the moment of prayer with study.

## Philosophy and Aims

Jewish education in America began in the mid-seventeenth-century with the settlement of the first Jewish immigrants in New Amsterdam. The rationale for Jewish education in the United States and everywhere else has been that Jewish religious training is a *sine qua non* for Jewish survival; that the study of Judaism—its sources, values and practices—makes one a better Jew, hence, a better person and a better American.

Jewish education strives to contribute to the spiritual

growth of both the individual and society. Concerning the individual, it endeavors:

1) to develop sensitivity to and appreciation of ethical, social, and spiritual values;

2) to impart a knowledge of the Jewish heritage which is necessary for meaningful and intelligent Jewish living;

3) to create a desire to observe Jewish traditions, and to identify with and become an active member of the Jewish community; and

4) to help Jewish children become good Americans through an understanding and appreciation of the essential harmony between the tenets of Judaism and the ideals and traditions of American democracy.

To society, Jewish education attempts to make its contribution through the social and religious practices of the individual, and the ethical, social and spiritual ideals developed and transmitted by the Jewish people through thousands of years.

In Judaism the emphasis upon the home as an educational agency is primary. Jewish education realizes that the home and the child's immediate environment largely define his feelings, mold his attitudes, and establish habits to which accrue his knowledge and experience. For this reason Jewish education attaches great importance to close school-home relationships and to parent education.

The basic elements of most Jewish school curricula— Hebrew language, liturgy, Bible, ethics, religious practices and observances, Jewish history, and the Land of Israel—are variously interpreted and taught in the schools of the Orthodox, Conservative, and Reform ideologies, the major religious groupings in American Jewish life.

*School Enrollment*

Jewish education has become increasingly popular during the last two decades. Between 1948 and 1963, for example, there was approximately a 150 percent increase in Jewish school population—almost nine times as much as the estimated increase in the total Jewish population, and twice as large as the enrollment increase in non-Jewish religious schools during the same period. Primarily for reasons of a slower birth rate, enrollment figures have remained stable between 1963 and 1969. It is estimated that about 80 percent of Jewish children receive some kind of formal religious schooling. In 1969, about 550,000 pupils, or 40 percent of all Jewish children of school age, 5-17 years, were enrolled in 2,700 Jewish schools. Approximately 42 percent studied in one-day schools, 45 percent were enrolled in two-, three-, four-, or five-day-a-week afternoon schools, and 13 percent were pupils in Jewish all-day schools.

*Auspices and Organization*

Although Jewish education is primarily the responsibility of parents, historically from the time Jews pioneered universal public education some two thousand years ago, the local Jewish community has voluntarily assumed a major role in the religious schooling of its youth. The assumption of communal responsibility of Jewish education does not mean the control of education since there is no central authority in Jewish religious life. In the United States this responsibility is demonstrated by the growing interest of the Jewish community in intensive Jewish education and by the gradually increasing financial commitment of synagogues, communal groups, and welfare funds to Jewish educational activity.

Each school is an independent, voluntarily organized educational unit with its own lay board and, in the case of day schools, its own constitution. It is supported by parents and lay members through tuition fees and other forms of contributions.

To help provide better educational services for Jewish pupils, to aid in coordinating educational efforts of individual schools and to provide educational supervision and consultation, local boards of Jewish education have been established in 35 Jewish communities. The oldest and largest of these agencies is the Jewish Education Committee of New York (organized as the Jewish Education Association in 1910), which serves some 750 Jewish schools in the Greater New York area. There are many national Jewish agencies, each serving specific groups and interests or providing special services. Chief among these are the American Association for Jewish Education, an overall national organization with which all local bureaus of education are affiliated; the National Council for Jewish Education, a professional fellowship of ranking Jewish educators; the Commission on Jewish Education of the Union of American Hebrew Congregations (Reform); the Commission on Jewish Education of the United Synagogue of America (Conservative); Torah Umesorah, the National Society for Hebrew Day Schools (Orthodox); and the Departments of Education and Culture, and Torah and Culture of the Jewish Agency for Israel. There are also a number of secular Jewish educational agencies.

In order to insure proper instructional standards, procedures for the certification of teachers and principals have been developed. The first Board of License was established in 1929 in New York. In 1940 the National Board of License was founded to organize and coordinate regional (local) boards of license. Presently, there are seven regional boards approved by the National Board of License. The Union of American Hebrew Congregations and Torah Umesorah maintain their own licensing procedures and standards.

Jewish schools draw their personnel from a variety of sources, primarily from seventeen Hebrew Teachers' colleges, twenty-one Orthodox rabbinical schools, and from

Israel. Many teachers currently employed in Jewish schools received their Jewish education and pedagogic training abroad, mainly on the European continent, and came to the United States immediately prior to or after World War II.

## Problems and Trends

During the first half of the twentieth century, Jewish education was significantly a male-oriented enterprise. The overwhelming proportion of children in Jewish schools were boys and most of the teachers were men. As a result of the growing recognition of the importance of Jewish education for girls, there has been, in the last two decades, a sharp increase of girls in Jewish schools. Currently, they comprise almost half of the Jewish school enrollment.

Moreover, there has been a dramatic increase in the number of women teachers in the Jewish schools. The underlying cause of this development is the transformation of Jewish education into a part-time profession. Out of a total teaching force of about 18,000, about half instruct one or two days a week (2-6 hours weekly) ; one-fourth are employed on a three-, four- or five-day-a-week basis (10-20 hours a week) ; and one-fourth may be considered full-time teachers (20 or more hours weekly). Most of the teachers in the full-time category either hold two positions (mornings in a day school and afternoons in a supplementary Hebrew school) or are engaged in a dual educational capacity as teacher-principal, teacher-cantor, or teacher-youth director.

The part-time nature of the Jewish teaching profession is one of the causes of the manpower shortage. Moreover, young, talented people, particularly males, are not attracted to a profession that lacks social status, does not provide the kind of economic security they desire, and does not afford wide opportunities for professional advancement.

The organized Jewish community is gradually becoming aware of the need for qualified educational personnel. Many bureaus of Jewish education, in collaboration with the local Jewish federations and welfare funds, are seeking ways of ameliorating the problem. On the national level, the Council of Jewish Federation and Welfare Funds (CJFWF), organized, in 1966, an Educational Planning Committee whose major focus has been on exploring ways of alleviating the manpower shortage.

The inability of Jewish education, over the last three decades, to recruit young promising people has resulted in a serious lack of educators adequately prepared to assume leadership responsibility. Two noteworthy attempts to train education leaders merit attention. These are: the 1969 summer in-service "crash" program for principals and consultants sponsored by the American Association for Jewish Education, and the doctoral program in Administration and Supervision of Jewish Education sponsored by the Department of Jewish Education of the Ferkauf Graduate School of Humanities and Social Sciences of Yeshiva University. From its end, the Jewish community is slowly awakening to answering the growing need for Jewish educational professional leadership by providing competitive salaries for people in supervisory and administrative positions.

Despite the concern and interest that Jewish parents traditionally have demonstrated for the education of their offspring, the average American Jewish parent relegates the total responsibility for the Jewish upbringing of his children to the Jewish school. This condition, coupled with the increased challenges of general education and the growing variety of cultural, social and recreational opportunities available to all children has affected adversely the involvement of Jewish youth in Jewish educational experiences.

Jewish education in the United States is largely an elementary school system. Lack of continuity has been one of the most serious problems in Jewish education. Less than 10 percent of the total Jewish pupil population is of high school age and the overwhelming majority of these students attend only a few hours weekly for a period of one or two years. During the 1960's, as a result of an intensive campaign to make "Jewish *secondary* education *primary*," there has been a slight increase in the number of children continuing beyond bar mitzvah and bat mitzvah. Several new communal and intercongregational high schools are being opened as the idea of continuation finds greater support in the Jewish community, particularly among parents who recognize the inadequacy of a Jewish elementary education in coping with the challenges of the college campus and society.

A major problem in Jewish schools is insufficient instructional time. Jewish children in one-day-a-week schools are exposed to 300-350 formal instructional hours during their Jewish schooling. This is the equivalent of four months of public school classroom time. The average pupil in a supplementary afternoon Hebrew school attends Hebrew classes for 600-700 hours—about 7-8 months of study time in a public school. It is difficult, indeed, to do justice to the variety of Jewish subjects within such time limitations. This is one reason that greater attention is being given to the Jewish Day School.

In order to cope with the time limitation imposed by the supplementary nature of Jewish education and to enrich the Jewish living experience of pupils, Jewish educators and educational institutions have been focusing their attention on Jewish educational camping. During the last three decades, many educational and Hebraic camps and camp systems have been developed. Chief among these are Massad Camps, Yavneh, Ramah and Morasha. In addition, many Jewish day schools sponsor residence camps and day camps featuring Jewish educational programs.

Another problem is the small school. The large majority of the Jewish school enrollment is found in schools with less than 200 pupils. Over half of all school enrollment is in schools with less than 100 children. In the smaller cities and towns the small size of the schools is inevitable. In the larger centers, efforts are being made to combine schools on a communal or intercongregational basis.

A number of significant trends are observable. New methodology is being introduced into Jewish schools, particularly in the teaching of Hebrew. New concepts in curriculum development have been developed by some groups. Attempts at programmed instruction have been made by others.

The influence of Israel is increasingly felt upon Jewish education. For one thing, the Sephardic pronunciation is gradually taking hold in Jewish schools. Currently, about one-fourth of all Jewish schools have shifted to the Sephardic pronunciation. Moreover, Israel is being increasingly programmed as a formal and informal subject. A commission on the teaching of Israel has recently been established by the American Association for Jewish Education. Many schools, school groups and organizations sponsor primer and year-round programs in Israel.*

Jewish education has undergone a rapid process of congregationalization during the 1940's and 1950's. About 86 percent of all Jewish schools are presently under synagogue auspices; 15 percent are communally sponsored. The congregational framework of Jewish education has had the effect of trisecting Jewish schools into three ideological movements, each with its respective set of goals, curricula, organizations, and patterns of communication. In recognition of this development, the American Associa-

---

* The Jewish Agency via its Department of Education and Culture and Torah and Culture and the American Zionist Youth Foundation are particularly active in this regard.

tion for Jewish Education, the umbrella agency of Jewish education in America, reorganized its board constituency to reflect among others, the religious organizational trends in Jewish education.

## Development of the Jewish Day School

The most noteworthy development in American Jewish education during the twentieth century is the growth of the Jewish Day School (popularly known by its Hebrew name, *yeshiva*) which offers a combined program of Jewish and general studies. Although the origins of the Jewish Day School can be traced back some two hundred years to the European setting, and to the eighteenth and nineteenth centuries in the United States, the modern American *yeshiva* is a relatively new institution. While the oldest existing day school was founded at the turn of the century, over 90 percent of the Jewish Day Schools were established since 1940. During this period, the pupil enrollment increased almost tenfold from 7,313 to approximately 70,000 students.

Unlike parochial schools which are controlled by a central church or parish, Jewish Day Schools are distinct educational units established and supported by parents and interested individuals, and communally conducted by autonomous, self-governing lay boards, responsive to the needs of the parents and community. Hence, heterogeneity is one of the characteristics of the day-school movement. Moreover, the Jewish Day School was not founded in opposition to public education since Judaism does not challenge the state's right to control education.

To the advocates of the Jewish Day School idea the combination of general studies and Jewish subjects under a single auspices is a vital necessity. In the first instance, the establishment of the day school is predicated on a deep-felt need for intensive Hebraic and/or Jewish religious schooling. Due to various sociological and cultural circumstances, the acquisition of the wide variety of information and experiences which constitute the Jewish heritage is not currently possible via supplementary Jewish education. Secondly, the American Jewish community strongly believes in the values of a sound secular education. The proponents of the day school believe that it is the best instrument for achieving this dual goal.

Almost all Jewish Day Schools consist of two divisions —a general studies department and a Jewish or Hebrew studies department. Since the instructional responsibilities in each division require full-time, college-level preparation, there are very few teachers who teach in both departments of the day school. Thus, pupils generally have two instructors—a Hebrew teacher and a general studies teacher. In the junior and senior high schools, where the programs are usually departmentalized, the students study under the guidance of two sets of instructors.

While their Hebrew curricula vary in intensity and emphasis, almost all schools are Hebrew language-centered and Bible-centered in the elementary grades. The concentration thereafter is divided between the study of Bible and Talmud and their major commentaries. Other subjects include Jewish history, Jewish life and observances, liturgy, ethics, and Israel. The general studies programs essentially use the same syllabi, textbooks, educational *realia,* and achievement tests employed by the respective local public schools.

The Jewish Day School began as an all-boy enterprise. Today, 65 percent of the schools are either coeducational or provide instruction for boys and girls under one auspices; 20 percent are all-boy yeshivot, and 15 percent are girls' schools. Slightly more than 90 percent of all day schools are Orthodox institutions, most of which are affiliated with Torah Umesorah. During the latter part of the

1950's, the Conservative movement, along with Hebrew culture and Zionist groups, began to show an active interest in the day school idea. The Department of Education of the United Synagogue of America encourages and provides guidance for the founding of new day schools. About 7 percent of the total day-school enrollment is currently in Conservative sponsored institutions. Significantly, a number of Reform Jewish day schools are also being planned.

## Summary

In sum, the picture of Jewish education in the United States is a mixture of progress, problems, and promise. The historical role of the Jewish school and the traditional Jewish attitudes toward Jewish learning constitute the frame of reference for Jewish education activity in this country. This is reinforced by the survival needs of the Jewish community and Jewish youth.

The problems facing Jewish education, resulting largely from parental apathy and the lack of sufficient communal support, have hampered Jewish schools from making noteworthy achievements. The rapid changes in our society presently indicate the need for new viable institutional formats for Jewish education. Most significant among the new developments in this direction are the Jewish Day School, the Jewish educational camp, and Israel-based programs.

Much progress still remains to be seen in a number of vital areas, chiefly: intensification of supplementary school programs, continuation beyond elementary school, the enhancement of the Jewish teaching profession; and the funding of Jewish education. In the long run, the resolution of these problems and the realization of the true potential of Jewish education as a creative force in American Jewish life will derive from the increased concern and support from both the organized community and individual parents and lay groups. If the community wills it and the parents demand it, the promise of Jewish schooling will be fulfilled.

*Part II*

# The Adult

trend becomes decisive. In short, if college success the
Jewish community, earlier pneumonia

in life on the attitudinal figures, the question of the
effect of college on Jewish values and values
and loyalty become one of extraordinarily importance to the
Jewish community. Add all this is reasonable, then, that
there has not been enough systematic or comprehensive
study of this question. The studies that do exist range
widely in quality, adequacy of research design, significance

*12*

# THE JEWISH COLLEGE YOUTH

## Irving Greenberg

The future of American Judaism is being shaped on the
college campus. This is not a public relations or alarmist
statement but a literal, statistically descriptive fact. In
1964, Alfred Jospe estimated that 80 percent of eligible
Jewish youth were attending college—up from 62 percent
in 1956 and compared to 27 percent of the eligible non-
Jewish youth. The main forces making for college attendance are affluence, expectations linked to status seeking,
and the desire for upward mobility through education.
Since these forces trend steadily higher in the Jewish community, we can foresee, in the near future, a condition of
"full college employment" among Jewish youth. (All but
a hard core of "unemployable," poverty-stricken, intellectually retarded, and emotional or psychological drop-
outs will be in attendance.) It is not just the elite, or the
leadership of the Jewish community of the future which
will be shaped by the college experience but the rank and
file foot soldiers as well. This is a fact unprecedented in
world history and is a reflection of the extraordinary
achievement of the Jews in the modern, free society. But
this also means that any effect which college has on the
values of other groups is somewhat marginal or, at least,
diluted. Although, since it is the elite of other groups
which are in attendance, the effect is much out of proportion to the number involved. In the case of the Jews, the
effect becomes overwhelming. A marginal, if significant,

trend becomes decisive. In short, if college sneezes, the Jewish community catches pneumonia.

In light of the attendance figures, the question of the effect of college or university experience on Jewish values and loyalty becomes one of extraordinary importance to the Jewish community. It is all the more regrettable, then, that there has not been enough systematic or comprehensive study of this question. The studies that do exist range widely in quality, adequacy of research design, significance of sample, freedom from bias, etc. Nor were these studies undertaken as part of an overall design to achieve coverage of all types of colleges, types of Jewish students, etc. The analyses and conclusions of this paper should be taken as educated guesses then. They are also heavily influenced by the personal observations and eperiences of the writer.

All of the studies we have point to one fact. By and large, college is a disaster area for Judaism, Jewish loyalty and Jewish identity. From Marvin Nathan's study of 1,500 Jewish students at 57 colleges and universities in 1931 to Meyer Greenberg's study of students at Yale in 1940 to the most recent studies by B'nai Brith, the trend is clear. Whatever the nature of the student's commitment, observance or loyalty, it tends to decline in college. (There is a minority which responds to the challenge by deepening its Jewish commitment. But it is a very small percentage and it hasn't been studied. It should be.) Observance of the Sabbath and/or *Kashruth* declines. Zionist students tend to reduce their support of Israel. Weak Jewish identities tend to shrivel or falter. (In Meyer Greenberg's study, a concept such as the Chosenness of Israel which calls for commitment in order to be believed and which seems to "flout" standard liberal norms, declines to where only 4 percent of the class is willing to affirm it.) Readiness to interdate or intermarry rises sharply. Perhaps it can be summarized in the following statistics.

Stanley Bigman's study of Washington, D.C., found the intermarriage rate to be 1.4 percent in the first generation, (foreign born), 10.2 percent in the second generation, (American born), and 17.9 percent in the third generation. If we isolate out the third generation college graduates, the rate leaps to 37 percent. (This statistic is more alarming than it should be. Washington is a city which concentrates marginal and alienated Jews. But the trend is clear and true in cities where the percentages are less frightful.) Let us take the trend as granted, then, and turn to the question: why?

The college years come during a key period of personality formation. Erik Erikson has suggested that it is one of the two crucial periods of personality integration of the individual. The first period is the first five years of life when the basic ego structure is formed. The second is the period of late adolescence when the social-cultural personality is formed. At this key period of life, the student comes to college. The search for self and self-definition, the establishment of loyalties and faithfulness, the trying of different roles and patterns—all characterize this phase. The student is highly suggestible and hungry for experience and influences. In the noncommuter college, the student goes into a setup where parental and family influence will be far away. He is most sheltered from the agencies of Jewish transmission—the parents, family, home, neighborhood and synagogue. He is really isolated from much adult contact in general. Contacts between students and faculty and administrators are notoriously marginal in most cases. As Dr. Seymour Halleck, director of student psychiatry at the University of Wisconsin said recently: "A student can spend months on a large campus without having a conversation with a person over 30." This means that the student is immersed in the group which is most suggestible, most willing to give up traditional values, most responsive to what is new as against

204 THE JEWISH FAMILY IN A CHANGING WORLD

what is continuous. The amount of personal supervision in most colleges is increasingly nil. The biological maturation of the sexual urge without official and legitimate ways of expressing it (such as marriage, which is out financially and emotionally for most students), the peculiar pressures and responsibilities of college can determine lifetime careers or success yet are clearly unrelated to direct action in the real world; the relative affluence without personal effort of more and more students—create an emotional ferment and restlessness (and in growing number the phenomenon of alienation) which made traditional commitment vulnerable. It should be pointed out that different colleges have different effects. One study of colleges suggested that there are three outstanding types of colleges:

1) those with a vocational-occupational orientation. These colleges with their matter-of-fact tendencies, their greater focus on conventional real life, their lesser intellectualism tend to have much less impact on their student's values. (These colleges tend to be less academic and they attract correspondingly fewer Jewish students.)

2) those with an intellectual-academic orientation. Here the school's stress on intense high-level study, the tendency toward a research directed to a cosmopolitan faculty, and the challenges posed by the humanities, etc., tend to create more impact on the student's values.

3) those with a particularly strong value-orientating impact. These schools tend to be academic-intellectual (although teaching and student participation may be more highly rated on such a campus relative to research). However, the key kicker is the presence of a strong value concern and a tradition of faculty and student involvement in questions of value and meaning. Frequently, the student subculture is particularly strong in creating groups involved in the subculture's values. These may range from social action involvement to bohemian circles, etc. Examples of such schools are Oberlin, Antioch, Swarthmore. In

the larger schools, Berkeley is a less pure form of this type. Needless to say, there are overlaps and cross-factors. Thus, Harvard probably straddles types 2 and 3. Commuter colleges such as the City University of New York tend to be academic-intellectual in orientation but vocational-like in their value impact since the student spends most of his social life in the home and neighborhood setting. Catholic or church-related colleges tend to reinforce traditional values for students. Obviously, then, some colleges will have more impact than others. Still, the general trend is again clear. All tend to have some impact on the values of the student. Most of the impact is in the direction of unsettling traditional values.

The college setting presents a challenge to all established consensual values which has not yet been fully apprehended by society. Most of society's codes tend to perpetuate themselves by being taken for granted. Being taken for granted depends in part on the unavailability of alternative codes, models of behavior, etc. The scientific and social scientific methods which dominate the college curriculum place great stress on challenging the given and the assumed. Moreover, the university atmosphere is like an exaggerated version of the modern cultural setting. It is a high-communication, opinion-forming and sharing situation. Many views and values are constantly being made available. This characteristic tends to undermine traditional patterns which depend on consensus and rarely are prepared to justify themselves in a market place of ideas and alternatives. The relative affluence of the college creates a setting conducive to hedonism. The multiplicity of codes creates a strong secularist and universalist orientation. Such values as patriotism and moralism which are heavily saturated with particularist and authority assumptions come under heavy pressure.

This general pattern has tended to attract people of a more alienated type or people with strong critical, hedo-

nistic and secularist bents. Thus the academic community or
"subculture" has a high concentration of personality types
critical or antagonistic to authority and relativistic in
ethics. It may be, of course, that this is intrinsic in the
culture of modernism and that college atmosphere is like
the rest of society—only more so. But the pure and highly
concentrated form of these trends make for exceptional
impact on personality and ethical values of the students.
There is also a built-in bias against the exercise of authority and discipline. Thus the administrator is frequently
on the defensive. Supervision tends to be steadily restricted. In effect, the student is left almost completely to
the influence of his peer group and the faculty critics. It is
no accident that the universities are bastions of antiwar
sentiment as they are of antipatriotic, antimoralistic sentiment. There is no implication here that the universities
are hotbeds of treason or immorality. Opposition to the
present war may be a more moral position. What is un-
clear, however, is whether the college community would
create a different attitude toward a more clearly justified
war or moral code. Of course, no society can operate without some consensual values. If it feels pressed enough by
the undermining of these values, it will tend to bring pressure for change. Thus, the severe parental backlash against
drugs has forced the universities to reverse their general
tendency to reduce supervision or enforcement of moral
codes. But the general problem that, in the college, society has created a subculture generally dissolving of
traditional values has not yet been fully perceived or
weighed. It may be that society will decide that it is beneficial for traditional norms to be dissolved. This certainly
has become the new American consensus toward the old
virtues of the Puritan ethic. The needs of the production
and distribution system as expressed in advertising particularly have led to the steadily more apparent destruction of traditional norms of asceticism, work orientations,

etc. However, this may be a more serious problem when it comes to questions such as the existence of the family, honesty as a code, and so on.

Be this as it may, this is the setting to which the Jewish student comes at a particularly impressionable age. The amazing thing is not so much how much undermining of traditional patterns there is but how much there isn't. Despite all the factors operating for change, a substantial number—probably a majority—go through college passively with a minimum of long-term effect on their central concerns. Nevertheless the trend and the influence of the minority who are affected are the stuff out of which massive cultural shifts are made.

When we see the effect of college on the newly arrived Jewish student, we see that the problem of college is an exaggerated version of the problem of Judaism in a free and open society. Until recent times, Judaism survived in a closed cultural setting with sharp distinctions between Jews and gentiles. The Jewish codes were self-evident and the alternative codes were culturally inferior and identified with the persecutors. Jewish existence was seen ascribed by birth. It was a diffuse commitment reflecting itself in every area of life and behavior. The particularist norms in Judaism became ever more prominent—in part as a necessary survival measure. Despite the massive transfer to the American setting, and the massive bleeding of Jewish loyalties and values which it caused, much of the surviving Jewish commitment and loyalty is still saturated with these tendencies. The universalization of Judaism and the weakening of traditional observance has left the surviving Jewish loyalties even more dependent on ethnic ties and tribal feeling. Parents have hoped to perpetuate a nominal Jewish identity for their children by concentrating on Jewish neighborhoods. But the further decline of discrimination and the open social setting of the university in particular has destroyed that possible escape.

The universal, secularist life style of the university is highly destructive of the remaining particularistic, ethnic loyalties of the student. The normative tone of much of religious life and teaching is undermined by the critical style of the college. The ethnic tribalism is seen as atavistic and as logically unjustifiable in the universalist atmosphere. Thus interdating and intermarriage are no longer seen as evil. It may be a blow for a better world where all men are equal. It has been pointed out by some observers that whereas intermarriage tended to be associated with character disturbances and emotional problems in the partners, this is no longer so. Many of the couples now may be quite normal and even idealistic types who approach intermarriage with little of the old inner conflict.

The life style of the Jewish community is still warm and sentimental in tone. Its organizational and fund-raising life is dominated by *kavod* situations, effusive and emotional situations and language and a generally saccharine medium. But this tone and quality is highly vulnerable to the cool, emotionally understated and highly critical style of the university. (Compare the style of a synagogue bulletin and a college student newspaper.) The "acids of modernity" create an "acidic" medium which is highly caustic in its effect on the Jewish student's feelings for Jewishness. The Jewish setting is seen as unsophisticated and bourgeois and there is an emotional recoil.

The net effect of the clash of the two life styles is to set up a pair of contrasting polarities in the mind and heart of the Jewish student. Judaism is identified with the group and ethnocentrism; secularism, with the universal concerns. Jewish society—its tone is warm and lush; the academic style is cool and spare. The Jewish is bourgeois; the academic—swinging. The Jewish community is the culture of organizations; college—its society is seen as the scene of privatism and self expression. Not surprisingly, the student tends to opt for the secular alternative.

In this connection, perhaps one word might be stated about the much bruited and possibly exaggerated sexual revolution on the campus. The change in sexual values not only may lead to a shift away from Jewish standards and, incidentally, reflect itself in interdating and intermarriage; it also tends to associate the new personality and identify with a swinging and more personal satisfaction oriented way of life. The Jewish identity remains equated with the more staid and conventional. For those who opt for the new values there is then the reward of this kind of performance being permitted. Even for those who do not fully identify with greater freedom or even promiscuity, there may be a fashion image created. If you will, Judaism is the old *Yiddisheh momma;* the secular—the mini-skirted swinger.

In addition to choosing the secular alternative, the student also withdraws from the Jewish community. It is true that this withdrawal may not be permanent, although intermarriage very likely may make it so, and intermarriage is rising in the college-educated population. However, even if the student does go back to a more normal pattern and rejoins the Jewish community after marriage he is likely to have incorporated negative emotional as well as intellectual orientations toward Jewish values. Thus, the quality of his Jewish life and the kind of community he is likely to create or participate in is probably going to be flawed or marred by serious ambivalence and even hostility to Jewishness. Thus, the weakening of values will lead to a weaker community and even more vulnerable offspring.

The emotional recoil of the Jewish student is intensified by the impact of the intellectual challenge of college. In the curriculum at the present times are a host of areas whose working assumptions and findings of fact are contradictory to traditional religions and Judaism in particular. Psychology, anthropology, sociology are obvious examples of this. Thus psychology may be operating with behaviorist assumptions or with psychoanalytic axioms. Both challenge traditional religions and Judaism moral assumptions. The chances are that if religion is studied in this area, it is as a human fulfillment (or repressive) system or through the eyes of Sigmund Freud in *The Future of an Illusion* which sees religion as a neurosis to be outgrown by man. The approach to religion in the history curriculum is likely to be far more historicist and relativist than that which the student has heard before. Sociology and anthropology offer highly relativistic orientations toward religion and moral codes. Not the least of the effect of these studies in the student is the powerful emotional psychic gain of having been "wised up." Once the traditional assumptions have been exposed or undermined, the student may tend to identify everything he has been taught earlier as "kid stuff" or phony or outdated. There is thus a moral and emotional recoil from it and from the authority of those who transmitted these teachings to him. Indeed, the college does not present itself as authoritarian. But the secular and relative orientations are quite ubiquitous.

Thus the student tends to accept them as indisputable, particularly when his sense of intellectual sophistication and discovery is being appealed to. This is the truth and not the existence of a liberal conspiracy which William Buckley was trying to get at in his lugubrious book, *God and Man at Yale*. What Buckley also failed to grasp is that all systems tend to perpetuate themselves by creating such an atmosphere. Still, it is a piquant development that under the cover of no values and openness so homogeneous a cultural atmosphere has been created. Religion and religious education will have to learn how to live in this atmosphere and develop commitment through such techniques if they are to survive in the new medium. This

creates a crisis for Jewish education—which I will discuss
further.

If the college atmosphere and culture is subversive of
all religious traditions and consensual values, it must be
said that Judaism suffers from double jeopardy. The university and its curriculum are secular and nonsectarian by
its own definition. Thus the student is apt to take its presentation of Judaism at face value. Judaism and Jewish
history are presented in passing in many areas of the college curriculum—such as the ubiquitous Social Science 1
or Humanities 1 courses. However, the presentation here
turns out to be essentially a secularized version of traditional Christian stereotypes of Judaism. The God of
Wrath of the Old Testament and the God of Love of the
New, the legalism and petrifaction of rabbinic Judaism
and the Faith and Love of Paulinist Christianity, the
particularism and henotheism of Judaism and the universalism of Christianity—these are a few of the short-
hand images of Judaism which are transmitted in the
secular course. The fact that Judaism tends to get no
serious attention after the birth of Christianity comes
through as a tacit confirmation of the Christian claim that
Judaism comes to an end with its birth. Christianity is the
warp and woof of Western culture, art, music, etc., and
the comparative absence of Judaism tends to confirm the
negative image.

Moreover, the few Jews who do rate in the college
curriculum—such as Spinoza, Freud and Einstein—are
models of alienation from traditional Jewish values and
a kind of universal, nonspecific existence as men in general. These stereotypes are particularly devastating because the student is unequipped to challenge them. At the
recent peak of enrollment in Jewish education, only 55
percent of Jewish children eligible were engaged in any
Jewish education. Even if we add a certain percentage

who may have been enrolled at one time and then dropped out, a large number have never had any Jewish education. (Many who are enrolled have only the most primitive and elementary kind of schooling.) Therefore, the only source of images and understanding of Judaism are the devastatingly negative stereotypes described above. Now the secularist world is not engaged in a conspiracy to undermine Judaism. But in all knowledge systems, there is much that is inherited or simply taken for granted. This information tends to persist until experience or new sources of knowledge or alternate images are encountered or provided. What has made the current cultural situation so explosive is that so many traditional stereotypes are vulnerable to the increased flow of information which breaks down presumptions and stereotypes.

Unfortunately, however, a Jewish scholarship has been lacking to challenge these circulating clichés. I am not speaking of apologetics or defensive scholarship either. But Jews of any loyalty or deep understanding of the tradition have been in the modern situation only a short time. Many of the first scholars and faculty of Jewish background tended to be those who were alienated from the Jewish community and were leaving it. Not surprisingly, they have been unable or unwilling to correct the image. (See the brilliant polemics of Walter Kaufmann as cultural critic of Christianity for an example of how the traditional stereotypes can be challenged or corrected.) Even if such a scholarship and such scholars were to be intensively developed it would probably take centuries before their circulation and currency caught up to the prevalent notions. Indeed, one is reminded of the American Jewish Committee sponsored study of other religions and groups in religious textbooks. Considering how many more students—Jewish and non-Jewish alike—read and absorb the secular textbooks in many different disciplines, I hope you will not consider it ironic to suggest that the money would be better invested in a study of secular textbooks with an eye to speeding up the process of revision. Even if such a study were done, the overcoming of the negative images would be more difficult. For the Christian community (and the secular) see the religious textbooks as inherently unscientific and subject to informed revision. And the leadership of the more liberal religious groups are in a paroxysm of guilt for the tragic anti-Semitic consequences of the negative images. The secular scholarly community would tend to suspect the motives of such a study as apologetic and to assume the scholarly and unbiased nature of the texts. Thus again the more liberal view would be more resistant to genuine openness. One need not add perhaps that there are extant many works of great and widely disseminated scholars which perpetuate these distortions. (Nathan Rotenstreich's book, *The Recurring Pattern,* is an interesting study of the anti-Judaic strand in the work of Kant, Hegel and Toynbee.) But the textbook clichés are probably far more devastating than the scholarly work.

The other side of the coin is the absence of serious works of a positive Jewish content and, in particular, the almost total dearth of college textbook level books in various Jewish areas. There is not a single first-rate one-volume work in English on Jewish history, *halacha,* Bible, or even theology. (Although the newly translated Guttman's *Philosophies of Judaism* is a big step forward.) Despite the growth of Jewish publication, any visitor to a well-stocked paperback bookstore cannot but be struck by the melancholy contrast of the range and depth of Christian works as compared to Jewish material. Of course, one factor is that Christianity has been working in the medium of Western philosophy and culture for centuries and a series of outstanding geniuses at least in Western languages have given it great literary and philosophical resources—certainly more than Judaism has. But part of the problem is that Jewish classics languish in neglect, untranslated and unavailable. Similarly, the excellent scholarship of some of the modern French Jews—Neher, Ashkenazi, Baruch—has not been translated. The other part of the problem is the failure to recruit and develop more positive Jewish scholarship or to underwrite the writing of the necessary textbooks. A constructive development is the program of the National Foundation for Jewish Culture. It is bearing some fruit already. But its scope and budget is most restricted. Tragically, the funds of the Memorial Foundation for Jewish Culture (reparations) have not been as fruitfully employed, as far as I can tell. In any event, there is a need for a program comparable to that of the Danforth Foundation and that of the Carnegie Foundation—of which see more below. Linked to this question is the fact that Judaism is not taught in the average college curriculum. Here, too, we have a combination of the traditional reticence in teaching religion, the liberal-secular flavor of the college, and the double jeopardy of Judaism's minority status. There has been a most promising growth of Jewish Studies chairs in the last decade. (See Arnold Band's survey in the 1966 *American Jewish Year Book*.)

However, the number of the chairs is still a drop in the bucket. The Jewish community should engage in a systematic double-barreled program—to underwrite such chairs and to get the private university and the state university to set them up from their own funds. While such chairs cannot be sold to administrations in the same way the U.J.A. operates, it should be possible to recruit the kind of people and set up the kind of approach needed to get more of these chairs. The real problem is that there is no center or office that is systematically interested, let alone working, in this area. Such chairs not only make more Jewish scholarship likely but their holders can, without serving as apologists, by their very presence stimulate the process of correction of the negative stereotypes circulating in the scholarly community. They raise the level of Jewish literacy of the student and they make available positive models of Jewishness on campus—which I will presently discuss.

A critical note should be added on the operations of the three leading Jewish theological seminaries: Hebrew Union College, Jewish Theological Seminary and Yeshiva University. On the whole they have failed to make Jewish scholarship sufficiently attractive in financial and working conditions and sufficiently mainstream intellectually to attract the best students. Therefore, they have failed to train sufficient scholars for the growing demand. (Yeshiva University has been particularly lacking in this area, considering the number of highly motivated and interested students who go through its college.) The leadership of these institutions has been too parochial in its concern for their institutional needs rather than those of the entire community. Thus, they have tended to see the university as competitor rather than a theater of operations. Perhaps they need to be transferred to university setting to be stimulated. This is something which many Christian seminaries are doing. (One may cite Harvard and Yale Divinity schools, which have a far closer relationship to their university's scholarship than does the Rabbi Isaac Elchanan Theological Seminary have to Yeshiva University. We should also cite the decision of Woodstock College [Catholic] to tie up with Yale. This might serve as a paradigm for J.T.S. and the H.U.C.) Ironically enough, the failure of the three institutions has created a situation where the new chairs in Jewish studies are competitive with these seminaries. There has been a noticeable bleeding of the few younger scholars which they have produced to the universities.

The failure of Jewish identity on campus must also be seen as a further revelation of the insufficiency and irrelevance of much of Jewish education in America. I have elsewhere made some evaluations of the failures of Jewish education. (See "Jews or Zombies: A Hard Look at Jewish Education," printed in the *Jewish Advocate*, September 30, 1966. An earlier draft was mimeographed in the proceedings of the American Association for Jewish Education annual Convention, 1966.) We can summarize the situation briefly. The last national count found under 600,000 students in some form of Jewish education. Of these, probably 85 percent are in elementary education. Of the total registration, almost one half are in Sunday school. This means a maximum of one or two hours a week for a very few childhood years. This is not to mention the wastage, absences, etc. The curriculum is primitive and weak conceptually. The personnel tend to be less committed or concerned for Jewish education. (The sheer limits of the medium suggest that more motivated people will seek out other forms.) About 40 percent plus of the students are registered in Talmud Torahs. Many Talmud Torahs have rabbis of synagogues as principals. Since there are hundreds of higher priority items in the rabbi's daily burden, supervision and planning tends to be nil or worse. The standard of professional principals tends to be lamentably low. This is hardly surprising in light of the historically low salaries, the absence of tenure, and the politics of synagogues. (Indeed, the qualified few are the miracle of Jewish education.)

The schools have been underfinanced and lacking in communal support and leadership as well as support from Federation. While the situation and salaries are improving, they are far from competitive with the public school systems. The caliber and support of Federations and the Bureau of Jewish Education leadership vary widely from city to city. Still, evaluation of the textbooks used shows a general pattern: immature and inadequate concepts, little or no sensitivity to the intellectual challenges which college will offer and, in general, little scholarly or research depth. This is perhaps not really possible in any other way in light of the fact that most students spend so few hours in Hebrew school and drop out by Bar Mitzvah. But even with this allowance, the material is shallow. The high school student today does research in primary sources. Even junior high school and elementary school children are capable of independent reading and projects that far transcend the depth and relevance of the Jewish curriculum. To engage in an unfair generalization, many of the Bureau consultants and textbook experts, are like the educationist masters of the public school system who are increasingly being ousted by the university-linked "new math," new textbook groups, the disciples of the Bruner approach, etc. What is needed, then, is centrally financed, university-level or university-linked center for research, evaluation and textbook and course construction. The Melton Institute is a good forerunner of what we are looking for, although it is my impression that it is a bit overtouted. We need a number of such centers if we are to break through in this area.

Given the limited number of hours, the Jewish school system must be considerably more efficient than the public school in transmitting knowledge and values. For the most part, it is less efficient. The failure of the Jewish Federations, by and large, and the Federation of Jewish Philanthropies of New York in particular, to give priority funds for Jewish education precludes the existence of such centers. The Talmud Torahs and other Jewish schools are financed by tuition, users' fees, and synagogal underwriting. The key to the quality achievements of the top universities is the large increment of foundation and government and private support—particularly unrestricted funds. The time has come for the Federations to give this top priority —the survival of their givers is at stake. There is a significant misreading of the future in the Federations' lack of support. It is true that the bulk of their funds—in particular, big gifts—come from people who have little, if any, Jewish education. Many of them have significantly ambivalent or negative attitudes toward various Jewish values and even Jewish identity. The Federations feel that they can ignore Jewish education, which, in any event, has little appeal to these big donors. But Federation counts on its continued mastery of the status and prestige-giving channels of the Jewish community to keep the gifts coming. This may indeed persist for a long time despite a decline in the Jewish community and religion. The fallacy is that ultimately the power to utilize prestige and status concerns depends on a residual consensus of the Jewish community that charity is an important and aristocracy-bestowing virtue. There is good evidence that this consensual ethic is hurt by the same factors on the college campus which weaken Jewish commitment. It is true that when they settle down into the Jewish community, people can be gotten to conform more in this area than in the cultural or religious areas of Jewish life. But when they do the inner identification is considerably weaker. At some point—such as the presence of an entire college-trained community, the inner weakening could lead to a massive breakdown of the charity consensus. In addition, there is the possibility of greater shifts to "pure" nonsectarian giving. (Marshall Sklare seems to detect some such incipient trends in his article, "The Future of Jewish Giving," *Commentary,* November, 1962.)

Let me cite one other major factor in the negative influence of the college years on Jewish identity: the absence during those years of positive models of committed and relevant Jewishness. The student is often away from home and his parents, as well as his synagogue and his rabbi (if he has one to begin with). In any event, the parent and the rabbi are likely to be saturated with the old ethic and style which are undercut by the college experience.

Few rabbis are free enough in time as well as capable enough intellectually to match the various challenges posed by colleges anyway. (Here the American "edifice complex" which guarantees that only one or two rabbis will have to service a huge congregation and building in order to make financial ends meet is also to blame.)

On campus the student finds few if any images of Jewishness that he can respect and identify with. The traditional heroes and thinkers of Jewish history and tradition are not available in light of the curriculum and course conditions described above. As far as living models of Jewishness are concerned, the first and foremost model is likely to be the Jewish faculty member. He is overwhelmingly likely to be a model of Jewish alienation. He tends to be a member of the liberal establishment on campus or even a radical. He is usually a confirmed member of the Enlightenment faith—longing for and living in a post-Jewish world where humanism, science and universal brotherhood shall reign supreme. Despite his own increasingly affluent circumstances, he is likely to be scornful of the bourgeois, organization-minded Jewish community. Intermarriage is highest among such people. The Jewish faculty member is concentrated in the style setting and pioneering fields of the university. His intellectual and academic achievements may be outstanding. His commitment to idealistic causes tends to be higher than non-Jews. It is small wonder that he can attract identification. Of course, in his own field, he is likely to work with assumptions which contradict the students' traditional views. Each of these men is a specialist in highly developed intellectual field.

Against this model, the Jewish community offers as an alternative—on many but far from all campuses—a Hillel director. Usually, he is a rabbi. Hillel has long made a valiant effort and been a pioneer on the college campus. However, there are some obvious limitations here. On most campuses, there is, at most, one full-time man. There may be thousands of Jewish students around. The Hillel man has to run the Foundation, supervise the physical facilities, counsel with students, arrange religious services, possibly provide kosher food, plan and execute dances, invite speakers, teach classes, etc. It is obvious that his time is highly limited for each student and cannot begin to compare with the time which individual students can spend with individual faculty members. Moreover, Hillel salaries are competitive only with the Orthodox rabbinate—and not with its best positions. There are advantages in not having to deal with laymen. But the fact is that Hillel has not succeeded in attracting the best people. In particular, the intellectual adequacy of the Hillel man is frequently in doubt. And even the intellectuals among Hillel directors could hardly be expected to meet the intellectual challenges of so many different fields. The academician also has the prestige of the college too. There is an additional and subtle problem, too. The Hillel man must be a *kolbonik*. But this may cramp the particular personal specialty which he is truly best at and which could move and inspire students. Thus a natural scholar may have to spend much or even most of his time arranging a dance or a program of various sorts. A social action activist may have to do much counseling or teaching.

The same problem shows up in another area. Hillel has been nondenominational in its approach. This is a very fine and laudable stress. It has kept the college campus free of some of the pathological institutionalism which besets American Jewish life. But there are real tensions in this approach. The idea of servicing all groups and not imposing one's own standards may lead to the suppression of the particular commitment which the man has to offer at his best. Try as he will to do justice to all, the man may end up doing least justice to the unique quality of his own mind and life. There is a need for exploration of the complexities of this dilemma. (This may include the imposition of his own approach by a systematic blocking of students seeking to express their own particular commitments in the name of preserving the community atmosphere.) Here, the developing and student-engineered particular religious groupings such as Yavneh, Atid, NFTY, could make a real contribution. In general, Hillel has responded with suspicion and covert obstacle-making in some cases. There were legitimate concerns of sectarianism and muscling in of outside organizations but this biased observer felt that Hillel's reaction reflected lack of thinking through the complexities and just plain insecurity.

In any event, the key to a breakthrough for Hillel's effectiveness is the development of teams of Hillel men on every campus. This would enable specialization—a teacher with a social action man with a counseling type or an Orthodox, Conservative, and Reform or a religious with a Zionist and a Yiddishist or secularist. Needless to say, these men should not be recruited as institutional representatives but with concern for maximum effectiveness and exemplary life qualities. The Hillel leadership is somewhat aware of the need for broadening but it pleads the limited budget and thinking of the laymen. This can be appreciated. But perhaps we can draw a harsh analogy. One is reminded of the Rumshinskis and the capos in the camps who felt that they could only work within the given framework to save a few individuals. The moral criticism we have of them is that when the mortality rate passes a certain point, working within the system becomes a form of collaboration which makes what is saved a thin cover which makes possible what is lost. The demand must be posed for an immensely higher level of support and financing, or else the leadership will be convicted of being too small for the necessary job. If this is true, the Jewish community should proceed to set up its own additional facilities.

Let me conclude by suggesting some things that can be

done to cope with this enormous crisis, in addition to the proposals included within the body of the paper. Many may have noted that steps are beginning along the lines of some of the proposals outlined above. In particular, there is a noticeable, if glacial, drift of the Federations toward greater involvement in Jewish education. But these steps are individual and uncoordinated. Nor have they been drawn up with a view to systematically identifying the problem and then filling the need. If this is the major arena of Jewish survival, then we are engaged in nothing less than a war for Jewish survival—and flowering. What is needed is a central location and center to develop and coordinate strategy. In light of what is at stake I would call it a Center for Jewish Survival. (My only objection is that it is not mere survival but the capacity to contribute and create that is at stake.)

The task of this Center would be to give central direction, financial aid, and a unified comprehensive program for a massive effort. Thus it could initiate or encourage efforts wherever possible. At the same time, it could direct efforts to the neglected areas or those where the most fruits would be forthcoming. It should also draw up a comprehensive research program to evaluate the problem, different types of response and their success, and what types of students are affected in which ways, and which backgrounds resist the negative effects best. One of the major advantages of having such an address for people to turn to is that the work in the field done by others becomes more efficient, overlapping and duplication are cut down, and the most productive approaches are identified and spread. Most of the people and agencies working in the college field for the Jewish community are besieged by day-to-day problems, limited financing and personnel, and, frequently, deficient imagination and conceptual apparatus. The Center would provide the setting for long-range planning, freedom of experimentation and conception. It should be pointed out that the freedom of Rand Corporation or Hudson Institute or other such "think tanks" has led to developments that have revolutionized American defense efforts—and saved money too!

In addition, the personnel of the various agencies now involved could be brought to the Center for "refresher" training and experiences. In time, the Center could build up consultant services to further improve the evaluation and the actual performance of the operating agencies. The evaluation function could be of tremendous importance. One of the great problems in the field is the absence of evaluation and, correspondingly, of recognition and reward of those who do better. A great upgrading of achievement could take place just by the natural process of recognition and advancement for the individuals and the approaches that work best. The financing of such a Center would demand Federation participation. Perhaps a group of Federations could participate as "shareholders" in the Center. Such a move would signal a shift in the attitude of neglect which has marked Federation policies until now. However, it may be the opportune time for this. The growing awareness of crisis and the greater stress on Jewish education is now showing up, at least in the rhetoric of the CJWF conventions. Moreover, such a Center could be evaluated and would not be tainted by the ineffectiveness of the past which is cited by Federations in justifying limited efforts in the field of Jewish education. It should be added that the nature of the problem (intellectual-spiritual, "life-style" problems, etc.) suggests that the Federations should allow maximum freedom of policy and approach to the personnel of the Center while checking carefully its productivity and results. The current Jewish organizational style and ethos would not be suitable for transfer to the college area intact. I would also venture a guess that the personnel needed are less likely to be in the established organizations. They might be best sought in the academic or academic-borderline fields where they would have developed a quality approach unaffected by the current financial and intellectual poverty of the Jewish educational field.

There are a number of major approaches that the Center should concentrate on. The first would be the enrichment of the Jewish content and experience on the college campus. One program would be modeled on that of the Danforth Foundation program. Correctly sensing that the high percentage of secular faculty has created the atmosphere and impact negative to religious values, the Danforth Foundation set up a fellowship program to attract religious people to the field of college teaching and research. The fellowship aids those who are religiously committed; it also attracts to the field of teaching people who were marginal and might otherwise have gone into other professions; and it gives recognition to bright, talented and religiously alive ( rather than conventional) people. Another advantage of the Danforth program is that fellows meet annually in a camp setting and continue to do so after becoming scholars and teachers. Thus they are strengthened and reinforced in their commitments even as they are broadened by contact with a wide spectrum of religious attitudes and approaches.

A similar program should be launched to recruit and attract Jewishly committed people to the field of college teaching. It must be stressed that it is not purely religious or traditional Jews that should be sought. Any model of commitment to Jewishness would be helpful and desirable. An advantage of such a program is that, once recruited, these people would be on the college campus with the financial support coming from the university and would not be a further charge on the resources of the Jewish community. Moreover, they would have the status and prestige of the university status as well as the freedom and time to specialize and compete intellectually in the open academic atmosphere. Their very presence and attitudes would be a big step toward the demolition of the secularized Christian stereotypes which characterize the college scene.

Another program would stress the development and publication of textbooks and college level courses in Judaism. Such courses would be suitable for inclusion in the college curriculum. Others might be useful for Hillel and other extracurricular Jewish educational experiences. The development of textbooks should go hand in hand with further establishment of chairs of Jewish studies at universities. Although the Jewish community might well provide seed money for such chairs, the goal would be absorption into the regular university budget and departments. This is important because, again, it would free Jewish community funds for other work. In general, there is a need for maximum utilization of self-sustaining techniques which function and compete in the open society. The other great advantage of chairs and courses in Jewish studies is that the student can take the courses for college credit. At the present time, even if the Hillel Foundation provides a course that is college level, the student cannot or will not do the necessary homework or research because he cannot afford the time on top of regular college courses. Naturally he will get less out of the course and will tend to take it less seriously. The same course given for credit will involve the student more and he will get correspondingly more out of it.

Indeed, we need colleges of Jewish studies to be set up on college campuses. There are colleges of Jewish studies in existence but they generally are isolated from the universities. They do not meet university standards or personnel qualifications (Ph.D.'s, research and publication, faculty teaching loads) and are sparsely attended. Bringing such colleges on campus would make them live, and force them to meet the standards of the universities.

The result would be a boon to Jewish scholarship. It would drive it toward development of an intellectual openness and an end to parochialism which would make it speak more effectively to students and college-educated adults. The arrangement between the Jewish Theological Seminary and Columbia University under which courses can be taken at the Seminary for college credit is a good prototype of what we seek. It has led to some students getting a degree in Jewish studies simultaneously (or for one extra year's work). The great advantage of having a college of Jewish studies is that it would provide a pool of scholars, a community, dormitory and religious facilities—all of which would raise the Jewish effectiveness considerably.

Another major approach to the challenge of college is in the upgrading of Jewish education. The Center would set up a center for Jewish education. This involves developing a curriculum which can eliminate the overlapping, repetition, puerility, and conceptual poverty which marks much of the Jewish educational system. The most desperately needed are sequences which are graded and non-repetitious. Most Talmud Torahs testify that students are successful, responsive and highly motivated during the first two years. During the third and fourth years there is a terrible drop-off as repetition and lack of depth take their toll. Children in junior high school and high school today do things once reserved for college courses.

Jerome Bruner's work has shown that the most advanced ideas can be broken down to basic components and taught to children. The work of the Physical Sciences Study Group led by Zacharias in the new physics and work in the new match or the upgrading of the social sciences must be matched in the field of Jewish education. The professionals and the Bureaus are too swamped by day-to-day problems as well as intellectually and financially limited to do the necessary job. There is a need for research in

Jewish education to weigh effectiveness, evaluate different types of school and upgrade teacher training.

Textbooks at high school level must be upgraded conceptually and, in particular, related to the intellectual challenges which college will pose. Materials for rabbis and educators are also needed. Few rabbis are equipped to handle the challenges in advanced areas without help and guidance. The technology of Jewish education is still relatively primitive. Yet such techniques should be more utilized in light of the shortage of hours and qualified personnel. This center would link in to the work of establishing college chairs of Jewish studies or the development of textbooks. Undoubtedly, personnel developed in one program could be utilized for the other. Universities are playing a greater and greater role in urban education and urban problem solving. The same techniques could be used in Jewish education and Jewish community work. The Center should try to draw upon the resources of Yeshiva University, Jewish Theological Seminary and the Hebrew Union College, too. (It could help these institutions grow internally in service of the Jewish community.)

Another major approach area is the realm of mass media. Mass media are even more effective than schools in shaping values and attitudes. Magazines, films and television reach more people and set styles and values. There have been notable individual efforts in this area such as the Eternal Light programs on radio and television. However, most of the television time made available to Jewish sources still is static and often cliché talk sessions. A Center could develop materials which could be shown on mass media as well as adapted for classroom and adult educational use. Films particularly appeal to the current college generation. The recruitment and support of efforts in this area can now be done on a financial shoestring. It would repay itself many times over.

228 THE JEWISH FAMILY IN A CHANGING WORLD

Since the goal is commitment as well as intellectual growth, there is a need to utilize "total environmental experience" situations. A few hours in a total environment situation have more impact than days in marginal settings. Examples of the total environment setting are summer camps, living in Israel, and Hebrew Day School education. Apparently, the reason for the great impact is that Judaism and Jewishness is experienced as a natural, even normative, highly respected, equal-quality component. The figures who exemplify Judaism or Jewishness are the elite of the environment. In short, believability and willingness to identify with the Jewish goes up sharply.

Moreover, total environment experiences create a living Jewish community which the student identifies with emotionally and intellectually. Such experiences coming during or parallel to those of college give emotional and intellectual reinforcement which equips the students to withstand counter-challenges. There has been a significant rise in the number of Jewish young people participating in such total environments. However, the number is still a drop in the bucket. It would be a great investment to step up scholarships and underwriting of costs to get more Jewish young people involved. We should not overlook the particular dynamic of Israel as a Jewish image at this time. Living in Israel can affect a lifetime. And there are many different possibilities available there—university, kibbutz, etc. Similarly, Federations will have to overcome their stereotyped rejection of responsibility of day schools on the ground that they are "parochial" or "sectarian." The solution is upgrading of quality and greater openness, not neglect. The very neglect and financial stringency of these schools frequently leads them to greater sectarianism. In addition, the Center could help enrich their effect by providing better textbooks, teacher training, etc. Besides, they work. It is time for appreciation and utilization of anything that works.

These have all been examples of the kind of work and development that our proposed Center could do. It could do all or some of these. It could go considerably further in many areas. But let me add what is assumed as underlying all these proposals. We will have to develop a new style of Jewishness. It will have to be considerably more open yet committed, more intellectually sophisticated and critical. It will have to be less organizational and more individual. It will demand greater self-fulfillment in Judaism and Jewishness and less working so that others can be Jewish. We will have to be more willing to concentrate our efforts on committed Jews and on particularistic activities. This does not mean exclusion or narrowness. But it means an end to mindless nonspecific Jewish loyalty and activity. Such a deepening would make Jews more capable of participating constructively in American society without thereby assimilating.

The Jewish community has been depending on a nominal Jewishness combined with neighborhood and social concentration to carry it through. College is destroying this possibility socially and culturally. Only a major upgrading in informed Jewish commitment and deepening of Jewish knowledge can save the day. It has been said that the British Empire was lost and won on the playing fields of Eton. The crown of Judaism and Jewishness will be won or lost on the campuses of America. These proposals are modest beginnings toward the reshaping of Jewish community effort and identity to meet the challenge.

## 13

# O YOU JEWISH COLLEGIAN

## Mark Jay Mirsky

In the letter which invited me to write this paper I received the following instructions:

> The chapter should have any footnotes that you deem necessary and a bibliography at the end. Since the material is to be geared to the intelligent layman it should not be too technical in content.
> We should like the chapter to be descriptive of the subject with which it deals and to provide statistical evidence and facts. We should also like your prognosis of the future developments in the area with which you deal.

It is my practice to begin the writing courses which I teach at the City College of New York with a simple in-class assignment. Insult me! To the cries of "We don't know you . . ." I reply that I'll allow fifteen minutes of damaging personal questions from the students. In lieu of these questions let me begin by providing you with some damaging information. These are the only statistics I can provide and they necessarily cast doubt on all I say. I have a meager Hebrew education, seven years to get through a six-year cheder. I refused to go on to Hebrew High School. I have never been to Israel. Though I make the rounds of synagogues occasionally, searching for one that will have some meaning for me, I am hardly a regular observer. My knowledge of Torah, Talmud, and the later rabbis is pretty much derived from English translation. I am a novelist, not a scholar. Even my role as one of the founding editors of *Mosaic*, the Jewish Student Journal, at Harvard was not a learned one. I collected fiction and poetry for the magazine. I'm not going to ponder before you the objective statistics of so many students who intermarried, so many who don't go to services, so many who will lead happy Jewish lives, etc., *ad infinitum, ad nauseam.*

I have had experience as a student and teacher at three colleges: Harvard, where I took my B.A.; Stanford where I was a graduate student, and four years later, a teacher; City College, where I now teach.

Not only am I useless as a statistician. I don't care *what* the figures say. Something stinks in our eyes. The brightest students fall away from observance, from attendance at Hillel, from the community of other Jews at college. Indeed, the atmosphere of a college encourages this. Ideas are in the air, heady ones. There are strangers next door in the dormitories, eager to talk, to exchange information. Opposites attract. Too often those of one's own community smell of one's parents. And it's time to revolt. The last people on earth an intelligent college freshman wants to be locked up in his room with are his parents. The rabbi, if he even sounds a bit in his sermon of that good homely parental advice, is impossible to face.

Invite Shlomo Carlbach, Theodore Bikel, show a movie of *The Dybbuk* . . . hundreds, even thousands, show up. But for the regular service? How many times has a rare smile on the rabbi's face greeted me as I stumbled in late, the tenth man.

If we were concerned with statistics, I could show you two sets. One for special events, the entertainment, (we can throw Rosh Hashonoh and Yom Kippur into this category, the uneasy guilt which drags multitudes into suburban temples exercises its strange undertow here too) and one for the everyday schedule of college Judaism.

If you see nothing wrong in this there is no sense in reading any more of this article. I predict that the situation will remain the same for another fifteen years, at which time either a miracle will occur or Hillel will be transformed, as so many Jewish organizations are, into a booking agency for ethnic entertainment.

And many are content with this. Let's tell the truth, most of the generation of my parents, the community which grew up in the twenties and the Depression are embarrassed by religion. The Temple is a Community Center, not a House of Study or Prayer. Most of the intellectuals in the American Jewish Community, the men who publish its periodicals, run the Welfare and Community Services—even the rabbis at the helm, are embarrassed by prayer, by services, by the thought of an ecstatic experience in a group of congregants. Instead of attempting to find a style of life in which an attempt would be made to speak to a Hebrew God, how many of the rabbis are engaged in the task of being amateur psychologists, psychiatrists, sociologists, etc. Sometimes they are scholars and often their information of Hebrew history is impressive.

Let it be spoken though, this life is drab. Joy, madness, an experimental, an alive intellectual, an existential life—is this not consonant with the practice of Judaism? Must it be cautious, sane to the point of inanity, mingling a few outmoded loyalties to medieval Judaism with the borrowed wisdom of the guidance counselor? How can such men command the respect of the brightest Jewish students or their professors?

Or their professors! You think that the most important person in the college community is the student? The college is oriented even in this era of student power toward the faculty. Do you think that the average professor who is Jewish is interested in Hillel? Strange to say, many are. For what reason, I'm not quite sure. At Harvard, where an energetic rabbi plagued them about showing up for Oneg Shabbats, quite a few became involved temporarily. However, few rabbis at the colleges really make an effort to court the faculty. Perhaps they are ashamed about the intellectual fare they are serving up. If a man's field happens to lie close to Jewish subject matter, there is a chance that he will involve himself with the Jewish community at college. Otherwise what are the inducements? What will bring the scientist, the student and faculty radicals, the men who are the great teachers and thinkers into a live and vital relationship to the community? We have to answer this question. Anything else is a "cop-out" on our love for Israel. We want a passionate congregation, one that can cry out as they did at Sinai, "Give us the law!"

At no point do the energies of American Judaism burn with a lower and more dismal flame than at the colleges. In a setting where we would, as the heirs of an unbroken intellectual tradition, expect to find the fiercest blaze, where we have a right to expect the daring, the creative, even the heretical, there is only the melancholy sight of a burned-out congregation outfitted in hand-me-downs, the scraps of the older Orthodox tradition and the worn-out programs of up-to-date Community Centers.

American Judaism can evade its failure to develop a life style, a community of shared laws, at the two ends of the candle, youth and age, where the priorities of need come first—nursery school, burial, old-age homes—even adolescence is in its first stages dependent on the dances and dating arrangements of the synagogue. Not at the college, though. Students do not need the Community Center. The Community, however, needs them!

The candy that used to bribe us to stay to the end of Shabbos Services is no answer; and the dances, parties, entertainments at Hillel are just so much more of this.

Even the countless lecture series on Jewish subjects are an evasion. Of what? Of a community!

What kind?

I'm not sure.

Only I know that, outrageous and impossible as they are, blundering, silly and woefully ignorant, America's hippies are closer to the ideals of ancient Judaism than we.

If we could combine their free-wheeling energy and innovative joy with some of the group spirit of the Chasidim. If we could experiment with the hunger in us all to touch and understand one another, the terrors and inhibitions we feel before the frank admission of our experience: we would be back on the road to that definition of the world which our ancestors called the Law. How it offends me to hear someone talking in fear about morals on the campus. Birth control has had a revolutionary effect on us all and we desperately need some sense of Law to guide us. But a Law that is defined not in terms of the understanding of an older generation but according to what seems to be the best way to live now. Judaism must admit to the possibility of its children experimenting. Standing some years ago in San Francisco's Candlestick Park in a wide pasture of trodden grass filled with improvised costumes, recognizing other teachers and students, many with only a strange hat or tie to mark their fellowship, I listened to the Rock groups and poets trying to draw the crowd up into a drugless ecstatic "trip." And as Allen Ginsberg sang the burning orange sun into its setting below the dark green rim of trees, hearing the crowd chanting with him, thrilling at its descent, I thought of our Jewish holidays, how powerful and dramatic they are and how I longed to be part of a crowd of fellow seekers trying to truly live their drama, to see the scapegoat of Yom Kippur go off into the bushes, to see the gates of Ne'ilah close, the daughters of Israel dance, to take home the stranger of Friday evening and have him enter the open door on Passover. Those strange off-beat communities which cluster in the hills of California attempting to find new ways to bring people together are important to us. It is no accident that the kibbutz developed in Israel perhaps the most successful of communal experiences. We in America must found kibbutzim here in which to live. Kibbutzim not for economic development but for the development of a way to live with daring that does not destroy us. Let us gather to rethink the laws by which this act is sanctioned and that forbidden.

We Jews at the colleges have no sense of responsibility to one another; we have no spontaneous delight in the services; we do not create—our Judaism is stillborn. Our forefathers, the great Talmudists, who had not a tenth of our intellectual "know how" were courageous to interpret and reinterpret daily as the conditions of their lives changed while we sit spellbound by the Law of four centuries ago knowing that the community must come together, must share a sense of lawfulness, yet unable to agree on what the strictures of righteousness are.

It is that sense of belonging to a lawful community that the majority of young Jews have lost. The Baal Shem Tov asks:

Why do we say: "Our God and the God of our fathers?" There are two sorts of persons who believe in God. The one believes because his faith has been handed down to him by his fathers: and his faith is strong. The other has arrived at faith by dint of searching thought. And this is the difference between the two: The first has the advantage that his faith cannot be shaken, no matter how many objections are raised to it, for his faith is firm because he has taken it over from his fathers. But there is a flaw in it; it is a commandment given by man, and it has been learned without thought or reasoning. The advantage of the second man is that he has reached faith through his own power, through much searching and thinking. But his faith too has a flaw: it is easy to shake it by offering contrary

evidence. But he who combines both kinds of faith is invulner-
able. That is why we say: "Our God," because of our searching, and "the God of our fathers," because of our tradition.
And a like interpretation holds when we say, "The God of
Abraham, the God of Isaac, and the God of Jacob," for this
means: Isaac and Jacob did not merely take over the tradition
of Abraham, but sought out the divine for themselves.*

The God of our fathers is only precious to us if he is
our God too, if our doubts and ideas help us to understand him.

And while we speak of the Holy Name let is admit
that American Judaism has been ashamed of God, that is,
the conception of a mystical unknown, a higher power.
Who calls out in the Conservative, Reform, or even the
modern Orthodox synagogue to God in expectation of an
answer? We do not tread the altar with a hope of mystery.
Yet it is this irrational hope that structures the service,
that has created most of the best prayers; if this intention
does not underlie our words then Yom Kippur, Rosh
Hashonoh, the Sabbath, our holidays, are in their present
form meaningless. The college student is not stupid. He
comes into the synagogue and sees that most of the
people are mumbling, droning, repeating by rote.

The English translation reveals to him the great emotion of the prayers, the rapt voice of its originators, yet
here is a congregation mechanically saying them, and
more often than not rushing to get through. As if one of
Hamlet's tortured soliloquies was being read like the
school child's pledge of allegiance. He sees that his fellow
Jews have assembled out of no love of what they are
doing, and if he has any intelligence, he suspects that
guilt, some inherited neurotic guilt, must have dragged
the congregation to a room where they stand and sit tor-

---

* M. Buber, *Des Baal Schem Tow Unterweisung*, pp. 16–19, quoted by
Nahum N. Glatzer, *In Time and Eternity*, Schocken, p. 86.

turing themselves by an hour or two of mindless recitation.

And outside the synagogue?

Dance concerts, theater, sentimental reminiscences; these are the achievements of our community in America. It is not the stuff to hold the allegiance of the brightest of my Jewish students. The Hillel seems too close to the community center of their high schools. You have to offer them something more exciting than Harvard or Stanford. You have to involve them, the best minds, in the process of making American Judaism. Perhaps you even have to turn it over to them.

And now I want to address myself to my students who ask me why. Why trudge to services and mumble through the prayers? The secular world, Marxist, Freudian, scientific, has more respectable dogmas, more exciting experiments, more practical results. The whole weight of your generation is thrust against this. It is your generation (not mine, comatose in the years before Civil Rights and Vietnam woke up the colleges) trooping under the banners of Love, trooping in clans, trying to stop directly and individually the madness of war and cruelty, intolerance and rigid materialism; it is your generation that needs and is closer to the older Judaism. The martyrs who died, the parchment wrapped around them, in the flaming embrace of the Torah, are more and more kin to this world. Throughout the Bible and its commentaries I feel an immediate and powerful celebration of justice, one that can even question God. I feel a joy superior to any we have today. I feel a courage that can ask the most terrible of questions and affirm its asking as the most important act of man. Mysticism, awe, even the psychedelics of sensation are there; let us open up this tradition of searchers and questions for a sense of inherent right and direction.

One of the great blindnesses of American Judaism has

been its failure to admit that a revolution has occurred in the past twenty years. The university which through much of its history was either a professional training ground or a polite finishing school for gentlemen has become the center of a communal structure in the United States. Around Harvard, Columbia, Berkeley, Michigan, have settled groups of people not directly employed by these institutions, attracted by the intellectual challenge and also, be it spoken in this era of Civil Rights and the Vietnamese War, ethical climate. One is insulated from the ugliness and commercial crassness of much of American society in the university community. There is a moral seriousness that has drawn much of the non-student population that lives there. This is precisely the atmosphere which drew men to Yavneh, to the great Talmudic centers in Babylon, North Africa, Spain, France, Poland. We Jews must create again such an atmosphere. We have forgotten that we are a community that receives its definition by an alive consideration of what it is to be a righteous man in the world. We are a radical people and, within America today, we must strike that radical posture.

If we talk about college and the Jew we are merely referring to a holding operation. Within the growing university community, however, it becomes possible to speak of a Judaism that can extend over a lifetime. Let us become again a community of scholars, not just of history but of the life around us. And in the light of this scholarship, perhaps we can redefine the Sabbath and the Holy Days so that they are the moments when we release joy and terror with one another. Into such communities perhaps we can draw the great secular minds of this century to help us create. Into such synagogues we can draw poets, writers, painters, philosophers, the minds that are defining the psychiatry, music, economics, the thought of this and the coming decades. I have seen, in the Civil Rights and Vietnamese protests, the most diverse men gathering for moral purposes with the university. These are the righteous men of this generation and if we Jews are to be a nation of righteous people, we must find our definition among them.

If we do, perhaps we will find a service written by our American Jewish poets that will not be like pablum in our mouths. Let us not bring wild men like Norman Mailer and Allen Ginsberg into the synagogue as objects of curiosity for a Sunday-night lecture series, let us see what they can do with the materials of Judaism.

And if you object, remember that Judaism at its great moments has been a tradition which has admitted to the outrageousness of human behavior. The Talmud is not ashamed to tell tales of its writers who were thieves, lechers, madmen. The Bible does not conceal the murders and adulteries of its great men. Our heroes have often fallen far from shining copybook standards.

Let us encounter one another. Can you imagine a service on Yom Kippur when we would actually fall on each other's chests and admit to sins we had truly committed, begging forgiveness. The bravest of Gestalt therapy offers no comparable experience.

Rabbi Trainin, who commissioned this chapter, told me in the heat of our interview he wished he had more time to think about the future of Judaism in America. Ah, Rabbi Trainin, shame on us all! Why aren't we thinking together? Why aren't we gathering in Jewish think tanks. Is the Rand Corporation going to outstrip a tradition that produced Marx, Freud, Einstein? Only let us no longer claim such men as sons of Judaism, but as fathers. Let the spirit, the breath, the wind, the *ruach* of this century blow through our study halls.

## *14*

# ATTITUDES OF JEWISH STUDENTS TOWARD INTERMARRIAGE

## Victor D. Sanua

In a much-quoted article in *Look* Magazine several years ago, Thomas Morgan reported that the American Jewish community will gradually disappear in years to come in view of the increase in their rate of intermarriage and their low rate of reproduction. It should be noted that most of the studies referred to in this article concerned Jewish communities in small towns or Jews living in large cities where they represent a very small minority. Statistics on intermarriage in New York City and its suburbs are not available even though, as indicated by A. Chenkin, 42 percent of the Jewish population lives in this area of the country. It would, therefore, be unwise to generalize from the high rates of intermarriage reported by studies conducted with small-town Jews, since approximately one-half of the American Jewish population is concentrated in one particular metropolitan area.

Many papers have been devoted to a discussion of intermarriage. However, the number of empirical studies in this area is limited. The first part of this paper reviews a number of studies of intermarriage published in recent years, while the second part of this paper reports on our own findings pertaining to the attitudes of adolescents and college students toward intermarriage.

*Review of the Literature*

Maria Levinson and B. Levinson reported that there

are two major reasons for marrying outside one's faith. One group, which they labeled "reluctants," consisted of subjects who had a strong Jewish identity and great dependence on their mothers but who attempted to establish adult independence through intermarriage. The investigators called this kind of intermarriage "neurotic exogamy." In the second group, intermarriage was not symptomatic of neurosis but resulted from a weakening of Jewish identity.

J. S. Heiss compared intermarried couples of various religious faiths with a sample of intermarried respondents on a series of premarital variables. He found that the intermarried report such premarital variables as: (1) lesser early ties to religion; (2) greater dissatisfaction with early relationship with parents; (3) greater strife in family orientation; (4) lesser early family integration; and (5) greater emancipation from parents at time of marriage. While all five of these variables were common to intermarried Catholic subjects, and two of these variables (weak ties to family, and religion) were common to the intermarried Protestant subjects, none of these was found to be significant for the intermarried Jewish subjects. The data, however, suggest that intermarried Jews differ from the intermarried non-Jew only in the strength of their family ties during childhood and adulthood.

Bernard Kligfeld reviewed the literature on the subject of intermarriage. His article includes thirty-seven references, but most of the studies mentioned were conducted in the forties and early fifties. His general conclusion is that Jews who intermarry are either unable to solve the problem of their relationship with their parents or they have given up their Jewish self-identification. The incidence of intermarriage among Jews in the United States is low in comparison to other religious groups but it is believed that this rate is gradually increasing. Kligfeld points out that there is much contradictory information concerning intermarriage and recommends an investigation to include a large and well-selected sample of intermarried families, studies in depth of both partners and personality evaluation combined with a thorough examination of their families and cultural background prior to marriage. He further recommends a study of the children of such marriages and the influence of parents of different religious backgrounds upon their self-image. Only such a well-controlled and intensive analysis could clearly point out who intermarries, why, and with what effect.

E. J. Mayer offers an hypothesis regarding the social causes of intermarriage and maintains that intensified anti-Semitism will increase the ratio of Jewish males marrying gentile females rather than gentile males marrying Jewish females.

Eric Rosenthal wrote an extensive article surveying the literature on the subject of intermarriage. He concludes his article by stating that the ethnic-religious bonds which hold the Jewish community intact are weakening and refuses to give credence to the suggestion that the third generation of Jews are returning to the practices of Judaism of the first generation. On the basis of his survey, he reports that the rate of intermarriage for third generation Jews is 17.9 percent and that 70 percent of the children of mixed marriages are lost to the Jewish faith. He also finds that intermarriage is more frequent among students living on college campuses. Moreover, the rate of intermarriage in small towns and rural areas is higher than that in the larger cities, and cites Iowa as an example, where the rate of intermarriage of Jews is 42.2 percent. In order to assess intermarriage properly, Rosenthal suggests that the Jewish community should assign the highest priority to a study of intermarriage in the New York metropolitan area which has the largest Jewish community in the country. Rosenthal (1967) repeated the same kind of study for the State of Indiana, and as in Iowa, the rate of intermarriage among Jews was found to be very high.

A. J. Prince, on the basis of 194 questionnaires answered by intermarried couples, found that Jewish males intermarry three times more frequently than Jewish females. Marriages between Jews and Protestants are more common (58.2 percent) than marriages between Jews and Catholics (41.8 percent). In Jewish-Catholic marriages, children are usually reared in the mother's religion, and in Jewish-Protestant marriages, children are raised in the Jewish faith in the ratio of two to one.

Marshall Sklare provides us with a short review of the most recent research studies and ideas on intermarriage. He concludes that the notions pertaining to the causes of intermarriage are beginning to look outmoded. The rate of intermarriage may not only be increasing because Jews are moving out into the general stream of society in increasing numbers, but also because certain tastes and ideas such as liberalism, always preferred by Jews, are becoming more prevalent with non-Jews; therefore, Jews are becoming more acceptable as marriage partners.

A major book on the subject was published in 1964 which was written by the well-known rabbi and social scientist, Albert Gordon. The book represents a most comprehensive survey available on attitudes of college students concerning intermarriage and the problems surrounding it in this country. The book does not discuss the attitudes of Jewish students alone toward intermarriage, but one chapter is devoted to a review of some of the literature on intermarriage among Jews. According to statistics collected by Gordon, the rate of intermarriage in the United States and in Europe is very high. He specifically mentions the Scandinavian countries, Germany, and Switzerland.

Gordon finds that even when Jewish parents have very weak ties with their religion, they become frantic when they hear that their child contemplates marriage with a non-Jew. Gordon points out that such a reaction is due to the fact that this type of Jew finally becomes aware of his far-reaching departure from the traditions and religious practices of his faith. The impending intermarriage of his child now leads him to the very end of the road, and consequently the loss of his identity becomes a shattering experience. Moshe Davis discusses in a recent paper the historical background of mixed marriages in the United States, Great Britain, Canada, Australia, Argentina, and France. In 1967, I reviewed the literature dealing with the relationship between psychological adjustment and intermarriage. I showed from the little evidence available that intermarriage may represent added risks to Jews and Catholics. However, there has not been a single study on the adjustment of the children of intermarried couples. With the high rate of intermarriage in the United States, where the majority of world Jewry lives, it is somewhat surprising that no researcher has ever been concerned about this problem. It is only recently that Berty Goldberg, a Belgian student, who under my guidance, conducted such a study among the small Jewish community in Brussels. In view of her limited sample, no generalization could be made except that most of the children of intermarried couples had no identification with Judaism.

For a number of years, under the sponsorship of the Commission on Synagogue Relations of the Federation of Jewish Philanthropies a number of meetings have been held to discuss the topic of intermarriage. Proceedings on two of these Conferences have been prepared (1964, 1968). Nathan Goldberg's chapter (1964) is of particular interest since he presents a masterful review of the empirical literature. Also under the sponsorship of the Commission, an extensive bibliography on intermarriage has been prepared by Marc A. Triebwasser (1968). While the Commission has been concerned with the problem of intermarriage for a number of years, thus far it has not been able to establish a research program to study this most important area of Jewish contemporary problems. Institutes of Jewish Contemporary Studies are to be found in Jerusalem, Buenos Aires, and Brussels, but none are to be found in the United States. Whatever institutes are available today are highly historical in their interests. We expect in our discussion to write at greater length on this point.

With the exception of Gordon's book which evaluates college students' attitudes toward intermarriage, there are no studies which have focused primarily on the attitudes of Jewish youth toward intermarriage. The present study is a modest attempt to fill the gap. We have not conducted a statistical analysis for significance and in view of the limited samples involved and in one area, New York, the reader is well cautioned not to draw definite conclusions from the findings. The present writer undertook the study to evaluate the Jewish identification of high school and college students of different ideologies and Jewish education. Discussion of this paper is limited to data obtained concerning their attitudes toward intermarriage.

Data in this area were obtained on the basis of four questions posed to the samples of adolescents and six different questions posed to college students. All of the latter questions were selected from the questionnaire used by Gordon.

## Discussion of the Study

### A. Procedure

The following groups of subjects were selected for this study, on the assumption that they would differ in their feeling of Jewish identity, and consequently, would also differ in their expressed attitudes toward intermarriage. It should be noted that all of the subjects reside in the New York metropolitan area.

1. Boys and girls members of Zionist youth organizations (*Hashomer Hatzair*, and *Habonim*) (70).
2. Boys and girls attending a public high school (48).
3. Boys and girls attending an All-Day School (Jewish Orthodox) (65).
4. Boys and girls attending a Jewish Reform afternoon school (60).
5. Boys and girls attending Jewish Community Centers (280).
6. Male students attending one of New York's municipal colleges (52).
7. Female students attending one of New York's municipal colleges (53).
8. Male students attending Yeshiva College (56).
9. Female students attending Stern College (57).

With the exception of the college students attending the municipal schools, who represent a selected group, all other subjects were administered the questionnaire as a group. This was done in order to control for the variable of selectivity, that is volunteering to fill out the questionnaire, which usually causes serious methodological weakness in such studies.

We do not know the extent to which the secular (municipal) college students who responded to the questionnaire differ from the total student population at their respective schools. Moreover, it is not known how these subjects differ from other Jewish students on their respective campus.

## B. Findings for Samples of Adolescents

The 75-item questionnaire concerning Jewish identification, which was administered to all groups of adolescents, included the following four questions pertaining to intermarriage:

1. The only solution to the Jewish problem is intermarriage.

2. A Jewish young man who really loves a gentile girl should give up his Jewishness if that were the only way he could marry her.
3. Intermarriage is bad for the Jewish people.
4. Generally speaking, it is not wise for a Jew to marry a gentile.

Subjects were given a choice of five alternative answers to each question: "Strongly agree," "agree," "?" (undecided), "disagree," "strongly disagree." When the study was first initiated, the sample was limited to adolescents attending Jewish Community Centers and the questionnaire at that time provided the subject with a choice of seven alternate answers: "Agree very much," "agree pretty much," "agree a little," "?" "disagree a little," "disagree pretty much," "disagree very much." Having found this seven choice method to be somewhat cumbersome, responses were limited to five choices in subsequent phases of the study. In order to compare the data obtained on adolescents attending the Jewish Community Centers with that of other groups adolescents, the range of responses was then reduced by combining the two responses at the extreme, thus yielding five alternatives. It should be noted that the sample of Jewish Community Center members were strongly urged not to check the "?" response, with the result that this group of subjects checked the alternate responses more frequently. The reader should bear in mind the aforementioned when interpreting responses for this particular group.

In Table I, we present the distribution, in percentages, of adolescents' responses to questions pertaining to intermarriage.

1. The only solution to the Jewish problem is intermarriage.

Table I shows that girls attending the All-Day School almost unanimously voice "strong disagreement" with the above statement. They are followed by girls attending the

TABLE I  *The only good solution to the Jewish problem is intermarriage.*

| Groups | Strongly Disagree | | Disagree | | ? | | Agree | | Strongly Agree | |
|---|---|---|---|---|---|---|---|---|---|---|
| | Boy | Girl | Boy | Girl | Boy | Girl | Boy | Girl | Boy | Girl |
| | % | % | % | % | % | % | % | % | % | % |
| 1. Day school | 64 | 98 | 21 | 2 | 15 | 0 | 0 | 0 | 0 | 0 |
| 2. Afternoon school | 81 | 73 | 19 | 23 | — | 4 | 0 | 0 | 0 | 0 |
| 3. Jewish Com. Center | 76 | 85 | 5 | 5 | 3 | 7 | 6 | 0 | 10 | 3 |
| 4. Public school | 36 | 58 | 36 | 16 | 24 | 26 | 4 | 0 | 0 | 0 |
| 5. Reform | 50 | 47 | 33 | 40 | 7 | 7 | 7 | 3 | 3 | 3 |
| 6. *Hashomer Hatzair* | 89 | 69 | 7 | 29 | 4 | 2 | 0 | 0 | 0 | 0 |

TABLE II  *A Jewish young man who really loves a Gentile girl should give up his Jewishness if that were the only way he could marry her.*

| Groups | Strongly Disagree | | Disagree | | ? | | Agree | | Strongly Agree | |
|---|---|---|---|---|---|---|---|---|---|---|
| | Boy | Girl | Boy | Girl | Boy | Girl | Boy | Girl | Boy | Girl |
| | % | % | % | % | % | % | % | % | % | % |
| 1. Day school | 50 | 73 | 14 | 21 | 36 | 6 | 0 | 0 | 0 | 0 |
| 2. Afternoon school | 45 | 47 | 16 | 27 | 32 | 23 | 7 | 3 | 0 | 0 |
| 3. Jewish Com. Center | 32 | 34 | 15 | 7 | 2 | 12 | 14 | 21 | 37 | 26 |
| 4. Public school | 4 | 42 | 44 | 10 | 20 | 32 | 20 | 11 | 12 | 5 |
| 5. Reform | 23 | 10 | 20 | 17 | 23 | 50 | 27 | 20 | 7 | 3 |
| 6. *Hashomer Hatzair* | 21 | 16 | 36 | 24 | 14 | 50 | 15 | 10 | 14 | 0 |

Jewish Community Centers while the girls attending a Reform school had the lowest percentage in the category of "strongly disagree" (47 percent). However, it should be noted that another 40 percent in the latter group checked the "disagree" response. As for the male respondents, 89 percent of the *Hashomer Hatzair* group checked the "strongly disagree" response. They were followed, in order, by the Afternoon School, and Jewish Community Center subjects. Those attending the public high school and those attending the Reform School had the lowest percentage in this category. However, a sizable percentage in the latter group also checked the "disagree" category in response to this question.

While only a very small minority "agreed" or "strongly agreed" with the above statement, this minority consisted exclusively of adolescents in the Jewish Community Center, public school, and Reform groups.

2. A Jewish young man who really loves a gentile girl should give up his Jewishness if that were the only way he could marry her, Table II).

In comparison to the previous statement, it appears that adolescents feel less strongly about maintaining their identity once the issue of "love" is injected. At this romantic age, many more adolescents, particularly members of the *Hashomer Hatzair,* Afternoon School, All-Day School, and public school groups, would be willing to give up their faith in order to marry the person they love; often they are ambivalent. Those attending the parochial schools, the girls in particular, voiced their disapproval with the above statement.

3. Intermarriage is bad for the Jewish people (Table III).

This statement as well as the one which follows differ from the previous two, since disagreement with these two statements indicates less concern about the survival of the Jewish group.

TABLE III Intermarriage is bad for the Jewish people.

| Groups | Strongly Agree | | Agree | | ? | | Disagree | | Strongly Disagree | |
|---|---|---|---|---|---|---|---|---|---|---|
| | Boy | Girl | Boy | Girl | Boy | Girl | Boy | Girl | Boy | Girl |
| | % | % | % | % | % | % | % | % | % | % |
| 1. Day school | 58 | 73 | 21 | 23 | 21 | 2 | 0 | 0 | 0 | 2 |
| 2. Afternoon school | 61 | 50 | 36 | 26 | 3 | 9 | 0 | 9 | 0 | 6 |
| 3. Jewish Com. Center | 28 | 34 | 12 | 7 | 1 | 8 | 16 | 14 | 43 | 37 |
| 4. Public school | 12 | 37 | 44 | 11 | 28 | 42 | 16 | 5 | 0 | 5 |
| 5. Reform | 23 | 23 | 27 | 27 | 20 | 13 | 27 | 27 | 3 | 10 |
| 6. *Hashomer Hatzair* | 32 | 31 | 36 | 14 | 14 | 29 | 7 | 12 | 11 | 14 |

TABLE IV Generally speaking, it is not wise for a Jew to marry a Gentile.

| Groups | Strongly Agree | | Agree | | ? | | Disagree | | Strongly Disagree | |
|---|---|---|---|---|---|---|---|---|---|---|
| | Boy | Girl | Boy | Girl | Boy | Girl | Boy | Girl | Boy | Girl |
| | % | % | % | % | % | % | % | % | % | % |
| 1. Day school | 57 | 83 | 14 | 11 | 29 | 2 | 0 | 2 | 0 | 2 |
| 2. Afternoon school | 62 | 62 | 29 | 23 | 6 | 0 | 0 | 15 | 3 | 0 |
| 3. Jewish Com. Center | 40 | 53 | 12 | 12 | 3 | 7 | 18 | 8 | 27 | 20 |
| 4. Public school | 20 | 42 | 32 | 21 | 24 | 37 | 16 | 0 | 8 | 0 |
| 5. Reform | 27 | 23 | 33 | 27 | 20 | 17 | 20 | 23 | 0 | 10 |
| 6. *Hashomer Hatzair* | 25 | 23 | 50 | 40 | 7 | 16 | 7 | 14 | 11 | 7 |

Both Day School and Afternoon School students generally agreed with the statement. However, approximately 20 percent of the Day School students were ambivalent in their response to the statement. Subjects who disagreed with the statement consisted predominantly of adolescents attending the Jewish Community Centers, of whom approximately 50 percent checked either the "disagree" or the "strongly disagree" response. This is somewhat at variance with their attitudes, as reflected in responses of this group to the first question, namely, that "The only solution to the Jewish problem is intermarriage."

4. Generally speaking, it is not wise for a Jew to marry a Gentile (Table IV).

Responses to this statement follow a similar pattern to the previous question. A great deal of ambivalent feelings were expressed by the All-Day School, public school, and Reform school groups, with percentage being even higher for the Jewish Community Center group who disagreed with the above (45 percent of the boys and 28 percent of the girls).

C. Findings for the College Samples

1. Do you date persons of a different religion?

As expected, students attending the Jewish Orthodox colleges rarely date someone outside their religion (see Table V). The majority, however, of the secular college students also date people within their religion, and date someone outside their religious group only on rare occasions. This compares with only 10 percent of the college population studied by Gordon who indicated that they would never date someone of a different faith. In drawing such a comparison, however, the reader should bear in mind that Gordon's sample represented students enrolled at 40 colleges and universities across the country. Our samples were drawn from the New York metropolitan area, which is densely populated by Jews, and moreover, the secular students were drawn from municipal colleges which have a high percentage of Jewish enrollment. These two factors would tend to minimize our subjects' opportunities for inter-religious dating.

TABLE V Do you date persons of a different religion?

| College Groups | Rarely | Some-times | Fre-quently | Almost always | Never |
|---|---|---|---|---|---|
| *Male students at a:* | | | | | |
| Secular college | 21% | 10% | 2% | 2% | 65% |
| Jewish Orthodox college | 4% | | | | 96% |
| *Female students at a:* | | | | | |
| Secular college | 28% | 14% | 2% | | 56% |
| Jewish Orthodox college | 12% | 2% | | 3% | 83% |
| Gordon's sample (students at 40 colleges & universities) | 21% | 39% | 20% | 9% | 10% |

2. Does your father, your mother object to your dating a person of a different religion? (See two separate Tables VI and VII)

Here again, subjects indicated that the majority of their parents would object to their dating someone outside of the Jewish faith. Approximately 14 percent of the parents of students enrolled in a secular college and 7 percent of the parents of students enrolled in the religious colleges would not object to their children dating people of a different faith. In view of the small number of students who would actually date someone of a different faith, there appears to be little conflict between parents and their children regarding religious dating patterns.

3. If any member of your family (including yourself) is married to a person of a different religion than your own please check which (Table VIII).

Except for the secular college girls, of whom 56 percent indicated that there is no intermarriage in their fam-

TABLE VI Does your father object to your dating a person of a different religion?

| College Groups | Yes | No | No differ-ence | No answer |
|---|---|---|---|---|
| *Male students at a:* | | | | |
| Secular college | 77% | 10% | 4% | 9% |
| Jewish Orthodox college | 96% | | 4% | |
| *Female students at a:* | | | | |
| Secular college | 83% | 10% | 7% | |
| Jewish Orthodox college | 89% | 9% | 2% | |

TABLE VII Does your mother object to your dating a person of a different religion?

| College Groups | Yes | No | No differ-ence | No answer |
|---|---|---|---|---|
| *Male students at a:* | | | | |
| Secular college | 79% | 11% | 2% | 8% |
| Jewish Orthodox college | 96% | 2% | 2% | |
| *Female students at a:* | | | | |
| Secular college | 88% | 8% | 4% | |
| Jewish Orthodox College | 92% | 5% | 3% | |

ily, approximately 85 percent of the other three college groups checked the same response. A sizable number of subjects checked "other." This was especially true for the secular college girls (22 percent). Respondents were asked to identify the particular relative who intermarried (i.e., brother, sister, uncle, aunt, etc.). The overwhelming majority indicated more distant relatives such as cousins.

The rate of intermarriage among subjects' closer relations such as brother, sister, uncle, aunt, is 16 percent (35 out of 220 college students). While our samples are not representative of the total Jewish population in the New York metropolitan area, these percentages do reveal an alarming trend in the rate of intermarriage among Jews. Estimates in the past, as to the actual figures on in-

TABLE VIII If any member of your family (including yourself) is married to a person of a different religion than your own, please check which:

| College Groups | Bro-ther | Sister | Uncle | Aunt | Niece | Nephew | Your-self | Other | None |
|---|---|---|---|---|---|---|---|---|---|
| *Male students at a:* | | | | | | | | | |
| Secular college | 2% | | | 2% | | | | 13% | 83% |
| Jewish Orthodox college | 2% | | 4% | | | | | 9% | 85% |
| *Female students at a:* | | | | | | | | | |
| Secular college | 2% | | 5% | 5% | | | | 22% | 56% |
| Jewish Orthodox college | 8% | | 2% | 2% | | | | 5% | 83% |
| Gordon's sample* | | (9%) | | (28%) | (1%) | | (2%) | | 60% |

* Gordon combined his figures for brother and sister, uncle and aunt, niece and nephew.

termarriage, have ranged from 7 percent to 17 percent. It should be noted that families who send their children to Jewish religious colleges are not immune to incidents of intermarriage in their immediate families, and the similar percentages obtained by the secular and religious college students bear this out. It is interesting to note that the

female secular students report a higher incidence of intermarriages among their relatives than the male subjects.

4. If your brother or sister married outside your own
   religion, would you?

A larger percentage of the religious college students
(male and female) indicated that they would "strongly
disapprove" of a sibling's intermarriage. This compares
with only 30 percent of the secular college girls who
checked the same response. This smaller percentage may,
undoubtedly, have been affected by the reported higher
rate of intermarriage found among the families of these
college girls.

How would our groups of college students compare
with a previous generation's attitudes on the subject of
intermarriage?

A survey of attitudes of Jews on the subject was conducted in White Plains. The Jewish community in this
suburb of New York is predominantly of middle and upper
class. According to this survey, 6 out of 10 parents would
"strongly disapprove" of their children marrying a non-
Jew, 3 out of 10 would "mildly disapprove," while 1 out
of 10 indicated "it would make no difference." Thus, 60
percent of the parents would "strongly disapprove" of
their child's intermarriage, while the rest do not consider
this to be a very grave problem. This attitude is in agreement with the one expressed by the male students attending a secular college in our study (56 percent).

5. If you found the girl (boy) for you and it developed
   that she/he was of a different religion from yours
   would you? (Table IX).

A large percentage of students attending the two religious colleges would tend to "break off" their relationship
in such a situation, while a sizable percentage of students
attending the secular colleges would continue to date persons of a different religion, or be undecided as to what
to do.

TABLE IX If you found *the* girl (boy) and it developed that she/he was of a different religion from yours would you,

| College Groups | Continue to date | Break off | Be undecided | Have partner convert to your religion | Offer to convert to partner's religion | No Answer |
|---|---|---|---|---|---|---|
| *Male students at a:* | | | | | | |
| Secular college | 16% | 42% | 25% | 17% | | |
| Jewish Orthodox coll. | | 62% | 20% | 14% | | 4% |
| *Female students at a:* | | | | | | |
| Secular college | 20% | 32% | 28% | 18% | 2% | |
| Jewish Orthodox coll. | 3% | 72% | 14% | 8% | | 3% |
| Gordon's sample | 45% | 8% | 21% | 14% | | 10% |

It has often been indicated in the literature that a college education would tend to change students' views and philosophies in a more liberal direction. In view of this, students were asked whether their college education has influenced their attitudes toward intermarriage.

6. Has your college experience affected your attitudes toward intermarriage so that . . . (Table X)

A decided change in the direction of more tolerant attitudes toward intermarriage is evident only for the female students attending a secular college. On the other hand, some of those attending religious colleges indicated that their college education has only intensified their negative attitudes on the subject.

TABLE X Has your college experience affected your attitudes toward intermarriage so that,

| College Groups | More acceptant | Less acceptant | Unchanged | Other |
|---|---|---|---|---|
| *Male students at a:* | | | | |
| Secular college | 10% | 12% | 74% | 4% |
| Jewish Orthodox coll. | 4% | 11% | 85% | |
| *Female students at a:* | | | | |
| Secular college | 20% | 2% | 74% | 4% |
| Jewish Orthodox coll. | 2% | 9% | 87% | 2% |

## Summary and Discussion

Our findings show that a sizable percentage of the groups of adolescents and groups of college students studied, appear to be unconcerned about the prospects of intermarriage. As expected, students enrolled in religious colleges tend to be more conservative in their views on this issue.

The most significant, and also disturbing, finding of the present study is the large percentage of intermarriage among our subjects' relatives. Despite this, the fact still remains that Jewish college students, compared to the college population at large, remain the group most reluctant to marry outside their religion. Gerhard Lenski indicated that in spite of their weak religious ties, Jews tend to express more negative feelings on the issue of intermarriage than Catholics.

The interpretation of the findings presented here is open, of course, to disagreement. Some may interpret the data to indicate that there is no threat to Jewish survival, while others may feel that the reported findings foreshadow the ultimate disappearance of the Jewish community in this country unless some drastic steps are taken to reduce the rate of intermarriage. As indicated earlier, the Federation of Jewish Philanthropies of New York has become actively concerned with this problem, and is trying to cope with it as well as arouse the Jewish community to the seriousness of this problem through meetings, publications, and mobilization of the resources of the Jewish Family Service. No one can predict, as yet, how effective these steps are. In order to cope effectively with such a problem, much group work would be necessary in order to reduce and prevent the possibility of adolescents' envisaging intermarriage. In an article entitled "Jewish Education and Jewish Survival," I reviewed empirical studies which tried to relate Jewish education and Jewish identification. It is believed that more effort should be spent in this area to insure the desire for survival.

Earlier in this chapter I pointed out the dearth of research on intermarriage among Jews. At this time, it would be worthwhile to discuss the general status of Jewish social research. I have written numerous reviews of social science studies on Jews and Jewish life in the United States. The observer is frequently awed and sometimes dazzled by the complex fabric of American Jewish life, and the abundance of thriving national and local organizations, the scope of philanthropic expression, and the responsiveness to national and sectarian challenges. Notwithstanding all this expression of energy and heightened social consciousness, there is a glaring gap in our knowledge of modern Jewish society. It is estimated that approximately $100 million are being spent each year on Jewish education. Yet research to evaluate the results of that education is almost nonexistent.

This lack of data on contemporary Jewry could be attributed to a number of conditions. The Jewish community in the United States is reputed for its high level of scholarship and learning. It is a well-known fact that a large percentage of behavioral scientists are Jewish, but very few of them are interested in devoting some of their energies to the study of the Jew. During my student days, I approached a Jewish professor and expressed my interest in studying the Jewish adolescent. The professor's reaction was that of surprise, since he did not believe that this was a worthwhile project. He felt that "Jews are not different." What makes his remarks somewhat incongruous was the fact that he had written a number of articles on the anti-Semite. Thus, while he felt that studying the anti-Semite was a worthwhile project, he could not conceive that studying the individuals who are victims of the anti-Semite was a fit subject for scientific study. This lack of interest on the part of Jewish social scientists has led Seymour Lipset to write the following:

The phenomenon of Jewish scholars ignoring the Jews as a field of study is not unique to sociology, although the gap is more glaring there, since the study of immigrant and ethnic groups has been so important in the field.

A second reason for the lack of research on contemporary Jewry is that the few existing Jewish foundations are managed primarily by historians who do not feel very comfortable with the modern technical social science research methods and therefore may be reluctant to acknowledge the importance of these procedures to study the Jew. Thus, it becomes easier for one to obtain financial support to study the accounting system used by the

Jews in the Middle Ages than to obtain funds to study the complexities of modern Jewish identification. This writer submitted to a Jewish journal a paper presenting some demographic information on the Jewish membership of a number of Jewish Community Centers. The Editorial Board rejected the paper, because they are more interested in "qualitative" rather than "quantitative" sociology. One of the purposes of the Journal is to foster a better understanding of the position of the Jews in the modern world. Papers dealing with Jews and which have only used the "qualitative" approach, do not, we feel, provide us with a comprehensive picture of the position of Jews in the modern world. It is probably for these reasons that Chancellor Louis Finkelstein indicated a few years ago that while he could get a hundred people or more whose profession it was to discover all that could be known about the Jews in the first century, there seemed to be no one who had the same duty for the Jews in the twentieth century. Note that it is England, with its relatively small Jewish population, that has the *Jewish Journal of Sociology,* which is the only outlet for empirical research on the Jew.

On the one hand, we have little support for Jewish social science by Jewish scholars, and on the other hand, there is also little interest shown on the part of Jewish defense and service agencies, who receive all of their financial support from the Jewish community. Money is more likely to be spent to support intensive research into the social and psychological characteristics of the anti-Semite, with little concern regarding the effect of this anti-Semitism on Jewish personality. Thus, it was recently shown that churchgoers tend to be more anti-Semitic than non-churchgoers. Another possible source of support for Jewish social science are the Jewish organizations devoted to social service. Since they are primarily social-work oriented, their evaluation of the effects of their services is usually based on subjective feelings, and there seems to be a de-emphasis on social science conceptualization. This is probably strengthened by the low priority which research is given in the education of the social worker.

In this chapter we have studied the attitudes of young people with different types of Jewish education toward intermarriage. Maybe we should expect Jewish educators to devote some of their energies to evaluating the results of their own teaching, in terms of its effect on the youth's views of himself as a Jew. However, this expectation is not realistic, particularly since funds for Jewish education proper are themselves limited. Since Jewish foundations and social service agencies may have the funds available but will not undertake the responsibility to develop the social science of contemporary American Jewry, the prospect that this endeavor will thrive in the near future is gloomy.

*15*

# INTERMARRIAGE AND THE JEWISH COMMUNITY

## Manheim S. Shapiro

In spite of our tendency to believe the contrary, patterns of courtship and marriage are influenced by the culture, expectations and standards of the community. It has become a commonplace in Western society to assert that the factor which leads to the marriage of any two people is "love," and that love itself is the product of some mysterious process subsumed under the term "chemistry." The consequence of relegating what happens in courtship and marriage to this unpredictable and uncontrollable mystery is the assumption that in an open society marriage and intermarriage are beyond the influence of the society itself.

Any examination of the facts, however, must lead us to conclude that this glib analysis of the forces which make for marriage is at least questionable. An extreme example was the public response to the announcement of Jackie Kennedy's marriage to Aristotle Onassis. It was clear both in the private gossip and in the public discussions that, for many, Mrs. Kennedy had violated the norms of what should lead to a decision to marry. It is interesting, too, that for these two figures so prominent in the public eye almost nobody resorted to that cliché so common in discussing the marriages of lesser personages, "Well, as long as they love each other . . ."

It is salutary to recall that the concept of romantic love as the necessary or even adequate precondition for marriage is, as history goes, relatively new. Indeed, even in some Western societies the idea is still not fully accepted, nor accepted at all. This is not to say that the idea of love is new; only that love as the primary reason for marriage is new.

Throughout world literature, there are references to occasions when a man loved his wife, or vice versa, but it was not assumed that this was necessary for marriage or, conversely, that marriage was a necessary consequence of love. The social standards for a marriage were summarized, as an example, by the factors which a *shadchen* applied in his professional efforts: family, wealth, stability, scholarship, reliability, and similar factors. If a bride or groom was also what we now call "attractive," that was an additional, but by and large fortuitous, element in the bargain.

Even today, in spite of what we articulate, these other elements still are as potent in determining marriages as is "love." But even if we were to accept the belief that marriages are made by love, we would still be left with the need to explain why X "falls in love" with Y but not with Z. To put it another way, if "love" is the product of "chemistry," then by the same token there must be an "analytical chemistry" which would enable us to factor out why certain reactions occur between any pair of people.

Of course, our understanding of human reactions is still in its earliest stages. Nevertheless, there are clues. In their compendium, *Human Behavior,* Berelson and Steiner provide us with some of these. They cite studies which utilize the taxonomic approach and inform us that of the marriages which are contracted in contemporary America, people tend to marry other people who are like themselves in the following social characteristics:

1. race
2. religion

3. socio-economic status and education
4. age
5. previous marital condition, and
6. residential propinquity

Each of these can be analyzed separately, but suffice it to expand upon the last of these. As recently as the 1950's, 25 percent of all the marriages contracted in the largest cities in America were between partners who lived within five blocks of each other and another 50 percent of all marriages were between persons who lived within twenty blocks of each other. This in spite of the social and geographic mobility of our times.

This tells us two things: first, that neighborhoods in America are still relatively homogeneous with respect to race, religion and socio-economic status; and second, that "love" it not as accidental as would be implied by all those terms like "chemistry," "falling" in love, being "smitten," and so on. The authors referred to above cite studies which establish the fact that "the likelihood of husband and wife sharing almost any characteristic is greater than chance expectation, whether this characteristic is a physical one, such as height or color of eyes, or an economic factor such as occupational background."

In short, what we are suggesting is that in order to look at mate selection realistically we must first of all rid ourselves of the superficial notion that this is entirely a matter of chance and beyond the influence of any factors other than some unfathomable "spark" which lights up when the young people meet. Some of the factors which contribute to the process we have already noted. What we have yet to recognize is that those who are similar in race, religion, socio-economic and educational characteristics have the potential of forming what we call a "community."

"Community," however, implies somewhat more than a mere aggregation of individuals of similar social characteristics. Among the other factors which make for community is a sense of cohesiveness among its members, whether this takes the form of common interests, mutual responsibility, shared values, expectations of patterned modes of behavior, or the sense of "common destiny." Additionally, a community is the vehicle for institutionalization, whether in the establishment of accustomed modes of individual behavior or in the establishment of forms of social organization which maintain both the relationships and the norms of behavior. Finally, a community possesses the capacity to compel conformity to its established norms through the implicit or explicit power to impose sanctions for violation of those norms.

It is against this background that we must look at some of the tendencies toward both intermarriage and intra-marriage among Jews in the United States today. It may be salutary as well to do this in a historical context which will point up by contrast some of what we confront today with respect to the communal effect upon marriages. Both in pre-Emancipation Western and Central Europe, and in pre-migration Eastern Europe, the Jewish community was capable of exerting great influence upon its members. Isolated perforce from the societies in which they lived, Jews evolved extremely cohesive communities. Their similarities to each other with respect to race, religion, socio-economic and educational background, and residential propinquity were salient in their self-awareness. Even when there were differences in one or another of these factors—say, socio-economic status or residential propinquity— the impact of the other factors served to emphasize their similarities to a greater extent than their dissimilarities. Furthermore, the perils latent in the attitudes of non-Jews tended to foster the sense of mutual dependence. The strength of the effect upon behavior of religious teachings and of established social custom made the community's norms and expectations clear. Lack of access to the civic services

and facilities of the total society compelled the establishment of internal institutions which were communally maintained and which accorded with the norms of communal
behavior. Finally, the community could, through social
condemnation, ostracism, expulsion or excommunication
(*cherem*) impose sanctions for violation of its accepted
standards.

In their effects upon marriage choice, these factors were
virtually all-powerful. A child grew up with the expectation that marriage to a Jewish partner was inevitable.
Association was, with certain exceptions which generally
did not impinge upon social contact, entirely with other
Jews. Marriages, as often as not, were arranged by
families rather than by individual will, and the family
was inclined to regard marriage to a Jew as the sole
available choice. One could continue this analysis by
dwelling upon other factors, but the import is clear without excessive expansion. We cannot, however, omit the
element of sanctions. In that world, intermarriage generally meant that the family would say *kaddish* for the
errant member and truly regard the individual as no
longer among the living, at least insofar as association
was concerned. Relatives and friends would also cut off
relationships. Institutions of the Jewish community effec-
tually closed off access. What is more, the probability of
condemnation on the other side, the non-Jewish world,
meant that the Jew contemplating intermarriage knew
that this portended giving up family, friends and institutional contacts and, in all probability, a marginal life outside any cohesive community.

There were, of course, exceptions to this general pattern, sometimes more and sometimes fewer, depending on
the time and the place. Even in the most effective communities there were occasional individuals who took the
fateful road of intermarriage. But, as a rule, the in-mar-
riage pattern was prevalent and its impact consistent.

The momentous borderline was crossed, however, with the enfranchisement of Jews or their migration; or, to stress its significance, the admission or the entry of Jews into the Western World. This represented in another way the incursion of modernity, to use sociologist Lucy David-owicz's formulation, into the relatively closed world of the Jewish community.

With this step (which in all its forms endured for about a century) a new way of life came about and the influence of almost all the factors we have described above was attenuated. With Jews rushing into Western society, the impact of a tight Jewish community was lessened. Neither the family nor the community as a whole exerted the same force, or was sure it wanted to do so.

In point of fact, quite the contrary was true, for a number of reasons. As a consequence of the long history of discrimination Jews had, like all minorities in this position, developed the propensity to feel that to be like the oppressor was indeed better. In their desire for equality, they had made the error of assuming that equality required similarity. As a measure to persuade others to accept them as equals, Jews and their institutions propagandized the notion that persons should be judged solely on "individual merit" rather than by group origins or affiliations, and succeeded in being most persuasive with themselves. Since higher status was clearly associated with the non-Jew, they sought contact with or entry into the non-Jewish group. (Indeed, many earlier intermarriages by Jews were clearly associated with the status drive.) Acquisition of Western education and the economic success brought the Jew closer to certain of his non-Jewish neighbors. Movement into second, third, and fourth areas of settlement brought Jews into residential propinquity with non-Jews.

Possibly more important than anything else was the loss, on both sides, of the community's power—or desire —to impose sanctions on intermarriage. Both Christians and Jews developed an attitude of tolerance toward intermarriage and a reluctance to impose communal sanctions upon those who undertook it. Intermarriage no longer means the abandonment of family and community or the need to live in a marginal world between or outside two communities. Indeed, it frequently means having the best of both worlds, or entrance into another community in which religion or ethnic associations is a matter of indifference or of antipathy.

In addition, along with the other social developments we have described, there emerged a shift in the community's values for individual behavior. Where there had been an emphasis upon communal duty and responsibility, the criterion for personal striving now became personal "happiness," whatever that may be. We can see this reflected in that familiar gambit of the parents of those who intermarry in saying, "Well, if she'll make him happy . . ."

The young person now contemplating intermarriage can now frustrate his distressed parents on two scores: that objection to such a marriage reveals the parents' hypocrisy about their professed belief that individual merit should be the sole criterion for judging people and that by attempting to prevent the intermarriage the parent is also preventing his child's happiness. And almost no Jewish parent, deprived of his primary tenets, unwilling to impose the sanction of terminating the parental relationship, and lacking the support of a common and effective community norm, can pursue the argument beyond feeble and unpersuasive protestations. As often as not, the parent is reduced to unprovable assertions that the intermarriage will eventually lead to unhappiness; but the mere assertions that it will or it won't merely produce an impasse in which the child almost always simply has his or her way.

This is, of course, a somewhat simplistic analysis of the situation. It omits certain qualifications and subtleties.

Nevertheless, it is in its essentials an accurate description of the process at work.

If these changes in the community of Jews are in fact components in the tendency to an increased rate of intermarriage, what may we derive from this with respect to the possibilities for retarding further increase in that rate?

To begin with, we need to examine in a new way some of the shibboleths which have been our guiding lights. For example, there is a need to overcome the uneasy embarrassment with which we recognize the tendency among Jews toward residential clustering. It may well be that in this pragmatic way the masses of Jewry are in fact taking measures for the preservation of the integrity of the Jewish people and its survival.

On a more abstract and theoretical level, we ought to recognize the possible fallaciousness of the glib assumption that "integration" is the best social organization for Jews, or for the society. For the immigrant seeking acceptance and equality, "integration" was the symbol of such "goods" and became, by inference and by rationalization, an ideal for the social structure. Now that we are no longer immigrants, we can perhaps come to a realistic view of pluralism, not merely as a technique for propaganda but as a viable and desirable form of social structure in which group cohesiveness and group distinctiveness are maintained.

This cannot be left, however, on theoretical grounds alone. For if we mean this, if we really care about intermarriage or other forms of group dissolution, then we must recognize that there are practical consequences of such a stance. It means, for example, that communal institutions and their functionaries must consciously work toward gaining acceptance of such an outlook among American Jews. They must, further, since they serve not only as advocates but also as models, make manifest in their programs their conviction that this is their view. Given the choice between programs which will serve the general good or the good of other groups and those which will serve the interests of Jews as a group, they must consistently give priority to the Jewish interest. This is not to say that Jews of their institutions must abandon their responsibilities to share in producing the general welfare. It is to say, however, that in considering that responsibility they must act, first of all, to give *priority* to specifically Jewish needs; and, secondly, to be willing to adhere to the principle that what is good for Jews (as distinct from General Motors) is good for society.

It is time to agree that a healthy self-interest is just as noble—maybe even more noble—as an abstract universalism that keeps professing an interest only in general social improvement. If we abandon or ignore the priority of our Jewish interest, we can hardly expect that our young will absorb a communal expectation of Jewish commitment and connection.

There are, of course, also many other aspects of acting out a Jewish communal standard and a communal atmosphere which will foster a tendency to think Jewish and to feel Jewish. The persons we place in positions of leadership, the modes of communal management and decision-making, the bringing together of groups of Jews must all be suffused with an awareness of the Jewish past, a motivation by Jewish ideals and Jewish interests, and a manifest concern for the Jewish future.

It is neither possible nor desirable to turn the clock back to that isolated Jewish community of the past. It is, however, both possible and desirable to re-create the sense of community around the sense of the Jewish. The greater the intensity we can lend to that process, the greater will be our chances to have at least some effect upon the extent of intermarriage among us.

What is more, in doing so we will lend strength and

support to what is at present only the intuitive and unsupported distress of the Jewish parent over a child's intermarriage. We will enhance the sense that to be Jewish and to be part of Jewry's continuation is a momentous opportunity. In the last analysis, we will even have reconstituted the possibility for communal sanctions, for although the individual's choice will continue to be a voluntary one, it may become an unbearable self-punishment to divorce one's self from so significant, exciting and dedicated a community. For it will have to be a community which has not only form but also content, which means what it says and which does what it means.

## 16

# THE INTERFAITH MARRIAGE AND
# ITS EFFECT ON THE INDIVIDUAL

## Louis Birner

To discuss the interfaith marriage and its effect on the individual, we must consider four problems: the problem of guilt, the problem of marriage, the problem of Jewish identity, and the problem of the individual adapting to the sledgehammer of modern-day history. A knowledge of these four factors may shed some light on the issues.

Every marriage is the joining together of two parties who, to some degree, have a sense of guilt. In general, guilt is our most difficult life problem. Two categories of guilt can be distinguished: guilt can be conscious or it can be unconscious. Freud stated that the unconscious variety of guilt can be defined as a need for punishment. The conscious variety of guilt is easier to define. We all have pangs of conscience and have endured anxiety, dread, and depression as a response to guilt feelings. Guilt is also timeless. Past guilt feelings can cloud our future, present, and the remembrance of our past. No doubt there is some sense of conscious guilt present as I discuss the problem of the interfaith marriage.

The need for punishment (unconscious guilt) is quite deceptive. We are not aware of it. Blissfully can we live our lives until one day we engineer either a major or minor piece of self-destruction.

There was the case of a very rational, methodical, unemotional lawyer who lived in suburbia and had an office in New York. He was considering divorcing his wife and was "intellectually undecided." One day his car broke down. He had to borrow his wife's car to go to work. Though he was a careful driver, he managed to have an accident and smashed his wife's car. He bought his wife another car. One day, soon after the car arrived, he managed to have another accident and smashed this car too. Symbolically, he was expressing his guilt toward his wife. Literally he risked his life to pay for the right to want to destroy his marriage. He was unconsciously guilty.

Unconscious manifestations of guilt are everywhere. Let me cite a few examples. A couple were recently married; a sum of cash set aside for the honeymoon and the marriage license were in the bride's purse. On the trip to the airport the bride lost the purse.

A graduate student had to present a talk about his research to an important university committee. He "forgot" about it, until a day after the appointment.

A promising young man lost the only copy of his thesis.

Unconscious guilt has conscious derivatives in the feelings of shame and doubt. Guilt can be denied, repressed, and projected. Guilt can claim a victory in the achievement of failure. Guilt can claim a victory by holding back and stopping one from finishing important pieces of work. The greater our degree of guilt, the greater our psychotic potential and need for self-destruction. The greater our guilt, the weaker our ego. The less guilt we have to contend with, the greater our level of mental health.

Two of the building blocks of psychoanalysis are the concepts of the unconscious and the Oedipus complex. Neurosis centers about the development and formation of the Oedipus complex. Books have been written about both of these topics. If we are to consider the interfaith marriage and its effect on the individual, we must talk about the Oedipus complex and the unconscious. The formation of guilt to a large degree rests upon how successfully one resolves his Oedipus complex. If we feel abnormal guilt on both conscious and unconscious levels, this reflects an Oedipal conflict that has not been successfully resolved. Let us consider for a moment how the Oedipus complex can alter one's perception of his Jewish identity. In the case of a male child, the more smothering and seductive the mother, the greater the guilt toward the father. In the classical Oedipal triangle one feels guilt primarily toward the parent of the same sex. There are a number of ways of handling this guilt. One can identify with the parent or reject as much as possible an identification with the parent of the same sex. Clear examples can be seen in cases where capitalists have communists for sons and vice versa, or in Jewish men who cannot stand Jewish women, or Jewish women who cannot stand Jewish men, or Jews who cannot stand Jewishness.

All guilt seeks expiation. Oedipal guilt can be expiated in many ways. One possibility is the interfaith marriage. I do not wish to imply that every interfaith marriage is based on an unresolved Oedipus complex. This is also true of the intrafaith marriage. No one ever fully resolves his Oedipal conflict. The factor of the Oedipus complex is primal in mate selection. When a Jewish man feels guilt toward his father, the Christian woman may serve as a psychological alibi. Through this type of mate he is giving up competing with and being like his father.

Psychoanalysis has uncovered some cruel facts about life. We are not the masters of our fate and our rationality is a poor defense against our unconscious drives. The decision to marry is not only, as the poets would say, "blind," it is also unconscious. The unconscious can be very insensitive to religious training. Mate selection is a testament to the degree of health or sickness in both parties. It is a testament to our past and our present experiences. It is a talisman of our concept of identity.

Let us consider past and present experiences. We live in a crazy world. History has been cruel to our group. Pressures are put upon us to Americanize and forsake our heritage. An accent can be made into horror. A "Jewish nose" can be seen as a reason to call the plastic surgeon. Education can mean the need for Protestantization in some Midwestern melting pot. According to the mass media non-Jewish types make up the world. This Americanization pressure can be minor compared to the family pressure. Many parents downgrade being Jewish through the expression of guilt and distorting Judaism as the royal road to suffering.

There is a healthy sense of identity, one can enjoy his past and take pride in it and choose to perpetuate it. This means that there must be a parental environment that is in touch with the past. I do not mean this necessarily to be only a religious practice but rather a happy sense and feeling about being part of a group and a historcial nation with a past, present, and future.

In situations where the Oedipus complex is resolved with some degree of health, Jews will tend to marry Jews. Certainly, severe neurotic conflicts can also find an outlet in the intrafaith marriage. In this case the ego lacks the freedom to make other forms of resolution.

We must also consider, if I may coin a phrase, the melted-down Jew. Yes, he is a Jew, but is a stranger to all things Jewish. He is responding to an identity crisis. His crisis is a need to be apart from the past. He cannot understand his past and is often unconsciously guilty about not being in touch with it. The melted-down Jew is reacting to parents who could not accept their Jewishness or each other. He can unconsciouly accept his parents' problems by rejecting their religion.

The sledgehammer of our present-day world is opening up new social possibilities. The interfaith marriage is made easy through mass travel and the breakdown of the ghettos and the communities. Protestation, defiance of tradition, and the rejection of the past are very popular.

Consequently, those of us who feel guilt and have poorly resolved our Oedipus complex have a new out. It is smart to be different. Thirty years ago an interfaith marriage could be seen as a rebellion. This rebellion has today become institutionalized. The point is, it is easier to marry out of one's faith today. A new tradition has been created.

The basis of all marriages is in the unconscious. Mate selection is a mirror of emotional health and pathology. The interfaith marriage seeks to do what other marriages do, but with one additional factor. It chooses a mate of a different identity. The difference in identity can be seen as a condition. Somehow the ego perceives a mate of the same religion as a threat. The person of the other religion gains value because of the difference.

If an interfaith marriage can reduce the person's sense of guilt and help both parties move in the direction of health it is a successful union.

Where there is contempt for one's past and identity, the interfaith marriage can be a highly destructive affair. The other party cannot be truly accepted, since the value placed on the partner is based on a quality the other can never attain. Let me cite an example: a rather anti-Semitic Jew married a rather anti-Irish Irish person. Each was the answer to the other's self-contempt. Each would tend to make the other guilty over nonreligious issues. But the guilt and self-contempt was there in terms of the religious and social identity.

We must face the fact that for certain people with major emotional problems the interfaith marriage may be the only out. Consider the overly guilty male in unconscious dread of incest. He can experience some sense of relief sexually with a member of a different faith or race. If one's guilt is severe enough, one can be pushed in the

direction of homosexuality. A very religious Jewish homo-
sexual once told me that the only girl he every thought of
marrying was Italian.

For the rather neurotic types, the interfaith marriage
is a stopgap solution to past problems. Granted, these marriages work, but they work at a high price. The price is
guilt and self-punishment. How common it is that a person
can marry outside of the religion to find a person just like
the dreaded mother or father.

There is a type of interfaith marriage that is requested
by one or both parents. The children are often brought
up with the idea that it is not good to be Jewish and that
being Christian is a highly desirable state. Unfortunately,
history has documented this neurotic projection and many
Jews have sought, themselves, or urged their children to
leave their religion through marriage. Consider the insanity of the Hitler period. Many people thought that
if the world hates Jews, why be a Jew? For the Christian
marrying the Jew a problem can exist in terms of motivation. Does the Christian see the potential Jewish mate on
a higher or lower level?

Where the Jewish mate is either exalted or down-
graded, problems will occur.

The spectrum of neurotic possibility in terms of marriage is vast. This same truth holds for those who chose
the interfaith marriage. With the interfaith marriage an
additional feature comes to the fore. The problem of
identity. Our identity is our psychological reality. Freud
spoke before the B'nai B'rith in 1926. Though an atheist,
he formulated his tie to his fellow Jews as an *inner
identity*. Freud also felt that his ability to stick to his
theories in the face of overwhelming objection and ostracism of the Viennese medical circle is a tribute to his Jewish background. The ability to hold on in face of rejection
is nothing new to the Hebrew nation. It is a part of Jewish identity. History can give many examples of this inner

278 THE JEWISH FAMILY IN A CHANGING WORLD

Jewish identity. According to Erik Erikson, identity can be seen as a link to the past, a sharing of a mutual relationship, a persistent self-sameness. Jewish identity also means a maintenance of an inner solidarity with a group's ideals and identity. Identity can mean a sharing with the past.

The identity quotient of an individual is a compilation of his historical time and his unconscious conflicts. Every step toward giving up the past creates the problem of loss, gain and substitution.

All interfaith marriages are based on a giving up. When this giving up occurs, a void is created. The interfaith marriage means a departure from tradition, and the possible quest for a new tradition.

One of the possible effects of the interfaith marriage is the creation of an identity absence. By this I mean that two people can live together adhering to no religion, holding no identity—much like Riesman's description of the alienated person. What is so insidious is that one of the possible effects of the interfaith marriage is that it can set the stage for the development of unrelated people and children. This type of marriage can lead one to being directed by the television, movie, and sales promotion campaigns. People can become pawns of daily pressure. The lack of past standards can lead to self-destruction.

Another effect of the interfaith marriage is the quest for new pseudo-religions. A friend, the product of a mixed marriage, who married into still another ethnic group, describes himself as a "West Side liberal." He is identified with certain progressive political beliefs. Countless examples of new pseudo-religions can be cited: the work religion, the political religion, the charity religion, and the intellectual religion, etc. In sharing this new form of religion there is an unconscious recognition of a loss of the old. Sometimes these new religions are workable substitutes.

One of the most dreadful "religious" developments (pseudo-religion) of late is the overly Orthodox rebel. Here is a devotee consumed with a passion, ready to destroy tradition completely. Many of these Orthodox rebels are college students. This type of rebel feels religious institutions and ethnic group indentification are worthless. Within this rebel group there can be a strong desire to validate liberalism through interfaith marriage, and if I can use one of their expressions: "to give up this false society."

Another effect of the interfaith marriage on the individual is the chance to discover marriage and to leave it or stay with it. We must not forget that one marriage can lead to another, and the second can be a new chance or possibility for better or worse.

There is a common problem to all marriages, which is, Does it help create and maintain a friendly relationship to one's past or does it lend itself to an isolation and rejection of these values? In the interfaith marriage the isolation and rejection from the past represent a distrust and can reflect a sense of inner despair. Where one can remain friendly to one's past and makes peace even with a cruel past, there is the hope of the interfaith marriage becoming a union that truly generates and provides a sense of caring and integrity.

In many interfaith marriages the husband and wife become involved in pseudo-religions. If these religions can give one a sense of belonging to something that leads to an emotional fulfillment there is hope of the person's making a substitute for the loss of identity and tie with the past.

The interfaith marriage can be a reaction to a particular form of guilt. If the marriage reduces the level of guilt that brought the parties together it is successful. Substitution for past identities has to be made by one or both parties. This is especially true of those marriages which produce children. Where the substitution moves in the direction of supporting the expression of love on an interpersonal and sexual level the marriage can be constructive. It can generate something healthy in the sense that love is supported and guilt is not catered to and reinforced. If we consider our present divorce rate, any type of constructive marriage, be it *interfaith* or *intrafaith,* if it can maintain itself in a loving way is worthwhile.

I spoke with a friend of mine who is a rabbi. I made the point that the Catholics and the Protestants are having quite a problem with the interfaith marriage and vast numbers are leaving their churches. The rabbi responded, "I don't care about Catholics and Protestants." In the old and familiar tradition we argued. Happily, we came to agreement. The interfaith marriage is a nationwide and worldwide problem. So far as the Jew in this country is concerned, it seems to be occurring with less frequency when compared to other groups. The same is true of the divorce rate. Statistically, we have fewer divorces. What does this mean? It means our inner identity is still with us and is carrying us through a grim and difficult period of history. I think it also is a token that we have used our ties to our past well. It speaks for us of a future. Many feel that the Jew can become assimilated and destroyed through the interfaith marriage. Let us remember that Hitler's ovens helped stimulate the birth of Israel and that Nasser helped create one of the finest armies in the world. The interfaith marriage is a challenge and we have the inner resources to deal with it and maintain ourselves.

One of the problems not spelled out but implied is what can the synagogues do to help maintain the Jewish community and reduce the rate of intermarriage? I do not know the answer, though I have some ideas about it. We have a tradition of survival and strength. I do not feel we will lose our identity. The interfaith marriage is nothing new in Jewish history.

It may well be that the rabbi, who has a history of being the community lawyer, judge, labor arbitrator, teacher, priest, and doctor may have to become a family therapist and a social worker. It may also be that the synagogue may become a part-time mental health center. One goal of such a therapeutic effort would be to maintain a loving relationship to our past. Where there is this sense of love there is also the need for perpetuation.

A final word about guilt. All mankind experiences guilt. But each group experiences guilt in a particular way. In certain forms of Christianity the sense of guilt seems lessened: Christ died for my sins and heaven is guaranteed. The Jew has no one to die for his sins and has no guarantee or insurance policy. He must do for himself. He must find his own answers. There is health in self-struggle. As Jacob wrestled for a blessing, so must we wrestle to claim the blessings of our past in this our present-day world.

I would like to close with a case history which deals with some of the problems presented here.

Sharon is the product of two parents who are first-generation American Jews. Both are well educated and are professionals. The parents traded in their backgrounds for the liberal, progressive pseudo-religion. High value was placed on all learning except religious learning. The mother and the father both have severe problems but function vocationally on a very high level. The mother can be described as a hysterical type and the father as a rigid compulsive. Sharon was rigidly brought up by rules and ritual, being dominated by both parents in different and similar ways. The father was cold and distant. The mother was smothering, clinging, and overly intense. Both parents were compulsively afraid about the worst happening to their child and had to know her exact whereabouts at almost all times.

She reached adolescence with feelings of guilt over her sexual role, being dependent and easily frightened. She, like the mother, was hysterical. Like both parents, she was overly intellectual and greatly committed to progressive ideals. Her parents were old-fashioned in one sense, that is, they instructed Sharon that it was a terrible thing to have sexual intercourse before marriage. When she started dating she had many sexless relationships with Negro young men.

Sharon, a brilliant young woman, majored in English at college and there met a young man of German Protestant background. He was a first-generation American and was suffering from an identity crisis. Carl felt an overwhelming sense of guilt about the German persecution of the Jews. This guilt was shared by his family. Consequently, Sharon's Jewishness was a very promising factor for both Carl and his family. Sharon's neurosis was also very attractive. As a lover and companion she was almost impossible. This was especially true when the relationship started to head in the direction of marriage. Consequently, Carl found an ideal woman in terms of expiating his own guilt. He found a troubled Jewish woman with whom he could suffer and try to help.

Sharon became so frightened about the possibility of getting married that she sought treatment. Her initial transference was that of a hysterical, crying, depressed woman. She demanded that the analyst reward her suffering with answers. One of the problems that presented itself early on in treatment was her weakened ego. She was very much pushed in the direction of following orders. She easily adjusted to a kind of intellectualized hippie existence. Particularly absent in her communications in treatment were the expressions of feeling and closeness.

Her chief complaint was her hysterical fear of marriage. In reality she was afraid of self-autonomy. As she became a little less hysterical, both families and the boy friend insisted on the marriage. After marriage they left the country to do some form of social work in a far-off country. The marriage was seen as the answer and therapy was terminated.

I would like to emphasize that this type of case is by no means unusual in this, our modern world. The parents of Carl and Sharon both reacted to a sense of guilt about themselves and their past identity. This problem was transmitted to the children. The children, in turn, had to face a world which offered them a new out. This new out is the giving up of the tie with the past.

In one of the recent student protests some students claimed that they should like to be taught only new and present-day material. The past, they claimed, has no relevance in today's world. Should such an attitude gather force we will be faced with a 1984 which will be without Bible or Shakespeare. Our identities will come from the computer, the television set, and government.

Carl and Sharon have the limitation of looking for a future without the benefits of a loving relationship with the past. This is a severe limitation. We face the problem today of keeping that past alive. In keeping the past alive, we are keeping ourselves alive psychologically. The delighting in our group and in our history can reduce our sense of guilt and preserve our mental health.

## 17

# REFLECTIONS ON INTERMARRIAGE

## Henry Enoch Kagan

There are three major factors involved in the increasing number of intermarriages threatening the survival of the American Jewish community. These factors are—the statistical, the sociological, and the psychological.

Putting the three major factors in the form of questions, we ask first, what are the statistics on the increase in intermarriage? Although this is not the major thrust of Dr. Victor Sanua's paper, we are indebted to him for reviewing the previous studies on intermarriage statistics. We also commend him for avoiding hysterical conclusions based on the high rate of intermarriages among small-town Jews. Most American Jews do live in large cities with large Jewish populations and, as Dr. Manheim Shapiro reminds us, propinquity determines more marriages than does romance. Nevertheless, the statistic on intermarriage is expected to rise because at least 80 percent of all Jewish males and females attend colleges where distance between Jew and non-Jew is diminished. Furthermore, marrying a Jew has become more acceptable to non-Jews. We should anticipate what Dr. Sanua states will be "an alarming trend in the rate of intermarriage among Jews."

If the Jewish affirmative conditioning agencies are to plan intelligently to modify the increasing separation from the Jewish community which usually attends intermarriage, the motivating forces at work must be studied in depth. Dr. Sanua's study, especially on the attitude of

college students toward intermarriage and how their attitude of approval or disapproval of intermarriage is related to the intensity of their Jewish education, is a study
in the right direction. His findings are not surprising,
since they confirm one hypothesis to account for intermarriage, namely, the loss of identification with the Jewish group. Dr. Sanua finds that the students with the
most intense parochial Jewish education show the strong-
est opposition to intermarriage, whereas the least concerned about intermarriage attend public school. Does this
finding suggest the establishment of more Jewish parochial
schools, in Reform Judaism as well as in Orthodoxy, as
part of a blueprint for stemming the tide of intermarriage?

Jewish-powered segregated schools may be premature
if this solution is based solely on attitudes tests such as
employed by Dr. Sanua. While attitude testing is more
informative than mere statistics, the attitude questionnaire
suffers from being fixed and loaded. Unless the questions
are validated for reliability and internal consistency by
comparison with control groups we cannot be sure without
this refinement that the attitude test conclusively differentiates between the attitude of the Orthodox and the
attitude of the secular respondent. Nevertheless, an attitude test is the first step in any study in depth of intermarriage.

A second hypothesis for intermarriage is the neurotic
interaction between parents and child. Dr. Sanua's test
does not expose this second factor, which I suspect may
be a more significant cause for intermarriage than the
weakening of Jewish group identification. Intellectually
and consciously the attitude-test respondents may say they
approve or disapprove of intermarriage, but would not a
better measurement be how many Jews trained in Orthodoxy and how many trained secularly actually intermarry?
Attitude does not necessarily indicate behavior. A study
in depth must search out unconscious motives, for all

marriages have unconscious motivations. We should ask how many of each of the extremes on the scale—Orthodox as compared to secular—unconsciously desire intermarriage. We are concerned here on two fronts and not only with preserving Judaism. We ought to be concerned about healthy marriages not merely with Jewish marriages.

The high incidence of divorce in the American family questions the general health of marriages in our society. In his sociological study, Dr. Shapiro poses our second question. We ask: Have the traditional Jewish family behavior patterns been completely altered by a century of acculturation with the typically dominant American middle-class family? Volumes have been written on the weaknesses inherent in the mobility, the individualism, and the decline of parental authority in the American middle-class family. As a result, the absentee father and the dominant mother in the child-centered middle-class family has turned upside down the former, healthier roles which are appropriate to each member of the family. Whether this process of deterioration can be reversed is the concern not only of Jewish but of every expert on the family.

Dr. Shapiro arouses our nostalgia with his review of the admirable communal values developed in the East European ghetto community regarding marriage and family. However, I doubt that the sanctions of that stable, homogeneous, medieval Jewish community or *shtetl* can ever be restored. The revolutionary mobile society of our day has radically reduced the authority of every religious establishment—Catholic and Protestant as well as Jewish—over the moral behavior of the individual.

In her preface to the study of the *shtetl* in *Life Is with People*, Margaret Mead, I am afraid, is overly optimistic when she writes, "With the traditional capacity of the Jews to preserve the past while transmitting it into a healthy relationship to the present, much of the faith and hopes which lived in the *shtetl* will inform the lives of the descendants of the *shtetl* in other lands." How much does the pseudo-sophisticated American Jew sitting in the audience seeing *Fiddler on the Roof* identify with Tevye when he says, "And how do we keep our balance? That I can tell you in one word—tradition . . . because of our tradition everyone knows who he is and what God expects him to do . . . ?" I suspect the American Jew identifies with the fiddler about whom Tevye says, "Without our traditions our lives would be as shaky as a fiddler on the roof."

As a fellow preacher, I appreciate Dr. Shapiro's sermonics, but preaching seldom changes attitudes. Preaching that in a democracy one should not confuse equality with similarity, and that a pluralistic society should avoid conformity for variety is the spice of life, has no effect on a young couple who think they are romantically in love.

**Despite its vulgarization** by the commercial purveyors of glamour, passionate romance still is a necessary catalyst even though it is ephemeral. We know that by itself romantic love does not have the lasting qualities of mature love which realistic marriage requires. Nonetheless, the irrationality of love is not changed by the most mature persuasion. Is not Cupid appropriately depicted as an *infant* with a bow and arrow? An infant desires having even more than the best of two worlds—Jewish and Christian—as Dr. Shapiro indicates romantic young lovers *imagine* they will enjoy. An infant wants the best of *all* worlds! Who will teach him that life has its limitations? Dr. Shapiro suggests that American Jews should welcome "residential clustering"—a nice phrase which semantically may be less pejorative than the word "ghetto." Whether they welcome it or not, the new migration of black men from farm to city which is rapidly transforming the core cities is forcing Jews into a multitude of Jewish suburbs. Yet, Jewish ghettos in America will not substantially reduce intermarriage for unlike being walled in as was the medieval ghetto, the children of our Jewish suburban ghettos commingle with non-Jews especially at the peak romantic period of adolescents at college.

Jewish community life obviously needs to be made more exciting, as Dr. Shapiro suggests. I question that as a result intermarriage will be rejected because it will create a self-imposed feeling of excommunication from an exciting community. Life presents a choice of many excitements to our youth who have no fears of an artificial illusory *cherem*. It may be more exciting and effective to spend our money on establishing Jewishly sponsored coed colleges where there is truly a conscious effort to show preference for Jewish applicants.

All such solutions are premature because they must undo what has been happening to the Jewish child in the home, which unconsciously leads it into intermarriage. The infant matures through a process of identification which begins first with another adult, preferably with one who is mature. Only later does identification with a group, if there is a cohesive group around, come into play. The child matures as it internalizes into its own life style the values of an adult.

We could use a few authentic American Jewish heroes with whom our Jewish youth might identify. Black youth in America, by identifying with black heroes, are regaining today their self-pride which reduces their immature ego desires for a white liaison. They identify especially with black athletes who express proudly and loudly their black loyalties. If athletics plays a secondary role to intellectuality or money power as status symbols for Jews, where are the authentic Jewish image makers in these two fields of ambition?

When a Jew who is intermarried can become a member of the Supreme Court of the United States, and when another Jew (deceased) who in fact was a prominent Zionist but intermarried became a Supreme Court Justice; when a prominent Jewish businessman who is intermarried and all of his children and grandchildren are officially raised as non-Jews is honored for his large contributions to Jewish charities and Jewish defense agencies; when a great medical genius who is intermarried and does not rear his children as Jews is honored by a rabbinical seminary—we certainly could use a few authentic Jewish American heroes. To our youth it appears that as long as a high status as a Jew is achieved it is all right to marry a Christian and even rear one's children as non-Jews. On this subject of identification, what loyalty is created in our youth when a prominent rabbi participates with a Christian clergyman in an intermarriage ceremony? There is a point where liberality becomes anarchy.

Our study in depth needs to explore this identification or lack of identification with a Jewish person. The place to begin is at the beginning—namely, with the child's interaction with its parents. It would be fruitful to collect case histories of those Jews who have been treated by psychiatrists for emotional problems which include marital breakdowns in intermarriage.

Two black psychiatrists, Dr. William H. Grier and Dr. Price M. Cobbs, include a number of cases of breakdown in interracial marriage in their recent instructive and well-written book about Negroes, *Black Rage*. Dr. Louis Birner concludes his psychoanalytic study of intermarriage with one case history. The Jewish girl in that case had two neurotic intellectual parents with whom to identify. Dr. Birner infers that her parents harbored guilt feelings for their total abandonment of Judaism, if that is what he means by "trading in their backgrounds for the liberal, progressive pseudo-religion." Instead of feeling comfortable as Jews they were compulsively rigid and conditioned their daughter with a frightened rigidity about sex, which is certainly un-Jewish. Her marriage to a German, guilt-ridden himself about the persecution of the Jews, could result in the all too frequent sadomasochistic partnership. When Dr. Birner states, "The marriage was seen as the answer and therapy was terminated," shall we read between the lines—that the therapy should have continued and the marriage been prevented?

Some unconsciously marry in order to destroy a marriage. This is self-punishment for irrational guilt. Dr. Birner tends to place all these irrational guilts into one Freudian basket. The comic-tragedy of the nursery triangle is not fated to the pessimism of Freud.

Some questions need to be asked before we categorically declare that the interfaith marriage for some is their only way out to secure forgiveness for their unconscious guilt of incest. It has not been proven that it is *not* incest with mother as long as the wife is *not* Jewish. It has not been proven that it is *not* incest with father as long as the husband is *not* Jewish. It is necessary to have some degree of freedom from both parents to have any kind of healthy marriage. Without adequate case histories we cannot state that three times as many Jewish males as females intermarry because the Jewish men want to victimize Christian women with whom they use their sex as a dagger for irrational revenge on their parents. I do not reject the fantasies of Oedipus, because Oedipus was a Greek and not a Jew, as Freud seemed to be able to identify with Moses only if Freud could prove Moses was not a Jew.

A dogmatic Freudian interpretation of Freud would assert that he had to identify with a non-Jewish hero to take unconscious revenge on his father from blocking Freud's infantile incestuous fantasy of sexual fulfillment with his very young mother. But Freud himself offered an opposite and equally pertinent cause for turning in his youth to a non-Jewish hero like Hannibal. He said he turned to a non-Jewish hero because his own father was a frightened, cowardly Jew in the face of anti-Semitism. Yet Freud became a Zionist, opposed intermarriage, and married a Jewess. This Jew did conquer his unconscious Oedipal complex by developing a strong, conscious Jewish ego. We should be more concerned with the loss of ego identity than with sexual vengeance in the psychological analysis of intermarriage.

It would be significant to know how many Jewish girls who think they are beautiful as compared to how many who think they are ugly intermarry. Our hypothesis is that there should be more ugly ones because the ugly girl has lost her feminine narcissism, has a low evaluation of herself, and feels unlovable. It would be significant to know how many Jewish males consider themselves inferior with a secondary social status because of being Jewish and therefore choose a non-Jewish sexual partner. They do not marry a Jewess because she is their Jewish counterpart and thus depreciated as much as they think they are. With weak egos sex is a form of self-debasement.

The sexual behavior of animals who feel inferior is instructive on this point. In chickens, males ranking lowest in the peck-order among the cocks suppress their sexuality to the point of psychologic castration. Dr. A. M. Guhl, professor of zoology, observed that one male failed to mate with the hens of the flock even when his peck-order social superiors were temporarily removed, but he did mate with strange hens from another flock. Dr. F. F. Darling confirms the significance of feeling important as a prerequisite in animal social behavior when he reported that the dominant bull water buffalo must have two other bulls to dominate before he is potent. (See *Sex and Internal Secretions*, edited by William C. Young, Williams and Wilkins, Baltimore, 1961, volume 2, p. 1247.)

Dr. Birner's uncompromising use of the Oedipal fantasy and his pessimism about ever resolving it leads him to assert that intermarriage must take place wherever there is unhealthy interaction with parents. He proposes to stem the tide of intermarriage by intensifying group identification. This happened with Freud, but every Jew is not a genius like Freud, and even he had to have some individual hero with whom to identify. Assuming that *group* identification can compensate for the absence of *individual* or parental identification in developing strong ego identity, the values which the group holds high must be internalized in the individual. When Dr. Birner says we are not the masters of our fate because we can never be freed from our unconscious, he removes the outstanding and most unique value in Judaism which differentiates it the *most* from all other religious cultures. This is the Judaic concept that we *are* masters of our fate. The Talmudic rabbis were realistic when they said one gets married and then falls in love with his wife. Though it may sound paradoxical, they are still realistic when they also said everything may be preordained but free will is nonetheless given.

As a rabbi and licensed therapist it is flattering to me to have one so Freudian-oriented as Dr. Birner suggest that the rabbi become a "family therapist" and the synagogue "a part-time mental health center." The New York Federation of Reform Synagogues has established such a Judaic-oriented psychological counseling center directed by a rabbi-psychologist licensed therapist in collaboration with religiously oriented Jewish psychiatrists. This collaboration can be effective only if both sides have a clear, unprejudiced understanding of what are the values and goals of Judaism as well as what are the *proven* methods of dynamic psychology.

One preventive measure against intermarriages is psychologically oriented group dynamic dialogues with Jewish youth under Jewish religious auspices at our Counseling Center. In these groups we point out the vital differences which are found in the Jewish attitude toward sex, marriage, divorce, birth control, and family values. In our premarital seminars limited to ten couples at our Counseling Center we deal with the challenge of self-esteem in marriage, love and lovemaking, the role of femininity and of masculinity, healthy attitudes toward in-laws, money and status. We are now planning small group seminars for young parents to sensitize them to the role they play in developing the ego identity of their children and to the superior emotional affect which the symbolic language of home rituals has over the no-religion home in creating ego identity.

The identity crisis we hear so much about is supposed to describe our alienated youg people among whom are so many Jews. To establish identity there is experimentation in sexuality which the contraceptive pill has made more permissive. Just because there is no ego identity, this experiment in sexuality usually fails. Despite all their open talk about sex, for all too many sex is degrading. Those who have an unconscious contempt for self can have more sensual pleasure with a member of the other group they regard as "lesser" or "degraded"—white with degraded black and now black with degraded white-or Christian with degraded Jew and now Jew with degraded Christian. As blacks regain their identity there will be not more but less interracial sexual intercourse, for now "black is beautiful," so as Jews regain their identity there will be less interreligious as well as interracial sexual intercourse with non-Jews.

For Jews this ego identity involves the recovery of Judaic moral values and their endorsement of sexuality. Is the radical difference between the Judaic and the traditional Christian attitude toward sexuality one of the unconscious reasons why very few Jews convert to Christianity in an intermarriage. There are Christians today who are accepting these Judaic values which enhance sexuality and free it from sinfulness. By earnest conversion they make their Jewish marriage succeed and in their success contribute to the preservation of Judaism.

Parents would not appear to their children ready to

acquiesce to their intermarriage as inevitable if the children believed their parents were committed to the values in Judaism worth preserving. Of 500 suburban parents interviewed, very few explain they would be unhappy because intermarriage would break the 3,000-year chain of tradition of a unique people and thus render the diaspora Jew an extinct fossil. Their only concern was with the personal happiness of their child since divorce is 2½ times higher among mixed marriages—and divorce is only higher among couples with no religion. In a number of studies, the chances for marital happiness are from four to eleven times less where couples differ in religion as compared to couples who agree on religion.

To parents as well as to our unmarried young the fundamental issue is whether there is anything worth preserving in Judaism. Is there? Unless you have some feeling about being chosen as a Jew, why should your child not choose to marry anyone? Just as we need an understanding of the psychological motives of intermarriage, we need a new psychological, not theological, meaning for that ancient, annoying (but most misunderstood) doctrine of the Chosen People. If to be chosen is a boast, our modern children reject it. If it is seeking of priestly status, they repudiate it. If it means a royal title, they abdicate. If they can be helped to see that, theologically, it once meant God reaching down to us, but psychologically it now is us reaching up to God, they may choose to consider such a chosenness as well as their private pleasure when they marry. "Chosenness" is not a boast but a burden; not a status but a standard; not a title but a task. Our Jewish youth yearn for a commitment and may even want to convince their loved ones to be sincerely converted to take on together with them this burden, this standard and this sacred task.

# 18

# THE ROLE OF PHILANTHROPY IN RELATION TO THE JEWISH FAMILY

## S. P. Goldberg

American Jewish philanthropy provided over $400 million in identifiable gifts in 1967 by more than one million contributors for Jewish needs and responsibilities. It was the peak performance in a generation of massive Jewish fund-raising, which had resulted in raising well over $3.4 billion dollars.

About three-quarters of the sum raised in 1967 was destined for needs of Jews in overseas areas, mainly for the overseas needs of the people of Israel in that year of crisis.

The Jewish Community in America used over $60 million for local Jewish welfare, health, education and related philanthropic needs, including over $20 million from the proceeds of campaigns of nonsectarian United Funds and Community Chests.

The impact of Jewish fund-raising on Jewish families was almost universal, except where extremely large population centers made complete coverage impossible. The number of families reached by these activities was far in excess of the number of families identified with any single national organization or any single wing of religious Judaism.

The level of giving to Jewish Federations was substantially higher, on a per capita basis, than was general giving to nonsectarian United Funds. This major difference was based on the inclusion of the overseas needs for the surviving victims of the Holocaust and the immigration of almost 1,270,000 Jews to Israel in the first twenty years of its existence.

This high level of giving required family decisions rather than the casual individual reactions when gifts are nominal. It involved all members of the family: the head of the household contributed at home, or through business or professional groups.

In recent years, women's giving has played a major role in community campaigns: the wife gave her supplementary gift to the Federation and to one or more national women's organizations; the youth through Keren Ami and Tzedakah drives in Jewish schools or Hillel drives on college campuses. Thus, giving extended to every age level in the family.

The basic objective for giving was to make possible the building of a normal life for Jews in need or in hazard both at home and abroad, wherever the shifting geography of human need required the provision of such aid.

The target of normality is the healthy Jewish family. The aim of building and strengthening of the Jewish family is sought through manifold services and agencies. Where agencies deal with pathology in individual and family development it is to retain or restore the family as the basic unit. The basic aim is to preserve the family as the fountainhead of the Jewish future.

Among the first to emerge historically was the need to make possible the beginning of a family by providing the bride's dowry where the family's economic status did not permit this. This has all but vanished in the United States with the relative attainment of affluence.

In earlier periods when children might be left at an early age without parents, provision was made for their care, at first in "homes," but in the last several decades in actual home settings, except where an institutional setting is essential.

To supplement the role of the home in building positive character attributes in Jewish youth, there was created the settlement house, which was succeeded by the modern Jewish Community Center serving all age groups.

The close interrelation of the family and the child is reflected in the pattern of Jewish family *and* child care service agencies as joint operations, except in a few of the larger cities. Jewish family agencies serve refugees and frequently handle intake procedures for homes for the aged. The aged, who are well enough to remain at their own homes, are serviced in community centers. They serve the needs of all economic groups concerned with family problems. Middle-class families are expected to pay service fees. Despite upward economic mobility, there still remain significant pockets of Jewish poverty in some of the larger cities.

Thus, there is a weaving together of the separate structures for Jewish services to Jewish families. Through the planning function of each city's Federation, the Jewish community treats the Jewish family as a whole, in sickness and in health, in youth and in age, as givers and as receivers rather than as separate parts.

There is a network of over 700 Jewish local welfare agencies (family, child care, aged), health agencies (hospitals and clinics), and community centers with most of these activities conducted in the larger centers of Jewish population.

Most contributions for these services come through Jewish Federations and Chests which operate as sources of central communal financing. Other sources of income affect and are affected by the level of these contributions.

Among family agencies, some of which are also child-care agencies, central communal funds (Jewish Federations and nonsectarian Chests) provide 75 percent of receipts; for child-care agencies, this figure drops to below 25 percent; for centers the figure is 37 percent, while but 10 percent is provided for homes for the aged.

There are four major patterns for division of financial responsibility for Jewish family agencies as between Federations and Chests:

1. *New York City:* The scope of the nonsectarian Community Chests (Greater New York Fund and United Hospital Fund) are relatively limited, compared with most other major cities. One of the results is that the Federation of Jewish Philanthropies of New York assumes a much higher financial burden for local Jewish services than occurs elsewhere. Thus, the FJPNY provides about two-thirds of receipts of its family agencies, whereas the Greater New York Fund provides less than 10 percent. In the case of child-care agencies, the FJPNY provides from 15 to 20 percent of receipts, whereas the Greater New York Fund provides 2 to 3 percent. (Public funds are a major source of receipts for child-care agencies but not for family-service agencies.)

2. *Lump-Sum Arrangements:* In about a half dozen major cities (including Chicago, Cleveland, Philadelphia, Newark, and Miami) the Community Chests provide a single amount for Federations for all local Jewish services. As a result, it is frequently not possible to determine how much of this lump sum is intended for specific services such as family-service agencies. However—taken as a group—the share of the large city Federation to Chest financing of all local Jewish services in these cities approximates that for large cities (outside New York City) where Chest grants are earmarked. Despite this approximation, there are variations in individual cities.

3. *Shared Financing:* There is shared financing between Federations and Chests in most of the cities outside New York, but there is a wide range in the relative shares of each of these sources of central communal financing. In cities with Jewish population of over 15,000, the Chest to Federation share of financing ranges from a ratio of 3 to 2 up to 10 to 1, with some cities receiving almost all of such central funds from Chests.

4. *Exclusive Financing:* In a small number of important instances, either Federations or Chests provide all central communal grants.

The impact of the philanthropic dollar in providing local Jewish services depends on the availability of other forms of financing. While most contributed dollars come from Federations or Chests, there are minor contributions from other sources. While these supplementary contributions represent less than 3 percent of receipts for family agencies outside New York City (9 percent in New York City), about 6 percent for aged care (2 percent in New York City), they amount to 25 percent for child care agencies (3 percent in New York City).

In essence, the Federation or Chest grant serves to make up a deficit or is earmarked for a specific program. The major share of income comes from payments for services: from individuals or families, from governmental agencies and from voluntary agencies.

Government plays a major role in financing child care and aged care services. It is minimal for family services. Child-care agencies in New York City receive two-thirds of their income from governmental grants, but only one-fifth outside New York City. Aged care facilities in New York City receive more than half their income from public agencies, while this proportion drops to below two-fifths outside New York City. In addition, Old Age Survivor Disability Insurance (OASDI) payments by residents account for a major portion of the payments made on their own behalf by clients.

Payments for service from beneficiaries is greatest for health services, for services to the aged, and for center services. These payments are a smaller but significant source of income for family and child-care agencies. They reflect partial "ability to pay" among those served as well as the extension of the scope of service beyond the most economically dependent families.

The variations in patterns of financing result from the

differences in development of central forms of planning and fund-raising, the relative affluence or lack of affluence of Jews particularly in larger centers, the availability of governmental funds for specific programs and the level of development of particular services.

The leverage provided by philanthropy makes possible a viable financial situation for many local agencies. Family, child-care and aged agencies, and centers had reported receipts of over $100 million annually with about $30 million derived from Jewish Federations and Chests.*

TABLE 1

Amounts Raised in Central Jewish Community Campaigns 1939–1968
(Estimates in Millions of Dollars)

| Year | Total[a] | New York City | | Total | Other Cities |
| | | NYUJA | FJPNY | | |
|---|---|---|---|---|---|
| 1939 | $ 28.4 | $ 6.6 | $ 6.0 | $ 12.6 | $ 15.8 |
| 1940 | 27.0 | 5.2 | 6.1 | 11.3 | 15.7 |
| 1941 | 28.2 | 5.0 | 6.4 | 11.4 | 16.8 |
| 1942 | 29.3 | 4.7 | 7.1 | 11.8 | 17.5 |
| 1943 | 35.0 | 7.0 | 6.6 | 13.6 | 21.4 |
| 1944 | 47.0 | 9.2 | 9.7 | 18.9 | 28.1 |
| 1945 | 57.3 | 12.6 | 9.8 | 22.4 | 34.9 |
| 1946 | 131.7 | 32.8 | 11.8 | 44.6 | 87.1 |
| 1947 | 157.8 | 38.2 | 13.2 | 51.4 | 106.4 |
| 1948 | 205.0 | 56.2 | 13.2 | 69.4 | 135.6 |
| 1949 | 161.0 | 41.9 | 12.1 | 54.0 | 107.0 |
| 1950 | 142.1 | 36.1 | 13.5 | 50.1 | 92.0 |
| 1951 | 136.0 | 34.6 | 13.6 | 48.2 | 87.8 |

* In addition, hospitals with receipts of over $330 million received about $13 million from Federations and Chests and Jewish schools with income of $70 million received $6.5 million from Federations.

a Total pledges exclude amounts raised annually in smaller cities having no Welfare Funds but include substantial multiple-city gifts which are duplications as between New York City and the remainder of the country. Estimates for some prior years were adjusted by NYUJA in 1967 to secure greater year-to-year comparability. Excludes capital fund campaigns of the Federation of Jewish Philanthropies of New York: $3 million in 1943, $13.5 million in 1945 and $16.5 million in 1949, and about $181 million in 1961—68 including government grants, other non-campaign income and endowment funds of beneficiary agencies. Also excludes most endowment funds and major capital fund-raising by Federations for local agencies outside New York City.

| | | | | | |
|---|---|---|---|---|---|
| 1952 | | 121.1 | 29.7 | 13.3 | 43.0 | 78.1 |
| 1953 | | 117.2 | 28.2 | 13.5 | 41.7 | 75.5 |
| 1954 | | 109.3 | 25.7 | 14.0 | 39.7 | 69.6 |
| 1955 | | 110.6 | 25.7 | 15.3 | 41.0 | 69.6 |
| 1956 | | 131.3 | 33.1 | 15.6 | 48.7 | 82.6 |
| 1957 | | 139.0 | 33.9 | 15.2 | 49.1 | 89.9 |
| 1958 | | 124.1 | 28.8 | 16.9 | 45.7 | 78.4 |
| 1959 | | 130.7 | 30.0 | 17.2 | 47.2 | 83.5 |
| 1960 | | 127.5 | 28.7 | 17.5 | 46.2 | 81.3 |
| 1961 | | 126.0 | 28.4 | 17.7 | 46.1 | 79.9 |
| 1962 | | 129.4 | 27.9 | 17.3 | 45.2 | 84.2 |
| 1963 | | 124.7 | 26.2 | 17.6 | 43.8 | 80.9 |
| 1964 | | 126.7 | 25.6 | 18.7 | 44.3 | 82.4 |
| 1965 | | 132.6 | 26.9 | 19.4 | 46.3 | 86.3 |
| 1966 | | 137.3 | 27.0 | 19.8 | 46.8 | 90.5 |
| 1967 | Regular | 145.7 | 29.2 | 22.0 | 51.2 | 94.5 |
| | Emergency* | 175.0 | 48.0 | — | 48.0 | 127.0 |
| 1968 | Regular | 153.3 | 30.1 | 22.5 | 52.6 | 100.7 |
| | Emergency* | 85.0 | 21.0 | — | 21.0 | 64.0 |
| TOTAL: | | | | | | |
| 1939–1968 | | $3,632.3 | $844.7 | $422.6 | $1,267.3 | $2,365.0 |

TABLE 2

Estimated Annual Level of Income and Costs in 1967
of Jewish Communal Services in U.S.

| | |
|---|---|
| A. Welfare Fund Contributions (*Excluding* Local Capital Funds) | 320.7 Million |
| B. Grants by United Funds and Community Chests | 21.0 |
| C. Other Contributions to National and Overseas Agencies (*Including* Capital Funds) | 95.8 |
| D. Other Income of National and Overseas Agencies | 90.3 |
| E. Hospital Income (Excluding A & B) | 448.0 |
| F. Family Service Income (Excluding A & B) | 3.6 |
| G. Child Care Income (Excluding A & B) | 13.2 |
| H. Jewish Vocational Service (Excluding A & B) | 5.2 |
| I. Aged Care Income (Excluding A & B) | 51.1 |
| J. Center Income (Excluding A & B) | 23.1 |
| K. Jewish Education Income (Excluding A) | 68.0 |

* Provisional Estimates. Excludes Israel Education Fund of the UJA with pledges of about $25.3 million in 1965–68. Total for both regular and IEF campaigns in 1967 was $324 million and $238 million in 1968. Subject to some adjustment for inter-city duplications. Includes some allowances by UJA for subsequent shrinkage.

## TABLE 3

### Distribution to Beneficiaries of Funds Raised (Excluding Israel Emergency Fund*) by Jewish Federations(a)
#### (Estimates in Thousands of Dollars)

| | TOTAL | | NEW YORK CITY(b) | | OTHER CITIES | |
|---|---|---|---|---|---|---|
| | 1967 | 1966 | 1967 | 1966 | 1967 | 1966 |
| TOTAL AMOUNT BUDGETED TO BENEFICIARIES(c, d) | $115,859 | $111,618 | $35,630 | $34,037 | $80,229 | $77,581 |
| Per cent | 100.0 | 100.0 | 100.0 | 100.0 | 100.0 | 100.0 |
| Overseas agencies | 66,281 | 63,516 | 18,805 | 17,727 | 47,476 | 45,789 |
| Per cent | 57.2 | 56.9 | 52.8 | 52.1 | 59.2 | 59.0 |
| United Jewish Appeal | 63,273 | 60,582 | 18,375 | 17,300 | 44,898 | 43,282 |
| Per cent | 54.6 | 54.3 | 51.6 | 50.8 | 56.0 | 55.8 |
| Other Overseas | 3,008 | 2,934 | 430 | 427 | 2,578 | 2,507 |
| Per cent | 2.6 | 2.6 | 1.2 | 1.3 | 3.2 | 3.2 |
| National Agencies | 4,661 | 4,578 | 400 | 391 | 4,261 | 4,187 |
| Per cent | 4.0 | 4.1 | 1.1 | 1.1 | 5.3 | 5.4 |
| Community Relations | 2,528 | 2,479 | — | — | 2,528 | 2,479 |
| Per cent | 2.2 | 2.2 | — | — | 3.2 | 3.2 |
| Health and Welfare | 26 | 36 | — | — | 26 | 36 |
| Per cent | * | * | — | — | * | * |
| Cultural | 513 | 491 | — | — | 513 | 491 |
| Per cent | 0.4 | 0.4 | — | — | 0.6 | 0.6 |
| Religious | 265 | 277 | — | — | 265 | 277 |
| Per cent | 0.2 | 0.2 | — | — | 0.3 | 0.4 |

| | | | | | | |
|---|---|---|---|---|---|---|
| Service agencies | 1,329 | 1,294 | 400 | 391 | 929 | 903 |
| Per cent | 1.1 | 1.2 | 1.1 | 1.1 | 1.2 | 1.2 |
| Local operating needs | 42,655 | 41,216 | 16,425 | 15,919 | 26,230 | 25,297 |
| Per cent | 36.8 | 36.9 | 46.1 | 46.8 | 32.7 | 32.6 |
| Local refugee Care(e) | 701 | 875 | — | — | 701 | 875 |
| Per cent | 0.6 | 0.8 | — | — | 0.9 | 1.1 |
| Local Capital Needs | 1,557 | 1,425 | — | — | 1,557 | 1,425 |
| Per cent | 1.3 | 1.3 | — | — | 1.9 | 1.8 |

* For gross estimated collections see Table 1. Net amounts comparable to data in this table will be available after actual shrinkage and collections are determined by experience: By early 1969, about $170 million of the 1967 Israel Emergency Fund has been collected in relation to pledges of about $175 million.

a Based upon communities which are currently CJFWF members and some smaller cities which are not CJFWF members but which had been included in the base group of communities used in 1948 when this statistical series was started. Minor differences in amounts and percentages due to rounding. Community Chest support excluded from this table but included in Tables 5,6.

b Figures for New York include the United Jewish Appeal UJA of Greater New York and Federation of Jewish Philanthropies. Local refugee costs in New York City are borne by NYANA, a direct beneficiary of the UJA nationally. Most overseas and domestic agencies which are normally included in Welfare Funds in other cities conduct their own campaigns in New York. The New York UJA included the following beneficiaries (in addition to the National UJA): United Hias Service and National Jewish Welfare Board (JWB). Data for New York UJA based on estimates of distribution of 1967 and 1966 campaign proceeds, regardless of year in which cash is received.

c The difference between this amount and "total raised" in Table 1 represents mainly "shrinkage" allowance for non-payment of pledges, campaign and administrative expenses, elimination of duplicating multiple-city gifts, and contingency or other reserves.

d includes small undistributed amounts in "total" and "other cities" columns.

e NYANA is included in UJA totals.

# Less than .05 of one per cent.

TABLE 3-A

Distribution to Fields of Service of Funds Raised (Exclusive of Israel Emergency Fund) by Jewish Federations[a]

| | TOTAL | | Under 5,000** | |
|---|---|---|---|---|
| | 1967 | 1966 | 1967 | 1966 |
| TOTAL AMOUNT BUDGETED* | $80,229,092 | $77,580,779 | $9,539,826 | $9,065,721 |
| Per Cent | 100.0 | 100.0 | 100.0 | 100.0 |
| Overseas Agencies | 47,476,169 | 45,789,015 | 7,331,545 | 6,957,354 |
| Per Cent | 59.2 | 59.0 | 76.8 | 76.7 |
| United Jewish Appeal | 44,897,892 | 43,282,083 | 7,009,112 | 6,657,784 |
| Per Cent | 56.0 | 55.8 | 73.5 | 73.4 |
| Other Overseas | 2,578,277 | 2,506,932 | 322,433 | 299,570 |
| Per Cent | 3.2 | 3.2 | 3.4 | 3.3 |
| National Agencies | 4,260,778 | 4,187,385 | 519,548 | 509,935 |
| Per Cent | 5.3 | 5.4 | 5.4 | 5.6 |
| Community Relations | 2,527,560 | 2,479,277 | 231,153 | 205,516 |
| Per Cent | 3.2 | 3.2 | 2.4 | 2.3 |
| Health and Welfare | 26,012 | 36,379 | 12,433 | 21,421 |
| Per Cent | # | # | 0.1 | 2.3 |
| Cultural | 513,043 | 491,049 | 63,834 | 59,12 |
| Per Cent | 0.6 | 0.6 | 0.7 | 0.7 |
| Religious | 265,496 | 277,297 | 127,769 | 136,02 |
| Per Cent | 0.3 | 0.4 | 1.3 | 1. |
| Service Agencies | 928,667 | 903,383 | 84,359 | 87,85 |
| Per Cent | 1.2 | 1.2 | 0.9 | 1. |
| Local Operating Needs | 26,230,150 | 25,296,890 | 1,519,630 | 1,442,73 |
| Per Cent | 32.7 | 32.6 | 15.9 | 15. |
| Local Refugee Care | 701,458 | 874,836 | — | 10 |
| Per Cent | 0.9 | 1.1 | — | |
| Local Capital Needs | 1,557,084 | 1,425,386 | 167,581 | 152,93 |
| Per Cent | 1.9 | 1.8 | 1.8 | 1. |

TABLE 3-A Continued

| 5,000–15,000** | | 15,000–40,000** | | 40,000 and Over** | |
|---|---|---|---|---|---|
| 1967 | 1966 | 1967 | 1966 | 1967 | 1966 |
| 2,101,433 | $11,570,129 | $11,738,697 | $11,238,883 | $46,849,136 | $45,706,046 |
| 100.0 | 100.0 | 100.0 | 100.0 | 100.0 | 100.0 |
| 7,800,930 | 7,522,247 | 7,549,712 | 7,201,811 | 24,793,982 | 24,107,603 |
| 64.5 | 65.0 | 64.3 | 64.1 | 52.9 | 52.7 |
| 7,403,574 | 7,131,721 | 6,995,976 | 6,670,569 | 23,489,230 | 22,822,009 |
| 61.2 | 61.6 | 59.6 | 59.4 | 50.1 | 49.9 |
| 397,356 | 390,526 | 553,736 | 531,242 | 1,304,752 | 1,285,594 |
| 3.3 | 3.4 | 4.7 | 4.7 | 2.8 | 2.8 |
| 694,839 | 714,213 | 722,810 | 694,787 | 2,323,581 | 2,268,450 |
| 5.8 | 6.2 | 6.2 | 6.2 | 5.0 | 5.0 |
| 371,617 | 384,951 | 451,030 | 434,290 | 1,473,760 | 1,454,520 |
| 3.1 | 3.3 | 3.8 | 3.9 | 3.1 | 3.2 |
| 7,321 | 7,418 | 3,258 | 4,540 | 3,000 | 3,000 |
| 0.1 | 0.1 | # | # | # | # |
| 70,364 | 69,264 | 294,065 | 283,815 | 84,780 | 78,850 |
| 0.6 | 0.6 | 0.6 | 0.6 | 0.7 | 0.7 |
| 103,252 | 103,769 | 4,950 | 6,300 | 29,525 | 31,200 |
| 0.9 | 0.9 | # | # | 0.3 | 0.3 |
| 142,285 | 148,811 | 547,806 | 520,815 | 154,217 | 145,907 |
| 1.2 | 1.3 | 1.2 | 1.1 | 1.3 | 1.3 |
| 3,099,178 | 2,875,065 | 18,640,018 | 18,225,791 | 2,971,324 | 2,753,301 |
| 25.6 | 24.8 | 39.8 | 39.9 | 25.3 | 24.5 |
| 63,875 | 74,395 | 543,818 | 584,102 | 93,765 | 216,239 |
| 0.5 | 0.6 | 1.2 | 1.3 | 0.8 | 1.9 |
| 440,705 | 379,638 | 547,737 | 520,100 | 401,061 | 372,710 |
| 3.6 | 3.3 | 1.2 | 1.1 | 3.4 | 3.3 |

Includes small undistributed amounts.
Jewish Population.
Less than .05 of one percent.
The difference between totals budgeted for beneficiaries and gross budgeted for all
purposes represents "shrinkage" allowance for non-payment of pledges, campaign and
administrative expenses and contingency on other reserves. The difference between what
community may budget for all purposes (its gross budget) and totals raised may
also reflect the extent that the budgeted amounts may include funds on hand from previous
campaigns (reserves, etc.). Minor differences in amounts and percentages due to rounding.

TABLE 4

Distribution of Federation Allocations* for Local Services
in 92 Communities, 1958, 1967
(Amounts in Thousands of Dollars)

|  | 1958 | | 1967 | | Index of Change 1958, 1967 1958=100% |
|---|---|---|---|---|---|
|  | Amount | Per Cent | Amount | Per Cent |  |
| Health | $ 7,064 | 23.5 | $ 7,151 | 16.9 | 101.2 |
| Family & child services | 6,704 | 22.3 | 9,950 | 23.5 | 148.4 |
| Centers, camps, youth services | 7,035 | 23.4 | 11,449 | 27.0 | 162.7 |
| Aged care | 2,203 | 7.3 | 3,481 | 8.2 | 158.0 |
| Employment & guidance | 1,007 | 3.4 | 1,526 | 3.6 | 151.5 |
| Jewish education | 3,535 | 11.8 | 6,125 | 14.4 | 173.3 |
| Refugee care | 836 | 2.8 | 573 | 1.4 | 68.5 |
| Community relations | 742 | 2.5 | 1,020 | 2.4 | 137.5 |
| Other | 499 | 1.7 | 578 | 1.4 | 115.8 |
| Chest to Fed. Local Admin.‡ | 409 | 1.4 | 543 | 1.3 | 132.8 |
| TOTAL** | $30,033 | 100.0 | $42,396 | 100.0 | 141.2 |
| Sources of income |  |  |  |  |  |
| Federations | $17,514 | 58.3 | $25,010 | 59.0 | 142.8 |
| Chests | 12,519 | 41.7 | 17,386 | 41.0 | 138.9 |

---

* Includes both Federation and Community Chest Funds; excludes New York City.
** Slight difference due to rounding.
‡ Administrative costs of Federations are not segregated between local and nonlocal programs.

## 19

# SOME SPECULATIONS ON THE EMOTIONAL RESOURCES OF THE JEWISH FAMILY

## Louis Birner

Any psychological study of the Jewish family must suffer the limitation of being speculative. One cannot make any hard or fast definition of the term "Jewish family." It is both self-explanatory and a mystery. The Jewish family of today is not the family of yesterday, in one and many ways. History frequently alters the Jew's perception of self and family. Clay can be molded into many forms but clay remains clay. Though the children of Israel can differ greatly in language, custom, and even in certain religious practices there is a uniqueness in their family structure that merits exploration and consideration. The special problems and strengths of being an individual in the Jewish family structure is the focus of this chapter.

The first sociocultural disappointment that a Jewish child faces is that he is a member of a minority group. Later on this disappointment can be enlarged through discrimination and historical knowledge. The past history of the Hebrews is both glorious and horrible. With an awareness of this history a sense of closeness with one's own can be and is an emotionally protective and reassuring feeling. This form of closeness has been traditionally forced on the Jews and has given to the Jew a sense of reassurance. Even in a foreign land a knowledge of Yiddish means the right to claim a friend. Within the family then there is a knowledge of a world that can turn cruel and the consequent yearning for and the receiving of certain emotional reassurances. The pattern of yearning for an emotional reassurance in the face of outside rejection is not unique or specific to the Jewish family. But the Jews deal with the problem of their rejection from the outer world in singular and specific ways. These modes of self-protection and regulation were an important part of the culture and family pattern. Hence the family structure itself is protective of the individual and also very demanding on the individual.

Perhaps the best classical sketch of the Jewish family lies in the *Halachah*, or the Jewish legal system. Two features of this law are essential in understanding the family: 1) It regulates the individual; and 2) it regulates the family.

*Halachah* is a stimulus for inner feeling and thought and generates a sense of responsibility for self and others. Above all, the law welcomes study, questions, debate and argument. With this type of background the intellectual probing of the most humble *shtetl* peasant can shine with brilliance. A person in the classical Jewish family received a special type of stimulation. He must know his law and he must look to himself and others for answers. In the old Jewish family one had a preordained training in dialectic and inward probing. According to the Bible the Jews argued with God. The law, the inner search and the apartness of the Jewish family from the community of Christians served to define the Hebrew social structure as a quasi-historical unit—to paraphrase Sartre.

Along with *Halachah* comes a sense of role and identity. Roles are defined, sexuality is accepted as an expression of closeness and not of guilt. Children are to be cared for not only by the family but by the community as well. The law even provides a system of charity whereby the general community can take care of the individual in case of bereavement or calamity. One cared for one's own and one was cared for by the community.

Another feature of the classical family is that of Jewish humor. Laughter is good even if it is at the expense of one's self or group. There is no compunction about criticizing self or others in humor. Jewish wit probes, reveals truth and shows the inner resources and the outer awareness of life. Wit and humor are almost universally shared phenomena among all Jews. This may help explain why so many great comics have been Jews.

Within the classical family there is a love of law and study. Learning is exalted. A daughter marrying a man of learning represents a great blessing for the family. Knowledge was and is the highest order of Hebrew heraldry.

Not only are the family law and morals reality-centered, they are also instinct-centered and the Hebraic concept of instinct foreshadows Freud in the concepts of *yetzer ha-ra* (evil impulses) and *yetzer tov* (good impulses.) It is and was accepted that all men had to battle with impulses. A primitive sketch of Freud's concept of Eros and Thanatos can be found in the Midrash. The rabbis on some level knew that the child was born with instinctual conflict and made penetrating insights into the nature of human conflict. Sex was seen as good. In the eyes of God the rabbis contended that a man was diminished if he remained celibate. Closeness, marriage, children, awareness, study, work, argument, and love of God were the sublimators of the instincts of the classical Jewish family.

Parental roles were defined and structured. The mother loved and played with the son. The father taught him the Torah and was concerned with the son's learning. Thus there seemed to be in the early childhood an attachment by the mother and a disengagement of the father. The child later made a rapprochement with the father through skill and learning. If the child felt guilt for all the affection of the mother during the father's absence (which was often in the *shtetl*) or for the father's aloofness he could redeem himself through excellence, for not only did the father discipline his conduct, the father taught his son the law. The father was an authority.

The case of the daughter represented a profound attachment to the mother in her family. She served in assisting the mother in her work and providing herself with the training that one day would make her a wife and mother. The mother's role was respected.

The religion, custom, folklore, humor, myth—in short, all the mainstreams of Jewish life have been and are today fertile grounds for psychoanalytic research and exploration. No single paper or book can deal fully with the forces that bind today's family structure to its past. Some generalizations about the classical family culture can be made. Jews could develop an intimate tribal feeling for one another. ("There is a mystic tie that joins the children of a martyred race.") They even symbolized their tie through the rite of circumcision. They developed a singular capacity for the expression of emotion in humor, wit, dialogue, and religion. They could develop a sense of continuous historical identity and inner reassurance. When the ghetto broke down the delicate balance of isolation and religious and cultural inspiration, there was a threat to the Jewish family structure.

If we consider some of the dynamics of the classical family it is easy to see that certain problems were created through its structure. The father was aloof or away. The mother would be intensely involved with the son and daughter. The Jewish mother then becomes a powerful force through her intensity. The father becomes a powerful force through his role and absence. To look at the problem in terms of the formulation of an Oedipus complex, one can see that for the son the guilt is directed toward the father. The guilt is usually assuaged through following the father's law and learning. The high value placed on learning tended to make the acquisition of knowledge ego syntonic. It lessened the son's guilt and gave him a sense of power. Every culture creates conflict, but in the classical family roads were open which reduced these conflicts. The old Jewish culture provided emotional releases and reassurances. Conflicts could be handled through assuming a role. The importance of role in mental health is first being understood today. With role comes a sense of certainty. Whatever degree of conflict the ego faces it can gather strength by having the certainty of something to do and following a particular direction. Role can enhance the sense of self-worth and give purpose to life.

The daughter was trained to help the mother and serve the family. For the daughter, then, marriage was a chance for identification with the mother and the right to continue her role as a woman. The classic family pattern of acculturation tended to develop a deep sense of intensity in the child. In the absence of the father, the mother displaced much of her love on the children. When this intensity is sublimated in the direction of learning and creativity we have a person of powerful motivation ready to become intensively involved in his study, work, art, etc. The feeling of guilt can help to direct this intensity. A man is judged by others and himself, and through his own work he may redeem himself. However, no one has the right to be self-satisfied, so a man must try all the harder. It is probably this intrinsic motivation which serves to light the minds of many of our scholars and artists.

The Jewish family of today no longer lives in isolation. Jewish familial patterns have been influenced by Christian society and national ethic. Language, education, and social mores have changed somewhat. However, certain of the Jewish classical family patterns remain.

A general sketch has been made of the Jewish family

in today's world in the sociological-psychological literature, in the novel, and in plays. The general outline of the
family has many similarities to the classical family.
Briefly, a picture is drawn of an overly intense mother
and a passive father. The son receives special emphasis.
He must be something. The mother is overly worried.
She is the guilt producer. The daughter, of course, should
marry a good Jewish boy and give the parents grandchildren. The son in today's world should be a doctor and/or
make money. The daughter should marry someone who
is a doctor or who has status. A modern-day joke can
illustrate this point. A headwaiter was seating Dr. Goldberg in a Jewish resort hotel. There were several women
at the table. "Ladies," he said, "this is Dr. Goldberg.
Don't bother to get up. He's only a dentist."

The extreme form of this achievement stereotype creates in the child emotional problems. In the Jewish family
of old these problems were stimulated, but a psychological
form of sublimation was presented in terms of the culture.
A Jew always had a role and a mode of expression. There
was never an identity or status crisis. If problems could
not be solved they could at least be argued. The Jew had
a sense of free will and destiny. His role was defined.

A recent popular book, *How to Be a Jewish Mother,*
presented a sketch of a modern-day monster-like woman.
She is intensely dominating, gives her son the highest
standards but makes him feel rather inadequate. She over-
feeds, she overworries, she pleads, she binds, ensnares
and terrifies her son. She is a guilt producer. In the extreme, this form of child-rearing is pathological. Yet
many Jews who have had a degree of this form of mothering tend to do rather well in the world. Clearly, on a
statistical basis the Jewish mother can raise her head high.
Generally, her children do amount to something. Per
capita, there are more Jews who go to high school and
college than Christians. Per capita, there are more Jews

in *Who's Who* than any other ethnic group. Jews frequently win the Nobel Prize. Areas of art, literature and science are often dominated by Jews. The art and science of probing the unconscious was discovered by a Jew—Freud, and his followers were mostly Jews. Since intelligence appears to be normally distributed genetically among ethnic groups, there must be other factors operating in the pattern of maternal upbringing that have perhaps escaped observation.

One factor that is most clear about the Jewish mother is that of commitment. This mother cares, tries to give *the best* to the child. What this commitment entails can probably be seen in the form of intense stimulation of the child in the earlier years. The mother's intensity no doubt invokes reciprocal intensity in the child. This intensity is stimulated constantly and directed in terms of a superego pressure when the child grows older. He must learn to use his head. In today's family there is an agreement by parents. College is important, success is important. Although a family may give up its religion and much of its heritage, a certain psychosociological remnant of the past remains in terms of the intensity, caring and striving of the parents. One can make this assumption on the basis that the significant emotional ties of the past and childhood unconsciously endure and are repeated in child-rearing. Many Jewish atheists carry more of the old tradition of their child-rearing practices than they realize.

The effect of the "Jewish mother" is that the child is overly stimulated and overly socialized. Much of his aggression can be neutralized and directed toward the area of achievement, or, to use the old expression, *naches*. The child must give pleasure to the mother. What may occur then in child-rearing is a type of emotional interaction that directs the child toward success and the dynamic force needed to achieve significant things.

The period of being a baby, an infant, and a young

child is especially important in the life of the Jew. Early childhood represents a freedom from anti-Semitism. The child's parents have a chance to relive through the child much of their own narcissism, as all parents do. Wordsworth said, "The child is father to the man." In Yiddish the child, especially the young, is called "little mother" or "little father." There is no doubt that the memory and reality of anti-Semitism puts an added budren on the parent of the Jewish child. The child is often worshipped and sacrificed for; pushed, yet held back; praised, yet severely criticized. Minority-group parents who have suffered persecution often have anxiety and guilt about bringing a child into this world. They want him to grow up and survive yet are afraid to have the child leave the home; they do not want him to be independent. Being persecuted, as most Jews have been, in one form or another, creates a significant degree of ambivalence about the self. One can feel inadequate and superior at the same time. The baby, then, can be like a Rorschach card on which the natural loving instincts are fused with a blending of masochism, overconcern, grandiosity, ritual repetition, and a deep intensity.

The maternally overstimulated child can generate a degree of emotional richness from his mothering. Developmental phases can become hallowed and harrowing history. The more time and emotion the mother puts into the child's rearing the greater the feelings of developmental conflict and satisfaction. Examples can clearly be seen in terms of the problems of eating. The first stage of human development and conflict is the oral stage. The mother who stuffs the child and takes great delight in this form of feeding can set a pattern of expectancy in a child. The ability to over-incorporate may later be used in endeavors of business, scholarship, and personal enlargement, e.g., "I have got to have it," or "I have got to know it," or "You must give it to me." These attitudes toward life can be stimulated in the cradle. The same parallel can be made to the anal phase of development. The overconcerned mother who feels that the child does not defecate enough, who uses laxatives and enemas to excess, can create a situation where the child is geared toward production. There are many possibilities that come from overstimulation on the part of the parents. Conversely, it is known that the understimulated child suffers in the area of intellectual and emotional functioning. Recent studies with deprived children whose mothers leave them most of the day to work indicate that they suffer from being understimulated. This understimulation or lack of maternal concern often leads to delinquency and intellectual underproductivity.

The first five years, then, can become a dramatic experience that sharpens the unconscious experience and serves as an emotional generator for intense involvement with life, self, and the unconscious.

The Jewish mother is verbal. She is often a guilt producer. However, she provides a way of expiation, such as, "You have got to be something." Therefore if the child becomes something he is forgiven. This form of guilt matched with this form of intensity can produce a child who becomes something or is ready to die trying.

The role of the father in this type of child-rearing is one which backs up the pattern of this form of maternal upbringing. The father, like the mother, lives under the *shanda* philosophy. There are things he *must* do. He must provide and care. He must work and teach his children. The greater the frustration the father feels about his being Jewish in a Christian world the more intensely he may react to his children. There is no doubt that he has anxiety about his son's potency. A successful son or daughter helps prove his masculinity, which has often been threatened by life.

The role of today's father is vital in that he works for

and cares for the children. However passive he may be, he seems to share the high standards with the mother and serves as a model of consistency. A sketch can be made of a style of marriage which leads the children to a sense of driving and striving in the directions of accomplishment. In the extreme, we have the Jewish family pattern that can lead to overproductivity and sometimes breakdowns.

A book that is illustrative of the form of driving can be found in Budd Schulberg's *What Makes Sammy Run?* Sammy has to succeed and yet he can never succeed enough. Many a Jewish college student is driven to despair because he lacks the particular skills to become a doctor. This is especially true if the family wants him to be a doctor.

*Portnoy's Complaint,* by Philip Roth, a bestseller, literally crucifies the Jewish mother. Portnoy eloquently describes the old maternal stereotype. He tells his analyst, Dr. Spielvogel, "I am the son of a Jewish joke. Only it ain't no joke. Please, who crippled us like this? Who made us so morbid and weak?" He goes on to explain about his sexual guilt, masturbatory guilt, castration anxiety, and the dread of retribution.

Portnoy is no doubt a masochist and a deceptive one at that. In many ways, although he will deny it, he is a successful and heroic person. Portnoy has made it as a professional. He is attacking life and seeking out adventure and engaging in self-struggle. He will make a good patient and stands a chance of resolving his problems. The book ends with the saddening fact that if he cannot sexually make it with a Jewish girl in the state of Israel he will not achieve mental health. However, he can at least begin to see his problem. Portnoy has probed and yelled and screamed, and for it all has at least found the beginnings of an answer. The author, Philip Roth, likes being Jewish and feels that he is enriched by the predicament of being a Jew. Although he does not state it directly, clearly his mother did a good job. Her son amounted to something. Let us not forget the father; he too can share in the glory.

No ethnic group in our time has the golden passport to the good, free-and-easy sexual life. Portnoy's sexual problems can be found in every religion and race. You do not have to be Jewish to feel a sense of impotence. Yet the author does something classically Jewish with his complaint—he makes sorrow and neurosis a form of poetry.

When the parental pressure is too severe and/or too inconsistent, a breakdown in the child can occur in many forms; underproductivity, dropoutism, a compulsive yet unfulfilling driving and complete rebellion. In certain instances this pressure drives the child toward a psychotic level of adjustment.

A common complaint today among counselors in college is that many students do not belong in an institution of learning. Yet these students feel guilt about leaving college. They are pushed to go, often, when it is beyond their intellectual and emotional abilities. Consequently, a son with an average IQ who cannot be the doctor can rebel in a number of ways and may even become one of the ever-increasing number of college suicides. It is also quite noteworthy that many of the rebels among the college left are Jewish.

When the parents generate intense concern and make strong demands on the child, productivity assumes a major role in the child's life. Where there is the unhappy combination of great demands, "Be smart," etc., and profound inhibitions, "Don't do it. You will be punished. You never do anything right, etc.," ego satisfactions that are to be derived from work and social interaction are short-circuited into severe super-ego pressures which inhibit the child. The child is at once applying the brake and putting his foot on the gas. He can go nowhere being pushed by parental ambition and locked in a parental restriction. However, where there is an avenue for approved success or even a vague promise of approval there is the promise of assuaging guilt and claiming again the deep involvements and pleasures of an overstimulated childhood. A certain Jewish doctor will work twenty hours a day and be delighted with his work. Within his memory is the image of a mother who would spend hours with him helping him learn about medicine before he was in kindergarten. The emotional drive of childhood kindled by the demands of his mother push him on in his work. (His father is an outstanding medical man.) Had he lacked intelligence or inclination, the same family pattern could have wrecked him.

Perhaps the most neglected person on the Jewish scene today is the daughter. Most often, father is seen as some type of patriarch and authority. Mother is well known. The son, of course, has a special focus. The daughter, however, may be and is often slighted.

In the very Orthodox families she is still prepared for marriage and her marriage is often still arranged by a broker. However, in the modern-day family she may suffer second-class citizenship. Where the son is worshipped by the parents, especially the mother, the daughter may feel an intense sense of inadequacy. The son's "being something" may overshadow the daughter's value. In short, being a male can be seen as the highest glory and being a female as a lower status. Where the daughter is robbed of maternal caring and concern she may not achieve that sense of self-satisfaction that comes with the feminine role.

A young Jewish woman came for treatment because of a severe depression. Her mother was pushing her brother through medical school. Her only desire for her daughter was marriage. The daughter had musical talent and wanted to pursue a career in that field. The family refused to give the daughter the money for her career and urged her to become a school teacher until she found a man to marry. This patient's feminine role was devalued by the mother.

In a recent paper, a description of this type of woman was drawn. She came from a background where the son was exalted and the daughter was undervalued. Two major characteristics were noted: 1) a profound need to be socially and intellectually adequate; 2) a profound fear of closeness.

In extreme form, the Jewish mother-father syndrome of today's world is pathological. The checks and balances of the old culture are absent. The pressures of Americanization can be disastrous. Success and social mobility may push the family and the individual beyond the limits of self-actualization to self-automation, and overregulation. It is noteworthy that the classical love of God provides for rest, meditation, and recreation. These values may be lost for many Jews today.

Recently there has been an awakened psychological interest in mothering as it relates to creativity and genius. Matthew Besdine, in a number of articles, has pointed out that the overly intense relationship can create the driving heroic forces necessary for great feats of work and creativity. Clearly, the Jewish mother drives her child and stimulates him. Perhaps behind many of the Jewish greats is the driving mother who demanded and the father who served as a model of work and consistency.

It is an anthropological fact that intense mothering does not necessarily stimulate intellectual achievement. We may speculate that for our achievement loving must be mixed with those values which push intensity into the direction of intellectual and creative accomplishment.

No family constellation in today's society is a perfect model for the burdens of maturing in a difficult world.

The Jewish family has found its particular solutions and is still waging many of the psychic battles that have hounded it throughout time. Perhaps to live in impossible situations the family and the community itself have to develop almost impossible achievements. This need to achieve may be a bond that joins the Jew with his past.

## 20

# THE JEWISH AGED: TRADITIONS AND TRENDS

## Sarah Lederman

Ever since Joseph sent his brothers back to bring their father out to Egypt, the Jews have cherished their elders and made them part of each migration. There is little evidence, however, as to whether early Jewish settlers of the American continent brought their parents with them. Certainly the crossing of the great, unknown Atlantic Ocean was a deterrent in this kind of family move. The earliest Jewish settlers seem to have been largely hardy, individualistic souls of Portuguese extraction. Thus they bore the Sephardic mores of the patriarchial family unit, one in which the elderly parent had a place of honor, a role in the kinship order. Consequently, those who grew elderly were cherished.

Tradition has set for the Jew the first communal activity; that of securing proper burial ground, a hallowed *beth-olam,* usually the concern of the elders. Thus it was in colonial America too. "From the first, wherever Jews were domiciled, plots were secured for burial purposes."[1] Old Jewish cemeteries are rich with headstones for elderly family members in the family plots. It might then be judged that these members lived within the family home.

The second large migration of Jews, those from Germany in the 1800's, especially 1840-50, were also hardy,

---

[1] Margolis and Marx, *History of the Jewish People,* Philadelphia, 1945, p. 605.

321

lone souls. These were the peddler barons who braved
their way westward. To them we owe the opening of a
continent, but family life was not really their best contribution. Only after settlement in the trader outposts, or by
setting up a local store, could these people fully meet
family obligations, grow old with dignity, and care for
those who shared their homes, and in doing so established
a community.

The first Jewish Home for the Aged as an institutional
setting was founded in St. Louis, Missouri, in 1855.[2]
Apparently it was to fill the need for lone German Jews
(for whom it was organized) and thus provide a haven in
a Jewish community toward which they could gravitate.
"By the middle of the nineteenth century, the pattern of
charitable effort as an expression of Jewish communal interest was becoming established. It was largely individual
and relatively unorganized, except as the synagogue itself constituted a force for a degree of amalgamation."[3]

The kinship loyalty common to these ambitious young
German settlers (1840-60) is well documented in the
recent best seller, *Our Crowd*. While the book describes
primarily the successful, many of whom would go home
for the *Brautshau*,[4] or bring their parents to the United
States, the less affluent could not enjoy these opportunities
but practiced the same family system wherever feasible
and in a more protective need for each other.

According to Dr. Jacob Lestschinsky, there were about
5,000 Jews in the United States in 1820 and some 100,000
German Jews entered during 1840-1870.[5] Such a popu-

---

[2] Morris Zelditch, "Trends in the Care of the Jewish Aged," in *Trends and Issues in Jewish Social Welfare in the United States, 1899–1958,* Philadelphia, 1966.
[3] *Ibid.,* "Historical Perspectives on Care of the Jewish Aged," address at National Conference of Jewish Communal Service, Atlantic City, N.J., May 24, 1955. Mimeo. reprint, CJFWF.
[4] *"Brautshau*—Bride Search." Cf. Stephen Birmingham's *Our Crowd,* N.Y.: Harper and Row, 1967, p. 45.
[5] Cf. Zelditch, "Historical Perspectives," p. 7.

lation begins to be a communal group wherein patterns can be established and new mores take over. Yet the consistent development of merchant-peddler plans (peddler with pack on back, later with horse and wagon) then trade outposts, and, finally, storekeeping, a variety of family businesses, left room for the parent, the older brothers, and even relatives to fill out work shifts and enter the "business." Many establishments took pride in the word "Sons" in the very name of the firm; there seems to be no question of close family living. In each part of the United States such evidence of storekeeping is seen. As people prospered, there apparently was still room for older persons to live with family members in enlarged households. "The oldest of the homes for the aged we now know, which clearly is on the record and continuous, is the Home for Aged and Infirm Hebrews in New York City, established in 1870 as a home for aged women only."[6]

"In 1870 the number of Jews in New York City was estimated at 80,000, or less than 9 percent of the city's population; as such they were no more than the object of casual curiosity."[7] This then would mean that for the Jewish family in New York City, the elderly unattached women, by 1870, had become a problem in the urban homes for the 9 percent largely German Jewish population of about 80,000. In a sense, New York City, with its layers of Jewry begins to pinpoint a problem: the need for care for elderly women, both the unmarried and the widowed, who were already outliving the men of the same generation.

"In the years between 1870 and 1905 more than a third of the Jews of Eastern Europe left their homes. Over 90 percent of these came to the United States and most of them settled in New York City.[8]

---

[6] Now known as Jewish Home and Hospital (present population, etc., will be treated later). Cf. Zelditch, "Historical Perspectives."
[7] Birmingham, p. 289.
[8] *Ibid.*, p. 290.

Beginning with 1880 enormous migrations of Jews from all Eastern European countries began to inundate the United States. Between 1870 and 1890, about 250,-000 arrived, followed by the tremendous wave between 1890 and 1925 when almost 2,200,000 East European Jews came to the United States. Only nine homes for the aged had been established before 1900 and eight more were built in the period from 1900-1909.[9]

Until new sections of New York City were developed at the turn of the century only country peddlers were to stray permanently beyond the familiar immigrant quarters. There was a compelling purpose to the pinched living. Virtually all immigrants saved to purchase steamship tickets for loved ones, and many mailed clothing and food parcels to dependent parents, wives, and children overseas. The power of home ties buoyed up the spirits of immigrants wedded to the sweatshop and peddler's pack; those precious pennies mounted to sums that would unite divided families. Among the early comers, women were relatively few, but the imbalance between the sexes soon was remedied. In 1890 an investigation by the Baron De Hirsch Society into the condition of 111,690 of an estimated 135,000 Jews on the lower East Side counted 60,313 children and 22,647 wage earners, with 28,730 unspecified, mostly women. Undoubtedly, the proportion of women and children in New York was far greater than it was elsewhere.[10]

"The great migration of Orthodox, Yiddish-speaking Jews from Eastern Europe after 1880 gave rise to homes for the aged where religious observances, including strict *kashruth*, were important."[11] In New York City such an Orthodox home was founded in 1897: the Home and

---

9 Zelditch, "Historical Perspectives," p. 9.
10 Moses Rischin, *The Promised City*, New York City: Corinth Books, 1964. Chapter on the Lower East Side, pp. 80-81.
11 Jacob G. Gold and Herbert Shore, "The New Look in Jewish Homes for the Aged." Reprinted from *Jewish Digest*, Feb. 1965, p. 18.

Hospital of the Daughters of Jacob (until this day able to provide for the strictly Orthodox, even to serving strictly *glatt kosher* food) was set up by a small group of determined women.

Sharing had become an American Jewish way of living. There was some part of it which related to the *shtetl* pattern of charity-giving at feasts and festivals, support of *halukkah* Jews in Israel, as well as the Zionist collections that marked every fermenting Jewish community in Eastern Europe. The long-time Biblical injunction of tithes and giving, developed after Maimonides taught his degrees of charity, portions to the poor on a personal basis, as well as the varied *kehillah* arrangements, were improved upon and enhanced by Jewish immigrants to America, who set up new systems of giving. American giving flourished under Aid Societies of every hue and conviction. For some families the urge to do for others took the form of giving shelter by boarding *landsleit,* someone else's children, or neighbors under stress. Jews who gained new skills in trades were welded together as they shared union actions, conflicts and strikes, lean months with meager benefits, and arrangements for loans and fraternal societies. Together, they envisioned more for themselves and their Jewish brethren by sharing the "gold" they did not really find in the "gold-paved" streets of the new land. The wages, when earned, were split many ways—a portion always found its way home, back to the countries of origin and the parents left behind. Sometimes it was easier to bring those older people and add them to a household so that another pair of hands or watchful eyes could be made productive at home. Thus, the elderly had a place in the already crowded homes of the earlier immigrants; they were needed and wanted.

Prior to the First World War, Jews came to the United States as individuals: parents sent for children, husbands for wives, siblings sent for each other and/or their parents. This person-by-person family exodus created the basic immigrant fabric typical of first generation family groups. Children born in this country or brought here while quite young, often recalled grandparents—newly arrived or living with them in three-generation homes—cherished, included, worked with, and supported by the family. Always the extended family consisted of active, visiting aunts and uncles, cousins, relatives by association, *schiffschvester* (shipboard-created relatives), *landsleit,* or distant relatives for whom a family pooled the hard-earned passage money and arranged for entry into the United States.

This family system was strengthened still further with the onset of World War I (1914-1918). For those already in America the war seemed to be happening not too far away, in their own backyards—not in distant lands! This was due perhaps to the influence of grandparents in the home who kept alive their homeland ties and maintained a continuity of survival, typical of the East European Jew.

By 1915 there were already about 1½ million Jews in New York City. The East European influx had serious impact on the established German-Jewish community comfortably ensconced in a variety of communities throughout the United States where their leadership was unchallenged. ". . . Americanized German Jews in New York [were presented] with the most pressing and painful problem they had ever faced, and a deep rift had developed between the Germans and the Russians, between uptown where the Germans lived, and the lower East Side."[12]

The Brooklyn Hebrew Home and Hospital (established 1907) had been organized by a group of community women for the Russian and Polish Jews who by then had settled in the Brownsville area of Brooklyn. This large

---

12 Birmingham, p. 290.

Orthodox home, like the earlier Home and Hospital of the Daughters of Jacob, was also in keeping with the tradition and mores of the East European immigrant. This seems to indicate that mothers and daughters, in accepting the role of caring for the elderly, were merely extending their homes and hearts to the aged who were lone and childless, or those too sick to be cared for in their children's homes. This was the community that cared. The woman, emancipated from her work and freed by her husband's mobility on the financial ladder, took her "doing" into the larger home for the elderly which she helped to create.

Some fourteen homes for the aged were thus established throughout the United States between 1910-1919,[13] indicating the urbanization of this mass immigration with the concomitant problems of family change, housing, and human needs. With the war patterns which changed family living, the place of the grandparent also shifted. Older Jews began to seek life outside their children's homes as a matter of choice. ". . . The nature of the family has changed, so that older persons are frequently unable to live with their children and grandchildren."[14] *Kashruth,* mobility and the different pace of life in the home affected the older person adversely.

Since the Jew is so clearly a resident of the large cities, Professor Urie Bronfenbrenner of Cornell put it succinctly that ". . . urbanization has reduced the extended family to a nuclear one with only two adults, and the functioning neighborhood—where it has not decayed into an urban or rural slum—has withered to a small circle of friends, most of them accessible only by motor car or telephone."[15]

---

[13] Zelditch, "Historical Perspectives," p. 9.
[14] W. Posner, "Problems of the Aging in a Changing Society." Address before the Queensboro Council for Social Welfare, October 19, 1950.
[15] U. Bronfenbrenner, "The Split-Level American Family," *Saturday Review* (October 7, 1967), p. 60.

In and among these pressures the Jewish family had to find a place for its elders, as sons and daughters with their families move in and out of two world wars, in and out of their social spheres, in and out of universities, in their consistent upward mobility. Parents, usually left behind, often preferred to live alone, independently—as family units of older people, the elder nuclear family! The widowed, who might have preferred to retreat to children—often far away—turned instead to a second marriage to re-establish a family unit, often in the familiar neighborhood.

But far more dramtic was the change in economy, the beginning of a system under social planning. The Social Security Act of 1935 proclaimed "liberty" for the person over 65. Its implementation by a variety of pension systems, retirement programs, etc., began to permit choice and some self-determination. The independence of the older person, who might even have to resort to Old Age Assistance supplementation to maintain himself, became a more recognizable phenomenon. With illness, children were half-expected to help, even if not asked, or urged to do so. Often the death of one parent compelled adult children to assume some degree of responsibility for the remaining parent. The benefits from 1935 to 1965 created an independent "senior citizens" community of attitude. Then the added changes of Medicare and Medicaid which began in 1965 furthered the movement to free adult children from the strangling responsibility of increased longevity, as well as to permit older persons greater freedom of choice in their way of life.

One of the by-products of the new legislation in behalf of older Americans has been the productive use of casework help to assist a family in fully understanding its rights and in determining the best use of existing resources. These developments grow more significant against the backdrop of a changing world, enabling legislation, social change, and economic responsibility. This was expressed in more personal terms by Eli Ginzberg, a manpower and human resources specialist: "There was a closer tie between my grandmother, who was a distinguished layman first in Kovno and later in Amsterdam, Holland, and a member of our family who lived in Jerusalem at the time of Hillel, than there is between my son and his grandfather. Two thousand years of capital, continuity, commitment, and relationship have been dissipated in less than eighty years."[16]

Homes for the aged were developed by immigrant groups, each in their own image for their own times. These accretions then mirror some of the developments in the care for the aged. However, institutions have a way of solidifying an epoch. Thus the Jewish Homes for the Aged tell us what our grandparents wanted rather than what our parents seek. The struggle to keep and maintain noble structures and community support calls for catering to the conservative and to the traditional rather than permitting innovation, too much creativity or newness.

In his 1955 address before the National Conference of Jewish Communal Service in Atlantic City, Morris Zelditch stated:

> The homes established by the German Jews were not acceptable to the newer immigrant group; they were not sufficiently kosher or religion-centered, nor did they provide a place in which the newer group could feel readily accepted among the old. Nor were the residents and leadership of the older homes quite ready to accept the newer immigrant group into these institutions. These were the communities of retirement, of older German Jews whose culture was of a higher grade to that of the newer group. Hence, there were established in most of the larger American communities special homes for the East European group; more Orthodox

---

[16] E. Ginzberg, "The Agenda Reconsidered," *Journal of Jewish Communal Service* (Spring, 1966), p. 282.

and designed for the admission of the Russian Jew and his fellow immigrants from Poland, Hungary, etc.[17]

But already there were cries in the wilderness which challenged *how* people are moved to care for their aging and whether even the institutions or rather the people who set them up, were truly serving the needs of the elderly. Dr. Maurice E. Linden, long a creative and thoughtful innovator for concerned work in behalf of the aged, spoke out:

> We neither revere nor crudely discard the aged. But our passive neglect of them has caused annihilation, just as surely as if our mode of action had been more direct. Witness youth who reject the protective caution of their elders as "conservatism and fuddy-duddyism." Is not the reactive suffering of the older group, thus hastily bypassed in the stream of life, murderous? Witness industry that arbitrarily regards age 65 as the end of usefulness. It is not the mandatory retirement thus achieved a ticket to nowhere? Witness the physician, yes, even the psychiatrist, the social worker, the counselor who, annoyed with problems difficult of solution, says, "Well, what do you expect of older people? They're rigid, unyielding, unmodifiable and cantankerous." Is not the resultant do-nothingness an invitation to indolence, stagnation and regression?[18]

More recently the dilemma of serving the elderly person whose place in the society of 1950-69, has been changing radically, was put rather succinctly by Dr. Norman Linzer:

> The emergence of the nuclear family, the lack of social and communal supports for the extended family, the role confusion that attends the aged whose primary functions are untenable, the loss of spouse and friends . . . these changes and others have created crisis situations for social, health and welfare agencies under Jewish communal auspices. Agencies and their professional

---

17 Zelditch. "Historical Perspectives," p. 9.
18 M. E. Linden, "Emotional Problems in Aging," *Jewish Social Service Quarterly* 31 (1954) :81.

staffs have been confronted with a growing population of mobile and chronically ill aged with a variety of needs.[19]

Thus the subtle changes, resulting from who people were and from where they came, were no longer as significant; the whole fabric of the life situation had changed. And the whole rather than its parts was affected.

When an attempt was made at a brief survey of Jewish Homes for the Aged (December, 1967) in New York City, eleven institutions cooperated. Three homes which usually operate in a strongly independent manner did not choose to give information nor did they welcome the person delegated to fill out the questionnaire or gather the information requested.

From the information gained it was clear that more than half of the New York City Homes for the Aged (six of the eleven surveyed) were founded in the first quarter of this century (1907-25). Two institutions, founded in the previous century (Jewish Home and Hospital, 1870; Hebrew Home and Hospital of the Daughters of Jacob, 1897) were already part of the Federation of Jewish Philanthropies. In fact, the six largest or most populous homes opened between 1870 and 1925. By 1968 five of these had become member agencies of the Federation family: Beth Abraham Hospital (for the chronically ill; 1946); Home and Hospital of the Daughters of Israel (1955); Home and Hospital of the Daughters of Jacob (1961); Brooklyn Hebrew Home and Hospital (January, 1968).

The hallmark of most of the responsible institutional settings has been the extension and pervasiveness of medical care coupled with additions to the physical plant, the "buildings." Somewhat less dramatic has been the sharpening up of standards for social service and other areas

19 N. Linzer, *The Jewish Family—Compendium for Social Workers in Jewish Agencies,* Federation of Jewish Philanthropies, New York City, 1968, p. 27.

of ancillary servicing as well as relatedness to actual and expressed needs in the community, e.g., dealing with the mentally impaired and making room for referrals and transfers from state hospitals.

The need for new approaches has been profoundly clear. In the 1960's homes for the aged and family agencies felt the need for a greater variety of beds for the elderly, 60 and older. There were many factors underlying these needs. Dr. Isadore Rossman, Medical Director of the Department of Home Care and Extended Services at Montefiore Hospital, put it thus:

> The steadily increasing need for nursing home beds for the elderly in the United States arises out of culture as well as medical changes. These include the rural-to-urban migration, smaller homes in which it is difficult to house three generations, and the partial abandonment of home and hearth by working wives. There also seems to be some weakening of the categorical imperative that one should not only honor his father and mother but also take care of them.[21]

The movement of the federal government into nursing home care via Medicare, operative since January 1, 1967, has revolutionized the concepts and the kinds of care with institutions set up by the Jewish community and by the proprietary sector. First and foremost is the sense of *right*—each elderly person has his rights by law and precedent. Secondly, as Jewish agencies participate in programs which make monies available outside the Jewish *kehillah* or voluntary contribution range, there is the need to comply with the inclusion of other population groups— a nonsectarian stance which will change the whole character of agencies, even those which have had a Jewish program and quality, unless the cultural difference is zealously guarded and meaningfully used.

20 Isadore Rossman, "Cultural Trends Increase Nursing Home Need," *Medical Tribune,* October 17, 1966.

Certainly the admixture now already begun may take some years to assess. But the setting up of laws which have diminished filial responsibility, because children truly could not carry the burdensome cost of care for the elderly who need any degree of extended medical or paramedical help, has accentuated the place of the older person outside the home of children. The care is more available *outside* the family home. Ancillary services are short and slow in coming.

Basic Jewish values are caught up in a cauldron of evolving medical patterns and facilities. There is a dearth of conviction and helpfulness on all levels. But this is the era of change and disequilibrium.

For the Jewish family, change is usually operative on a variety of levels: in the differences of thinking between parents and children as they affect cultural attitudes, means of expressing religious mores and practices and in the very ways for which parents seek to stay on in their own homes, in their old neighborhoods, and children seek to bring them nearer to their new locations either in a new community or in suburbia. In most cases the change is traumatic (with illness), leading to added problems in planning and finding the proper resource. Through some community developments groups have yielded some amelioration of problems, family agencies are making slight headway in service aspects, and homes for the aged are looking for added ways of helping the changing Jewish family.

## 21

# ASPECTS OF BEREAVEMENT IN THE CONTEMPORARY JEWISH FAMILY

### Bernard Kligfeld and George Krupp

With the stage set by advances in research and communications, basic and universal topics relating to family life have quite recently become prime objects of scientific investigation. Superficial probing has yielded to empirical study, as man's most intimate feelings regarding the death of a loved one are being scientifically investigated.

To the professional whose task is to help individuals and families in stress, this new knowledge can be most useful. For as family life educators and counselors well know, a well-integrated family in which the roles of members are clearly perceived and in which there is adaptability, tends to rally in time of stress and surmount its obstacle.

This paper concerns itself with the improvement of family life education and counseling techniques through the application of recent knowledge acquired from clinical observation and research.

One concensus that has emerged from current studies of bereavement and death is that the problems of coping with loss are universal, and that mourning can best be understood as a process of striving to adapt. In the bereavement crisis, the dynamically oriented psychologist detects self-defense mechanisms which operate to protect the ego; these are critically tested. Whether the response is adaptive or maladaptive significantly influences the future of the individual who sustained the loss.

One is trained to adequately cope with loss in the process of ego development through close interpersonal relationships in the family. This training has its inception from the beginning of a child's life, as his relationship to his mother involves him in the experience of "primary loss" (Abraham, 1924, Melanie Klein, 1934).[1]

The growing child experiences many losses in family life: temporary absences from the mother, withdrawal of the breast or bottle, loss of attention of the mother following the birth of a sibling, and the loss involved in the child's resolution of his oedipal feelings. The pattern of responses to these losses may include feelings of rage, hopelessness, impotence and worthlessness, as well as being the forerunner of guilt.

This loss reaction as shaped by subsequent experience appears to be evoked on the occasion of bereavement. The mourning process sets in, tending to move the bereaved into ultimate acceptance of the death by integration of this concept into his personality. New relationships are established with other persons in the environment which enable the individual to go on functioning despite the loss. The mourning process has been extensively described and discussed by Freud (1917), Lindemann (1944), Bowlby (1960, 1963) and Krupp and Kligfeld (1962).

In the study of the effects of bereavement, several basic and, in some ways, contradictory facts about present-day Western family life have great significance. First, there is a trend throughout the world toward greater freedom for the individual within the family (William J. Goode, n.d.).

[1] This term refers to the feelings of the infant when he is faced with the temporary absences of the mother. The meaning is determined by the relationship previously developed and established with the mother figure, mediated through the experience of warmth, oral satisfaction, and tactile sensations of being firmly and securely held for a sufficient time.

336 THE JEWISH FAMILY IN A CHANGING WORLD

In all areas of social living, the family has less control. Mass media provide behavioral sanctions which are sometimes inimical to family solidarity. Ease of mobility augments exposure to influences outside the family. Increased freedom for the individual loosens intrafamily ties and weakens the family institution as a source of comfort. However, our society increasingly emphasizes a long period of child-parent dependence,[2] and also the uniqueness and worth of the individual. As a result, intense, meaningful interpersonal relationships develop. People are thought of less and less as members of an amorphous mass in which any one person is of relatively little significance. This appreciation for individual uniqueness and worth, along with intensity of involvement and dependency, increases the sense of grief when loss occurs. Another factor making for increased difficulty in dealing with loss is the gradual change in family structure in many parts of the world, from the extended family to the nuclear family. The extended family may be defined as a system in which the ideal of society is that several generations should live under one roof. One of the strengths of such a family organization is maintenance of its identity and property, and its collective responsibility when one of its members dies.

In primitive societies with extended families, the trauma of death is not likely to be extremely disruptive. In such primitive families, the parent-child and husband-wife relationships are often extended to other relatives (for example, the replacement of the father by the mother's

---

2 As dependence upon another is increased, there is a consequent increase of ambivalence. We have found that the more ambivalent the relationship is to the deceased, the more difficult is the process of mourning. (Ambivalence is the core of anxiety and of neurosis, consisting of the alternation of positive and negative feelings. These feelings may be partly hidden from awareness, or only one polar feeling may be conscious. Whereas everyone is always more or less ambivalent in his object relations, the problem arises when, within the ambivalence, there is an excessive amount of hatred with guilt.)

brother among the Trobrianders, and the levirate, well-known from the ancient Hebrew family, and found by Murdock in 127 of his sample cultures). Our Western society provides no such compensation for the "thinning out" of interpersonal relations. This is not to say that strong emotional ties and intense relationships are absent in the extended family, but the ready availability of close substitute objects may render the pain of separation more bearable.

The immediate or conjugal family is a small nucleus, consisting only of parents and their children. The individual in such a family who suffers a loss is thrown more upon his own resources in the absence of the socially determined familial supports that are present in pre-literate societies, and other cultures with strong, emotionally binding traditions (Krupp and Kligfeld, 1962). Sussman (1959), denying the isolation of the nuclear family in our society, found a pattern of kin-related families who, though living at a distance from each other, rendered assistance in time of critical, or even long-term, illness. To the extent that such assistance is substantial and persistent, it mitigates the loss, much as in the extended family. We have found, however, in our experience, that the role of the deceased, especially if a parent, is very rarely taken up by relatives. The nuclear family must usually fend for itself socially and psychologically after an initial period of high involvement by relatives.

In addition to the change in family structure, a shift in the role of religion, especially with respect to family life, has an important effect on bereavement reactions. In our society, the influence of religiously set norms of behavior has progressively weakened. Our American culture has been judged to be basically secular. Conflicting theological systems, along with unrealistic ethical dogmatism, combined with liberal theology that cannot provide a forceful, unequivocal answer to many moral questions, are seen as basic fixtures of the religious scene in America (Genne & Genne, 1961, p. 32). Religion, indeed, has tended to become an instrument of family life rather than the regulator of it. Here and there, Roman priests dare to break the age-old church tradition of priestly celibacy. A diminution of sacramental functions is seen in the secular lectures, entertainment and social activities that take up much of the time spent by congregants in many houses of worship. The authority of religious sanctions has weakened and a corresponding curtailment within the family of the patterns of interpersonal relationships tends to occur in association with it.

In most societies, a whole complex of universally accepted ritual and rite surrounds familiar family events such as marriage, birth, divorce, illness, and death, establishing with great clarity how these life crises are to be met. These religious and civic rituals have the social function of establishing group norms and enhancing the feeling of comity and mutuality among the participants. Rituals of death and mourning serve to channel and legitimize the normal expression of grief and, at the same time, rally the emotional support of the bereaved by friends and relatives who participate. They also serve to publicize and formally establish new status and roles that are incident to the loss, and to help the participants to accept philosophically the relationship of this event to all of life and to the universe.

Thus the ceremonies of such societies as the Kota, Cocopa, and Hopi focus on reintegration of the bereaved into the religious and social system. There is a rallying of resources that prevents the kind of isolation and difficulties which occur in the bereaved in the American scene where ritual is less important (Krupp and Kligfeld, 1962). In *Shiva,* the seven days of mourning prescribed by Jewish tradition, the expression of grief is channeled into a socially approved form by means of overt, prescribed signs. The visits of friends and family provide repeated occasions for "leave-taking." The fact that the *Shiva* lasts for an extended period of days and that it is customary for visitors to repeat their visits enables the mourner to release the object gradually, firmly, and definitely (Kidorf, 1966). One of the most important components of *Shiva* is the services that are conducted in the home which serve not only to structure feeling, but more importantly as a reaffirmation of group solidarity with the mourners. The service says in effect: "While we do not forget the deceased, we turn our attention to each other who are alive—to the problems of living and to the future." Parts of the service tend to attract the attention of the participants with the answers to questions of meaning and purpose. To the extent that the urgency of these questions is assuaged, the participant is guarded against a feeling of such hopelessness and despair as would prevent him from turning to the pursuits of life. Jewish ritual connected with death and burial tends to emphasize the factuality of death: plain coffin, the shrouds, interment and the Orthodox custom of the family remaining to see the coffin lowered. The deprivation of usual daily comforts during the *Shiva* period helps to alleviate guilt feelings. The extended period of the recital of Kaddish for eleven months may psychologically serve as a defense against the possibility of being overwhelmed by effects, if time for "working through" has not been granted. The Kaddish itself, which according to rabbinic interpretation is an expansion of the words of Job "The Lord giveth and the Lord taketh away; blessed be the name of the Lord," is a formula of resignation and submission to the overwhelming nature of the universe in which we find ourself and indeed a proclamation of its majesty. To recite the Kaddish with this in mind serves, then, as a sublimation of the separation experience into an act which is part of the divine drama. The experience of loss is thus ennobled.

This process, as Kidorf suggests, may serve to absolve the mourner's implication in the death. "It was God, not the mourner who caused the demise; and He did so not because the mourner willed it but in the normal course of duties of God" (Kidorf, 1963). The extended period of Kaddish may also provide for the process of introjection of the lost object. "Apparently, for a normal person it is easier to loosen the ties with an introject than with an external object" (Fenichel, *Psychoanalytic Theory of Neuroses,* New York: W. W. Norton & Co., 1945, p. 393, quoted in Kidorf, 1963).

This Jewish ritual tends to become devalued as Jewish families move away from traditional observances.

In our society, each family tends to create its own rituals, picking and choosing from tradition, such as one does with purchases in a department store. The result, while it caters to the individual's esthetic taste, is robbed of some deep social significance and impact on the emotions. Lacking emotional impact, the power of ritual to console the bereaved individual and help him redefine his position in the family and the community is reduced.

It may be seen from the preceding discussion that the reactions of a bereaved individual in our society are influenced by the many conflicting forces at work in present-day family life. On the one hand, our conjugal family structure and the emphasis on individual importance foster intense emotional ties within the family which increases the pain caused by the death of a loved one. On the other hand, such factors as greater mobility, mass communications, and lessening of authority within the family tend to weaken family ties. Simultaneously, the decline in religious authority and the decreased use of ritual have robbed the bereaved of important supports in coping with his grief and reintegrating himself into society. In the face of all these conflicting influences, it is to be expected that many persons fail to adjust adequately to the stress of bereavement, and that their maladjustments cause further serious disruptions of family life.

At this time we shall consider several actual clinical cases of inadequate adjustment to bereavement which will demonstrate some of the dynamics involved. We shall comment on the implications for management and education. The first case illustrates how ambivalence obstructs the mourning process and how consequent unresolved mourning may interfere with family life even leading to divorce.

Mr. A., thirty-eight years old, came for counseling with what appeared to be a marital problem. His relationship with his wife had deteriorated; divorce was being contemplated.

In treatment, it was revealed that his father had been a dominating person with whom he frequently had been in conflict. The father had suffered from a respiratory ailment which caused him to wheeze audibly. The son, from time to time, would yell at his father to "shut up" when he heard the labored breathing at night.

While still in college, the young man had fallen in love with a girl whom he decided to marry. His father had forbidden the marriage, however, because one of the girl's parents was of a different religion.

Mr. A.'s father became very ill, and while the young man was traveling to his bedside, he wished his father would die. When he arrived home, the father was dead. He felt no particular reaction at that time, but at the cemetery, he broke down with severe crying.

Subsequently he devoted himself to his mother rather than to his girl friend. He apparently felt a strong obligation to take care of his mother. He told the girl that if they married, they would have to move in with his mother. She refused to marry him under the circumstances, and in a sense he felt relieved.

When he was twenty-eight, he married a thirty-two-year-old professional woman who was willing to move into the house with his mother. However, two years later, the wife persuaded the mother to move out. Two children were born; on the surface everything seemed all right. However, the wife complained that she was not taken care of, and that Mr. A. cared more for his mother than for her.

Some months before he came for counseling, the mother suffered a thrombosis which necessitated a leg amputation. Mr. A. insisted that his mother move back into his home. The relationship between Mr. A. and his wife rapidly deteriorated and finally the wife insisted on a divorce. At this point, Mr. A. came for help. His wife had agreed to stay with him provided he sought therapy.

In treatment, he recalled the experience of his father's death and began to acknowledge the unresolved bereavement and feelings of guilt connected with it. He also began to understand how these feelings caused him to devote himself excessively to caring for his mother and, at the same time, take his father's place. With his mother's recent illness, the old oedipal conflict was reactivated along with feelings that his wish was somehow responsible for his father's death. Fortunately, his wife's action in demanding a divorce had started him on the way to resolving his conflicts. When he became aware of his chronic unresolved bereavement and feelings of guilt, Mr. A. was able to develop a more mature relationship with his mother and move her out of his home, which was better for all concerned.

In this case, we have seen how in a marital problem a neurotic maladaptation to a significant loss is an important component of the total situation.

It has been established that ambivalence toward the deceased object tends to render the "work of mourning" increasingly difficult in proportion to the degree of ambivalence. Often, as in this case, guilt feelings with reference to the death are the summation of an unexpressed powerful hostility toward the object. It is too threatening to acknowledge hostility openly and the mourner converts it into depressions, guilt, and disturbed behavior. The guilt focuses attention back on the mourner himself so that he is rendered unable to contemplate the loss and openly acknowledge it. Unresolved bereavement can be a potent factor leading to a disruption of family life. Infantile incorporations or identifications in reaction to a loss usually prevent the normal resolution of bereavement; this in turn renders the development of a mature marital relationship almost impossible, as shown in the case of Mr. A.

The sufferer from incomplete mourning is unable to move on to new patterns of relationship and instead, employs various mechanisms to retain the lost object.

A consequent threat of new significant loss may reactivate infantile responses since the pattern of coping with the loss, once established, tends to repeat itself. As Paul and Grosser (1965) pointed out, in cases of incomplete mourning, "effects and attitudes toward the lost person have remained essentially unchanged and recent losses evoke similar patterns." They report that as families began to participate in "operational mourning certain typical phenomena appeared, including a temporary family disorganization similar to the personal disorganization which occurs "in the process of relinquishing a deeply entrenched defense mechanism." It is only after this phase has been evinced that further progress can be made toward acquiring "ability to bear and accept the affects attending termination of treatment."

Once there is awareness of bereavement, the background is permitted to emerge in a clean and clear way. The intellectual imparting of information in such a case is not nearly as important as the visceral recognition of emotions together with training in ways to handle them on a mature basis. A residue of unrecognized incomplete mourning may cause the loss of a parent to continuously disrupt the pattern of interrelationships that has been established in a family and which the various members had counted on as a source of security.

As long as half a century ago, Freud (1916) noted the factor of depression in mourning as an expression of suppressed anger. The psychic function of anger is to permit the continued involvement with and search for the lost object (Bowlby, 1962).

Let us consider an illustrative case, that of Mrs. B., a woman in her forties. She had been referred for treatment with her nine-year-old son by the school psychologist because of the boy's learning problem and disturbed behavior at home. Mrs. B. declared that she was very tense and moderately depressed, and that these feelings disturbed her relationship with her son. Mrs. B. reported that her father had died when she was a child, and when she was an adolescent her mother had remarried. The stepfather brought two children with him.

A year and a half ago, Mrs. B's mother died and she took it badly. She began to quarrel with her stepbrother and stepsister, thus alientating her stepfather as well. The overt focus of alienation was a trust fund left by the mother. The stepbrother and stepsister wanted the money to go either to the stepfather, or to the entire family. Mrs. B. was very angry because it seemed unjust to her. The money had come from her first father. There was a breakdown in family communication with the result that Mrs. B. felt she had now lost not only her mother but her stepfather, stepbrother, and stepsister as well. This was an important root of her depression.

In effect, then, Mrs. B. was still mourning her mother. Now she felt bereaved of the rest of the family as well. Under treatment (operational mourning), Mrs. B. was able to recognize intellectually and, more important, emotionally, some of these components of her depression. She gradually became less depressed and was able to be a better mother with improvement in her child's behavior at home and learning ability.

Thus, in the case of Mr. A., as he achieved operational mourning, he was able to go back to his wife. Mrs. B. came to forcefully recognize the various aspects of her depression and could become a better mother to her child now that she was less depressed. Both cases illustrate disturbance of family relationships by unresolved mourning.

When a loved one dies, the family functions of the deceased individual need to be redistributed among the other members of the family. One source of friction arises when the surviving members are unable or unwilling to take on the functions they fall heir to. On the other hand, in many cases an individual will attempt to cope with his loss by identifying with the deceased and taking over his functions. This serves two purposes. On the superficial level, "necessary" activity is resumed after the interruption by death. On the unconscious level, the individual is able to deny his loss by keeping the deceased alive through identification.

The following case illustrates a disruption of family process by an abnormal continuation of mourning in which a widow, through nonuseful identification, prevented herself and her children from replacing the lost husband and father.

Mrs. C. was widowed unexpectedly two years before she was seen in treatment. During her marriage, she had been quite helpless and dependent on her husband, leaving it to him to deal with extrafamilial matters. But after his sudden death, she found herself able to speak in a commanding tone to auto mechanics, gardeners, etc. To her surprise, she began to keep the checkbook balanced and bills paid, something she could never do before. All this is constructive.

At the same time, however, even many months after her husband's demise, she could not think of removing his clothes from the closet. And every day, at about the hour he used to come home, she would feel chest pains that mimicked those of his heart illness.

Her continuation of her bereavement and her identification with her late husband thus had a deleterious effect on Mrs. C.'s family life. For one thing, her protracted preoccupation with the deceased served to drain away time and energy that should have been directed toward effectively rearing her children.

This preoccupation makes it impossible to accept her loss and continues to prevent her from looking for another mate and thus re-establishing a more normal family situation, in spite of opportunities to remarry.

Another form of neurotic bereavement reaction which rabbi, counselor, and psychiatrist encounter is the fixation of the breaved individual at an immature level and his refusal to develop beyond the stage of maturation which he was when the loss occurred.

A loss may occur at a point in a child's life at which the psychosocial development is arrested because of the unbearable pain of the loss combined with the absence of the socializing influence of the deceased parent.

Let us now consider the case of Miss D., a thirty-two-year-old woman who was referred for consultation because of increasing fears, anxiety, depression and difficulty in leaving her home in order to go to work.

Miss D.'s father, a successful manufacturer, had died when she was fourteen. There had been a relatively good relationship between the girl and her father during the adolescent reactivation of the oedipal period, whereas with her mother there had been conflict. At the time of her father's death, she had been slim and pretty, but now she is heavy, with an infantile look and behavior (as of about thirteen or fourteen. She speaks in a whining, plaintive tone and is querulous. She has found it necessary to quit college and cannot keep a job. From time to time, her father's coronary symptoms seem to be repeated in her, with chest pains and difficulty in breathing.

Her father used to tell us that he wanted her to grow up to be a model and then he would give her a job. Now that he is dead, she cannot grow up. Her greatest pleasure is currently to go to the beauty parlor, which she says is the only place she is relaxed. In the beauty parlor, she is a model. She feels safe there. Her whole demeanor is to keep herself fixated at about a fourteen-year-old level. She says, "It seems as if my father had just died a few days ago." She writes poetry to "someone sitting above," and worships and idealizes this someone.

A somewhat similar reaction has been noted with respect to some concentration-camp victims. In court, seeking restitution, they present problems to their attorneys. They look very young and relatively unaffected by their harrowing experiences. Dr. Niederland (1965), who had made an extensive study of concentration-camp victims, felt they were identifying with a happier period of their lives, seemingly fixated at an earlier period of development. Educators and counselors need to be aware that fixation of this kind makes it difficult for an individual to learn, to mature, and to grow, emotionally and intellectually.

Unless the mourning is dealt with in such cases, the therapy cannot progress either. The patient is using up psychic energy to retain the fiction that the parent is still alive. The childlike attitude toward the therapist, the doctor, the teacher, exhibits this retention. The relationship to these figures is the same as the relationship to the parent when alive (Krupp, 1965).

A fairly common reaction to bereavement is anger, which may, however, be disguised in many ways. Mrs. E., a recent widow, was extremely angry about her single situation. She felt that in social relationships she no longer counted. Her pain was not so much because of the loss of her husband per se, as because, by dying, he had robbed her of protection, status, and social interaction.

Mrs. E.'s anger made her resentful of her married friends and was interfering with her relationship with her son. She had reported one occasion when she went to a concert with her son and his girl friend. When some friction arose between mother and son about a trivial matter, the girl asked, "By the way, has the will been probated yet?" Mrs. E. felt that the girl was actually saying, "You have lost your man, now let mine alone." Mrs. E. was angry and resentful. In the course of her therapy, Mrs. E. learned to face the fact of her anger and to understand it, so, it gradually diminished freeing her to get her own man and to remarry.

It is an important thing to be able to treat such cases of poor bereavement adjustments as have been described in this paper, but it is equally as important to consider how such maladjustments can be prevented in others. A number of considerations can be kept in mind for improved ways of preparing a person for loss and enabling him to cope with it when it occurs.

In this day and age, in our society, the average person has little first-hand experience with death. In an earlier time, it was a rare person who had not been present, at least once, at the death of a relative. Today, deaths usually occur in hospitals, and the bodies are immediately removed to funeral homes. In view of this, perhaps the time has come to stop protecting our children from the facts of death, and instead to expose them to it in small, controlled doses, so that they are not completely devastated when they first experience bereavement as adults.

One of the most interesting new ideas dealing with preparation for bereavement is the concept of early "immunization" to later life stresses, much as one is immunized against physical disease. Dr. Gilbert Klerman (1965), Director of the Center for Preventive Psychiatry, has suggested that exposing children to small doses of painful life experiences may aid in building a kind of immunity against later, more stressful experiences. Thus, adults in contact with children would bring into the open such small tragedies as the death of a household pet or a classroom turtle, and then later discuss larger tragedies such as the death of a grandparent. Discussing such occurrences, says Dr. Klerman, helps prevent the development of morbid fantasies and builds strength to face later losses.

A similar suggestion was made in a study by Marjorie McDonald (1965) of children's reactions to the death of a playmate's mother. She states, "In order to experience, tolerate and master his feelings, the child must be able, through identification, to experience the traumatic event 'on trial'—as though it had happened to himself. This 'trial' trauma is best felt in miniature dosage." She continues, "The child's personality structure gains in depth through the experience. This, of course, has considerable prophylactic implication."

The role of social institutions as an aid to social living must be recognized and valued so that they may function effectively. Religion, particularly, may supply a way of dealing with the stresses in the individual or in the family resulting from loss. The role of religion as prophylaxis in helping man deal more effectively with emotional stress may serve as a most important contemporary social function.

Ceremonies can be used to dramatize the position of the individual and the interest of the group in the event that is being marked. The ceremonies can be occasions when the group strength is mobilized not only to maintain itself, but primarily to support the individual and to make clear a new and important and legitimate status in the group. Ceremonies are particularly important when they express universal principles and manifest life's aspect of continuity as a counterforce to the fear of death, and as an aid to living in the wake of breavement.

In Judaism, the bereaved is required to recite a blessing over the bier of his dead, and to recite a doxology, the Kaddish, during the year of mourning. These practices force the mourner into affirmation in the presence of the congregation, and usher him into a rich system of remembrance. Perhaps what families need most of all to meet the stresses of contemporary society are values that are worthy of being held strongly and that can be affirmed even in the face of death.

From all this, it can be seen that the subject of bereavement must be considered fully by those who deal in any way with family life and its problems. No family escapes bereavement; sooner or later it comes to all. It is an important part of the function of those who are professionally involved in working with families, with the help of the enlarging body of information researchers are making available, to see that families are prepared to deal with bereavement and to maintain their cohesion and viability despite the inevitable occurrence of death.

# BIBLIOGRAPHIES FOR CHAPTERS
## 2, 4, 5, 8, 9, 11, 12, 14, 16, 20, 21

*Chapter 2*

Adoption

Andrews, Roberta G. "Casework Methodology with Adoptive Applicant Couples." *Child Welfare,* December, 1963.

Bernard, Viola W. "Adoption." *Encyclopedia of Mental Health,* 1963.

Billingsley, Andrew. "Black Children in White Families." *Social Work,* October, 1968.

Biskind, Sylvia E. "Helping Adoptive Families Meet the Issues in Adoption." *Child Welfare,* March, 1966.

Bradley, Trudy. "An Exploration of Caseworkers' Perceptions of Adoptive Applicants." *Child Welfare,* October, 1966.

Chevlin, Myron R. "Adoption Outlook." *Child Welfare,* February, 1967.

Child Welfare League of America. *Standards for Adoption Service,* Revised 1968. New York: Child Welfare League of America, 1968.

Fradkin, Helen, and Krugman, Dorothy. "A Program of Adoptive Placement for Infants Under Three Months." *American Journal of Orthopsychiatry,* July, 1956.

Hylton, Lydia F. "Trends in Adoption, 1958-1962." *Child Welfare,* July, 1965.

Jenkins, Alma C. "Some Evaluative Factors in the Selection of Adoptive Homes for Indian Children." *Child Welfare,* June, 1961.

Kirk, H. David. *Shared Fate: A Theory of Adoption and Mental Health.* Glencoe, Ill.: The Free Press, 1964.

Kreech, Florence. "Services to Adoptive Parents after Legal Adoption." *Child Welfare,* July, 1959.

————. "Supervision of the Child in the Adoptive Home." *Child Welfare,* March, 1955.

Maas, Henry S. "The Successful Adoptive Parent Applicant." *Social Work,* January, 1960.

Madison, Bernice Q. "Adoption: Yesterday, Today and Tomorrow." *Child Welfare,* May, 1966.

Marmor, Judd. "Psychodynamic Aspects of Transracial Adoptions." *Social Work Practice,* 1964.

Polier, Justine Wise. "Religion and Child-Care Services." *Social Service Review,* June, 1956.

Sandgrund, Gertrude. "Group Counseling with Adoptive Families After Legal Adoption." *Child Welfare,* June, 1962.

Schaechter, Marshall D. "Observations on Adopted Children." *A.M.A. Archives of General Psychiatry,* vol. 3, no. 7, July, 1960.

Smith, I. Evelyn (ed.). *Readings in Adoptions.* New York: Philosophical Library, 1963.

Smith, Rebecca. " 'For Every Child . . .': A Commentary on Developments in Child Welfare 1962-1967." *Developments in Child Welfare,* 1962-1967.

Toussieng, Povl. W. "Thoughts Regarding the Etiology of Psychological Difficulties in Adopted Children." *Child Welfare,* February, 1962.

Turitz, Zitha R. "A New Look at Adoption, Current Developments in the Philosophy and Practice of Adoption." New York: *Child Welfare League of America,* 1965.

Services to Unmarried Parents

Blatt, Marianne, Balmford, Edith F., Anderson, Portia

M., et al. "Brief and Intensive Casework with Unmarried Mothers." *Child Welfare*, 1963.

Bernard, Viola W. "Needs of Unmarried Parents and their Children as seen by a Psychiatrist." New York, 1948.

Chaskel, Ruth. "The Unmarried Mother: Is She Different?" Reprinted from *Child Welfare*, 1967.

Child Welfare League of America. *Standards for Services to Unmarried Parents*. New York: Child Welfare League of America, 1960.

Eisenberg, Dr. Morton. "Out of Wedlock Pregnancy—Aspects of the Mother-Child Separation Crisis." National Conference on Social Welfare, May 21, 1963.

Kinsel, Virginia Travis. "The Unmarried Mother Who Keeps her Baby." National Conference of Social Work, 1960.

Levitt, Esther G. "Repeated Out-of-Wedlock Pregnancies." Child Welfare League Eastern Regional Conference, February, 1959.

Leyendecker, Gertrude T., Evan, Sarah, Rindfleisch, Roberta. *Services to Unmarried Mothers*. New York, 1958.

Rall, Mary E. "Casework with Parents of Adolescent Unmarried Mothers and Potential Unmarried Mothers." New York, 1961.

Rowan, Pannor, Evans. "Casework with the Unmarried Father." *Child Welfare*, 1968.

Sauber, Mignon, and Paneth, Janice. "Experiences of the Unwed Mother as a Parent." New York: Community Council of Greater New York, 1965.

Vincent, Clark E. "Illegitimacy in the Next Decade: Trends and Implications." Reprinted from *Child Welfare*, 1964.

Wright, Helen R. "80 (Eighty) Unmarried Mothers who Kept their Babies." May, 1965.

Young, Leontine. *Out of Wedlock*. New York: McGraw-Hill, 1954.

*Chapter 4*

Alksne, H. *A Follow-Up Study of Treated Adolescent Narcotic Users*. New York: New York State Interdepartmental Health Resources Board, 1959.

Dai, B. *Opium Addiction in Chicago*. Shanghai: The Commercial Press, 1937.

Glaser, D., Director of Research, New York State Narcotic Control Commission, personal communication, 1969.

Jaffe, J. and Brill, L. "Cyclazocine, a long acting narcotic antagonist: Its voluntary acceptance as a treatment modality by narcotic abusers." *International Journal of Addictions* 1 (1966) :1, 99-123.

Jandy, E. C. and Floch, M. *Narcotic Addiction as a Factor in Petty Larceny in Detroit*. Detroit, Bureau of Governmental Research, Report no. 145, 1937.

Knight, R. C. and Prout, C. T. "A Study of Results in Hospital Treatment of Drug Addictions." *American Journal of Psychiatry* 108 (1951) :303-8.

Lambert, A. "Report of the Mayor's Committee on Drug Addiction to the Honorable R. C. Patterson, Jr., Commissioner of Correction, N.Y.C." *American Journal of Psychiatry* 10 (1930) :433-538.

Metzner, R. (ed.). *The Ecstatic Adventure*, New York: Macmillan, 1968.

O'Donnell, J. Addiction Research Center, U.S. Public Health Service, Lexington, Kentucky, personal communication, 1969.

Pescor, M. J. "A Statistical Analysis of the Clinical Records of Hospitalized Drug Addicts." *Public Health Reports*, Supplement no. 143, 1943.

Snyder, C. R. *Alcohol and the Jews*. Glencoe, Ill.: The

Free Press and Yale Center of Alcohol Studies, 1958.

Metzner, R. (ed.). *The Ecstatic Adventure,* New York: Macmillan, 1968.

## Chapter 5

Drapkin, Israel, and Landau, Simha. "Drug Offenders in Israel: A Survey." *British Journal of Criminology* 6:4, October, 1966.

Friedman, I., Peer, I. "Drug Addiction Among Pimps and Prostitutes, Israel 1967." *International Journal of the Addictions* 3, no. 2, 1968.

Horowitz, M. "A Survey of Procurers in Israel, 1961-63." *The Israel Annals of Psychiatry* 4, Autumn, 1966.

Rosenbloom, Joseph R. "Notes on Jewish Drug Addicts." *Psychological Reports* 5, Southern University Press, 1959.

## Chapter 8

Ackerman, Nathan W. *Treating the Troubled Family.* New York: Basic Books, 1966.

————. Beatman, Frances L., and Sherman, Sanford N. (eds.). *Exploring the Base For Family Therapy.* Family Service Association of America. N.Y., 1961.

Caplan, Gerald. *Prevention of Mental Disorders in Childhood.* New York: Basic Books, 1961.

Epstein, N. B., and Westley, W. A., "Parental Interaction as Related to the Emotional Health of Children." *Social Problems* 8 (1960).

"The Family as a Unit in Mental Health," in Proceedings of the Third World Congress of Psychiatry, Toronto, 1963.

Laing, R. D. and Esterson, A. *Sanity, Madness and the Family*. New York: Basic Books, 1964.

Leader, Arthur L. "Current and Future Issues in Family Therapy," presented at Family Service Association of America Biennial Meeting, Miami, Florida, Nov. 20, 1967.

Mitchell, Celia. "The Use of Family Sessions in the Diagnosis and Treatment of Disturbances in Children." *Social Casework,* June, 1960.

Sherman, Sanford N. "Family Treatment: An Approach to Children's Problems." *Social Casework,* June, 1966.

## Chapter 9

Munk, Mosheh, "Education for Family Life" (Heb.). *Ha-ma'yan* 7, no. 1 (Tishri, 5727).

"Sex Education" (a series of reprints from various journals and representing different points of view). In *Child and Family* 7, no. 1 (Winter, 1968).

A great deal of material has appeared in the popular periodical literature and also in the *Staff Bulletin* of the Public Schools of N.Y.C. For information on the reaction against Sex Education in the schools, see the front-page article in *The Wall Street Journal* of April 11, 1969.

## Chapter 11

### A. Books

Dushkin, Alexander, and Engelman, Uriah. *Jewish Education in the United States*. New York: American Association for Jewish Education, 1959, 265 pp.

Gannes, Abraham. *Selected Writings of Leo L. Honor*. New York: The Reconstructionist Press, 1965, pp. 27-143.

Janowsky, Oscar (ed.). *The Education of American Jewish Teachers.* Boston: Beacon Press, 1967, 354 pp.

Pilch, Judah (ed.). *A History of Jewish Education in America.* New York: American Association for Jewish Education, 1969, 233 pp.

Schiff, Alvin I. *The Jewish Day School in America.* New York: The Jewish Education Committee Press, 2nd ed., 1968, 294 pp.

B. Articles and Pamphlets

Dushkin, Alexander. "The Pattern of Community Thinking in Jewish Education." *Jewish Education* 35 (Spring, 1965): 136-47.

Eisenberg, Azriel. *Problem No. 1—The Hebrew High School.* New York: Jewish Education Committee Press, 11 pp.

*Jewish Education for Modern Needs.* New York: American Jewish Committee Institute of Human Relations, May, 1963, 13 pp.

Millgram, Abraham E. *Parents Can Become Real Partners in Jewish Education.* New York: American Association for Jewish Education, Feb., 1962, 22 pp.

Pilch, Judah. "Changing Patterns in Jewish Education." *Jewish Social Studies* 21 (April, 1959): 2.

Ruffman, Louis. "The Jewish Education Committee of New York." *Jewish Education* 35 (Spring, 1965): 148-65.

Schiff, Alvin I. "Israel in American Jewish Schools." *Jewish Education* 38 (October, 1968): 6-25.

———. "The Manpower Crisis in Jewish Education." *Jewish Education* 38 (June, 1968): 12-29.

———. "The Reconstruction of Jewish Education." *Jewish Education* 39 (April, 1969): 19-25.

*Chapter 12*

Fein, Leonard J. "Dilemmas of Jewish Identity on the

College Campus." *Judaism* 17, no. 1 (Winter, 1968), pp. 10ff.

Greenberg, Irving. "Escape from Freedom: Jewish Identity in America." *American Jewish Historical Quarterly* 55, no. 1 (September, 1965), pp. 5-21.

————. "Jewish Values and the Changing American Ethics." *Tradition* 10, no. 1 (Summer, 1968), pp. 42-74.

Greenberg, Meyer. "The Jewish Student at Yale: His Attitude Toward Judaism." *YIVO Annual of Social Science* 1 (1941):217-40.

Hassenger, Robert. *The Shape of Catholic Higher Education.* Chicago: University of Chicago Press, 1967.

Himmelfarb, Milton. "The Jewish College Student and the Intellectual Community." *Judaism* 17, no. 1 (Winter, 1968), pp. 3-9.

Jacob, Philip. *Changing Values in College.* New York: Harper, 1957.

————. "Jewishness and the Younger Intellectual." A Symposium in *Commentary* 31, no. 4 (April, 1961), pp. 306-57.

Nathan, Marvin. *The Attitude of the Jewish Student in the Colleges and Universities Towards His Religion.* New York: Bloch Publishing Co., 1932.

Podhoretz, Norman. *Making It.* New York: Random House, 1968.

Sutherland, R. L., Holtzman, W. H., Koile, E. A., and Smith, B. K., eds. *Personality Factors on the College Campus.* Austin: The Hagg Foundation for Mental Health, 1962.

*Chapter 14*

Chenkin, A. "Jewish Population in the United States 1962." *American Jewish Yearbook* 64 (1963): 57-76.

Davis, M. "Mixed Marriage in Western Jewry: Historical Background to the Jewish Response." *Jewish Journal of Sociology* 10 (London, 1968): 177-220.

Goldberg, Berty. "Les enfants issue de Marriage Mixte: Identité et Adjustment, Psychologique." *Memoire de Licence en Sciences Psychologiques,* Université Libre de Bruxelles, 1968.

Goldberg, N. "Intermarriage from a Sociological Perspective," in *Intermarriage and the Future of the American Jew.* Proceedings of a Conference of December, 1964. New York: Commission on Synagogue Relations, Federation of Jewish Philanthropies of New York, 1964.

Gordon, A. I. *Intermarriage: Interfaith, Interracial, Interethnic.* Boston: Beacon Press, 1964.

Heiss, J. S. "Premarital Characteristics of the Religiously Inter-Married in an Urban Area." *American Sociological Review* 25 (1960): 47-55.

Kligfeld, B. "Intermarriage: A Review of the Social Science Literature on the Subject." Presented at the Central Conference of American Rabbis, Detroit, Mich., June, 1960.

Lenski, G. *The Religious Factor: A Sociological Study of Religion's Impact on Politics, Economics, and Family Life.* New York: Doubleday & Co., 1961.

Levinson, Maria H., and Levinson, B. "Jews Who Intermarry: Socio-Psychological Basis of Ethnic Identity and Change." *Yivo Annual of Jewish Social Science* 12 (1958-59): 103-30.

Mayer, E. J. *Jewish-Gentile Courtship: An Exploratory Study of Social Process.* Glencoe, Ill.: The Free Press, 1951.

Morgan, T. B. "The Vanishing Jew." *Look Magazine,* May 5, 1964.

Prince, A. J. "A Study of 194 Cross-Religious Marriages." *Family Life Coordinator* 11 (1962): 1.

Rosenthal, E. "Studies of Jewish Intermarriage in the United States." New York: *American Jewish Yearbook* 64 (1963): 3-53.

————. "Jewish Intermarriage in Indiana." New York: *American Jewish Year Book* 68 (1967): 243-64.

Sanua, V. Social Science Research Relevant to American Jewish Education: Fourth Bibliographic Review, *Jewish Education* 32 (1962): 99-114; Fifth Bibliographic Review, *Jewish Education* 33 (1963): 162-75; Sixth Bibliographic Review, *Jewish Education* 34 (1964): 187-202; Seventh Bibliographic Review, *Jewish Education* 35 (1965): 238-56.

————. "Social Science Research Relevant to Jewish Group Service Agencies." *Program Aids* 24 (1963): 106.

————. "A Survey of the Needs of Jewish Social Science Research." *Journal of Jewish Communal Service* 40 (1963): 48-57.

————. "A Review of Social Science Studies on Jews and Jewish Life in the United States." *Journal for the Scientific Study of Religion* 4 (1964): 71-83.

————. "The Relationship Between Jewish Education and Jewish Identification." *Jewish Education* 35 (1964): 1-14.

————. "Patterns of Identification With the Jewish Community in the U.S.A." *The Jewish Journal of Sociology* 6 (1964): 190-211.

————. "Jewish Education and Jewish Survival: A Review of Empirical Studies." *Hachinuch* 28 (1966): 214-32. (*Review of Educational Psychology*, Jerusalem.)

————. "The Jewish Adolescent: A Review of Empirical Research." *Jewish Education* 38 (1968): 36-52.

————. "Jewish Education and Attitude of Jewish Adolescents." 1967 Convention of Educators' Assembly, United Synagogue of America, published in *The*

*Teenager and Jewish Education,* New York: United
Synagogue of America, 1967, pp. 112-37.
Sklare, M. *The Jews: Social Pattern of an American
Group.* Glencoe, Ill.: The Free Press, 1958.
————. "Intermarriage and the Jewish Future." *Com-
mentary,* April, 1964, pp. 1-7.
Zurofsky, J. J. ed. *The Psychological Implications of In-
termarriage.* Proceedings of a Conference of April,
1966, New York: Commission on Synagogue Rela-
tions, Federation of Jewish Philanthropies of New
York. 1966.

*Chapter 16*

Books
Mead, Margaret, and Wolfenstein, Margaret. *Childhood
in Contemporary Cultures.* Chicago: University of
Chicago Press, 1955.
Sartre, Jean-Paul. *Anti-Semite and Jew.* Translated by
George J. Becker. New York: Schocken Books,
1948.
Zborowski, Mark, and Herzog, Elizabeth. *Life Is with
People.* New York: Schocken Books, 1965.

Periodicals
Besdine, Matthew. "The Jocasta Complex, Mothering
and Genius." *The Psychoanalytic Review,* Summer,
1968 and Spring, 1969.
————. "Mrs. Oedipus." *Psychology Today.* January,
1969.
Erikson, Erik H. "Identity and the Life Cycle." *Psychological Issues* 1, no. 1, 1959.
Gilbert, Arthur. "A Rabbi's Theory of Instincts." *Psychoanalysis* 3, no. 3, 1955.
Grinstein, Alexander. "Profile of a Doll." *The Psychoanalytic Review,* Summer, 1963.

Linzer, Norman. *The Jewish Family—Compendium for Social Workers in Jewish Agencies.* New York: Commission on Synagogue Relations, Federation of Jewish Philanthropies, 1968.

Original Sources
*Code of Jewish Law.* Translated by Hyman Goldin. New York: Hebrew Publishing Company, 1927.

*Chapter 20*

Birmingham, Stephen. *Our Crowd.* New York: Harper and Row, 1967.

Bronfenbrenner, Urie. "The Split-Level American Family." *Saturday Review* (October 7, 1967), p. 60.

Ginzberg, Eli. "The Agenda Reconsidered." *Journal of Jewish Communal Service,* 42 (Spring, 1966) : 282.

Gold, Jacob G. and Shore, Herbert. "The New Look in Jewish Homes for the Aged." Reprinted from *Jewish Digest,* February, 1965, p. 18.

Linden, Maurice E. "Emotional Problems in Aging." *Jewish Social Service Quarterly* 31, no. 1 (1954); 81.

Linzer, Norman. *The Jewish Family—Compendium for Social Workers in Jewish Agencies.* New York: Federation of Jewish Philanthropies, 1968.

Margolis, Max L. and Marx, Alexander. *History of the Jewish People.* Philadelphia: Jewish Publication Society, 1945.

Posner, W. "Problems of the Aging in a Changing Society." Address before the Queensboro Council for Social Welfare, Oct. 19, 1950.

Rischin, Moses. *The Promised City.* New York: Corinth Books, reprint, 1964.

Rossman, Isadore. "Cultural Trends Increase Nursing Home Need." *Medical Tribune,* October 17, 1966.

Zelditch, Morris. "Trends in the Care of the Jewish Aged." In *Trends and Issues in Jewish Social Welfare in the United States, 1899-1958.* Philadelphia: Jewish Publication Society, 1966.

————. "Historical Perspectives on Care of the Jewish Aged." Address at National Conference of Jewish Communal Service, Atlantic City, N.J. (May 24, 1955). Mimeographed reprint.

*Chapter 21*

Abraham, K. "Notes on the Psychoanalytic Investigation and Treatment of Manic-Depressive Insanity and Allied Conditions." *Selected Papers.* London: Hogarth, 1927.

Bowlby, J. "Grief and Mourning in Infancy and Early Childhood." *Psychoanalytic Study of the Child* 15, 1960.

————. "Pathological Mourning and Childhood Mourning." *Journal of American Psychoanalytic Association* 11, 1963.

Freud, S., "Mourning and Melancholia." *Collected Papers,* Vol. IV. London: Hogarth Press, 1925.

Genne, Elizabeth Steel, and Genne, William Henry, eds. "Foundations for Christian Family Policy." Proceedings of the North American Conference on Church and Family (April 30—May 5, 1961), N.Y. Dept. of Family Life, National Council of the Churches of Christ in U.S.A. (1961), p. 32.

Goode, William J. "The Family as an Element in the World Revolution." New York: Institute of Life Insurance (n.d.), p. 19.

Hill, Reuben. "Social Stresses on the Family." In *Source Book on Marriage and the Family,* ed. Marvin B. Gassman, New York: Houghton Mifflin, rev. ed. 1963, pp. 303-14.

Kidorf, Irwin W. "Jewish Tradition and the Freudian Theory of Mourning." *Journal of Religion and Health,* April, 1963, pp. 248-52.

————. "The Shiva: A Form of Group Psychotherapy." *Journal of Religion and Health,* January, 1966, pp. 43-46.

Klein, M. "A Contribution to the Psychogenesis of Manic-Depressive States." *Contributions of Psycho-Analysis, 1921-1945,* London: Hogarth, 1948.

Klerman, G. "Scientific Depression." Proceedings reported by Sidney Levin, *Journal of the American Psychoanalytic Association,* April, 1965.

Krupp, George. "Identification as a Defense Against Anxiety in Coping with Loss." *The International Journal of Psycho-Analysis,* 46 (1965) : 303ff.

————, and Kligfeld, Bernard. "The Bereavement Reaction: A Cross-Cultural Evaluation." *Journal of Religion and Health* 1, no. 3 (April, 1962) : 223-46.

Lindermann, Eric. "Symptomatology and Management of Acute Grief." *American Journal of Psychiatry,* Sept., 1944, pp. 101-144.

McDonald, Marjorie. *Psychoanalytic Study of the Child* 21. New York: International Universities Press, 1965.

Murdock, George P. *Our Primitive Contemporaries.* New York: The Macmillan Co., 1934.

Niederland, William G. "Scientific Depression." Proceedings reported by Sidney Levin, *Journal of the American Psychoanalytic Association.* April, 1965.

Paul, Norman L., and Grosser, George H. "Operational Mourning and its Role in Conjoint Family Therapy." *Community Mental Health Journal* 1, no. 4 (Winter, 1965) : 339-45.

Sussman, Marvin B. "The Isolated Nuclear Family: Fact or Fiction?" In *Source Book on Marriage and the Family,* edited by Marvin B. Sussman. New York: Houghton Mifflin, rev. ed., 1963, pp. 48-53.

# Index

365